THE EFFECTIVE INTERVIEWER

THE
EFFECTIVE
INTERVIEWER
A Guide for
Managers

John D. Drake

American Management Association

Library of Congress Cataloging-in-Publication Data

Drake, John D., 1928–
    The effective interviewer: a guide for managers / John D. Drake.
        p.   cm.
Rev. ed. of: Interviewing for managers. Rev. ed. c1982.
    Bibliography: p.
    Includes index.
    ISBN 0-8144-5920-X
    1. Employment interviewing.   I. Drake, John D., 1928–
Interviewing for managers.   II. Title.
HF5549.5.I6D7   1989
658.3' 1124—dc20   89-45449
                                                                CIP

Printing number

10 9 8 7 6 5 4 3 2

For my parents,
John
and
Louise

Preface

This third revision of *Interviewing for Managers* represents a departure from the past. In the earlier editions, the focus was entirely on employment interviewing and allied issues, such as sourcing, recruiting, and selling the candidate. Although these topics still account for a major portion of the present text, the coverage has been broadened substantially to include how-to information on just about every kind of interview that managers are called on to conduct. New chapters describe specific models for screening job applicants, reference checking, job coaching, terminating employees, and exit interviewing.

While I believe that this book will be of help to human resources professionals, it was written with the operating manager in mind. The interviews are described in nontechnical terms and provide practical, hands-on techniques that managers can adopt for use in job situations. For reading ease, footnotes and references are kept to a minimum.

The heart of this book is the employment interview, especially the critical hire/not-hire interview. I have provided a complete system for assessing job candidates—from determination of what is needed to succeed in the job to effective ways of making the hiring decision.

A unique feature of this system is the Hypothesis Method, a methodology for interpreting the meaning of data gathered during the interview. Because interpreting data is the most difficult aspect of assessing others, a clear-cut procedure is presented for conducting the interview so that past history can be readily projected to future job behavior.

Several chapters deal with current trends that are affecting how interviews should be conducted. One of these focuses on the erosion of the traditional concept of employment-at-will and on ways to avoid "negligent hiring." Appendix D is devoted to the new immigration laws and what can be done to avoid violations and fines.

For human resources professionals, a procedure is presented for making exit interviews more productive. It has been used by many companies with excellent success.

For organizations involved in campus recruiting, a complete game plan is provided. It deals with how to organize a recruiting effort that will most effectively tap this source of candidates. In addition, a model for conducting the campus interview is provided; it is the product of much research and field experimentation. Operating managers and other nonprofessional interviewers find it easy to learn and to apply in campus situations.

Almost all the material in this book is based upon my consulting experience with clients over a twenty-five-year period. It is a compilation of what I have seen work well in the difficult world of running a business. My objective is simple: to provide a practical guide that will help managers to be more effective in conducting those interpersonal exchanges that often spell the difference between success and failure in managing.

I wish to acknowledge the thoughtful suggestions from my partners at Drake Inglesi Milardo, Inc. Their professional experience added significantly to the scope of this work.

I have enjoyed writing and revising this book; I hope readers will find pleasure and profit in applying its contents.

John D. Drake, Ph.D.
Kennebunkport, Maine

Contents

THE
EFFECTIVE
INTERVIEWER

Chapter 1

Listening—The Essential Skill in All Interviews

Regardless of the kind of interview—hiring, coaching, or firing—at some point during that interview it will be important just to *listen*. Listening helps an interviewer to understand (often more than is initially apparent); conveys respect for the other person; minimizes the possibility of reacting inappropriately; and enables others to share themselves. *People will be open, and continue speaking, for as long as they believe that an interviewer is interested and wants to hear what they have to say.* Conversely, all it takes to stop the flow of communication is a turn of the head, a frown, or a raised eyebrow.

Because listening skills are essential for all the interviews described here, it is appropriate to tackle this topic first.

Five Ways to Listen

Listening is an art. It doesn't lend itself to specific patterns, because how one listens depends on the individual personality and situation. However, there are some techniques that can be employed to help us listen and, at the same time, encourage others to talk. Here they are:

1. Asking questions
2. Accepting responses
3. Restating and reflecting feelings

4. Pausing or being silent
5. Using nonverbals

The art of good listening lies in using a mixture of all these techniques and in never using any particular one many times in a row or any one technique to the exclusion of the others. They are well worth mastering because their application has great relevance to successful communication, whether in business or personal life.

Asking Questions

The most frequently used listening tool is that of asking questions. To encourage verbalization, however, the interviewer should avoid beginning the question with such words as "do," "have," "is," "was," "would," "did," "had," "are," "were," and "could." These and other closed-ended words usually produce yes/no answers or rather limited responses.

In most cases, a better way to phrase a question is to begin the sentence with words such as "what," "why," "how," or "tell me." They are particularly useful for initiating discussion on a particular topic. For example, in job coaching: "*How* do you think you could improve on that area of your work for next quarter?" In an employment interview: "Please go on now and *tell me* something about your job experiences."

One reason that open-ended questions are helpful is that they convey a strong interest in what the other person has to say on the topic. In effect, use of open-ended questions says to the interviewee, "I care about your ideas. I recognize that what you think is important, and because of that I'm willing to give you the freedom to flesh out your thoughts as you choose."

During employment interviews, open-ended questions allow the interviewer to learn not only about the applicant's history and qualifications but also about *how* the applicant responds. For example, how well does the applicant structure his answer? Is his answer scattered or systematic, terse or relaxed, superficial or complete? As much can be learned from the applicant's *way* of answering as from the content of the reply. Also, the open-ended question usually creates a relatively nondefensive climate; it gives applicants an opportunity to structure their answers in their own manner.

Problems With the Use of Questions Even if the interviewer uses many open-ended questions, a consistent or exclusive use of questions for obtaining interview data is not recommended. As was suggested at the beginning of this chapter, the use of a variety of listening tools is most effective. However, because so many interviewers find questions the most natural way of eliciting data, there is a tendency (particularly with novice interviewers) to rely too much on them. Let's examine, for a moment, some of the difficulties encountered when questions become the primary means of encouraging the applicant to talk. Overreliance on questions:

1. *Reduces input from the interviewee.* There is significant evidence to suggest that the amount of verbal response diminishes in proportion to the number of questions asked in a series. The first open-ended question is apt to get a fairly detailed response; with the second, the elaboration will decrease. As the interviewer proceeds to ask several questions, one after the other, the interviewee may mentally hear the interviewer saying, "Look, there are certain things I want to know, and if I want to know them, I'll ask you." As a consequence, the interviewee becomes increasingly passive, or merely reactive, and is not motivated to extend himself.

2. *Often puts others on the defensive.* At its worst, questioning can become an inquisition and cut off almost all conversation. Even at its best, questioning tends to arouse caution. Whenever the interviewer asks a question, the interviewee understands that the topic is one of importance and so becomes careful and guarded in responding, particularly if the issue is at all threatening.

3. *Makes it easy to be fooled.* The extensive use of questions, especially during employment interviews, makes it easy for applicants to create a positive impression. In effect, when interviewers rely on questions, the interview becomes a series of discrete thought units. Here is a typical example.

INTERVIEWER: How were your grades in college?

APPLICANT: Oh, pretty good. I was in the upper third of my class and I made the dean's list last semester.

INTERVIEWER: How about extracurricular activities—were you involved in any?

APPLICANT: Well, I was quite active. I got a letter in track and was active in intramurals. In fact, our fraternity won the softball league championship. I also belonged to the radio club and was chairman of the soph hop.

It can be readily seen that for each question the applicant has the opportunity to select a reaction; the applicant is given the time to analyze the question, sift through alternative answers, and pick the one that will put him in the best possible light. One can also note from the foregoing dialogue that it is quite evident to this applicant that extracurricular activities are important to the interviewer. Consequently, he strives hard to resurrect as many positive facts as he can.

It is interesting to contrast this question approach with normal conversation in which the participants tend to exchange ideas, building one thought upon the other. Interviewers will learn much more about how candidates think and behave through a relatively unstructured conversation than they will by giving applicants an opportunity through set questions to carefully select those responses that will make them look good.

4. *Burdens the interviewer.* A final problem with relying on questions as the central technique for listening is the burden it puts on the interviewer. Most inexperienced interviewers have the problem of not knowing just what to ask. Many interviewers become so preoccupied with formulating the right questions that little time is left to analyze the answers or obtain a meaningful understanding of the individual in front of them. Questions are helpful in controlling the decision but ought to be used in conjunction with other techniques.

It should also be recognized that interviewers who rely on questions to stimulate discussion assume that they know the right questions to ask. They inquire about the topics believed to be relevant, but in so doing may overly control the interview and thus divert time and attention away from other unthought of, but possibly more meaningful, topics.

In brief, this is not to say that the interviewer should avoid asking questions. The point here is that significant problems can arise when all eggs are put in the question basket.

Accepting Responses

Another tool that aids listening and, at the same time, encourages conversation is to accept what is being said rather than to pass any kind of judgment on it. Accepting is a way of expressing interest in what is being said, and ordinarily it stimulates expansion of the topic at hand. For this reason, some professionals refer to such techniques as "expanders."

We can accept another's comment either verbally or nonverbally. Typical nonverbal responses are a nodding of the head (not as in sleep, but to indicate acknowledgment), maintaining periodic eye contact, and giving undivided attention to the person.

Verbal acceptance can take many forms, but the most common are responses such as: "uh-huh," "go on," "I see," "I understand," and "that's interesting."

Restating and Reflecting Feelings

One of the most effective tools available to the interviewer is restatement. In effect, the interviewer listens to the other's comments and then attempts to restate them in his own words. This action usually encourages the interviewee to expand on what was already said. Here are two examples:

INTERVIEWER: Do you see any possible difficulties you might have in getting started on this job?
APPLICANT: Well, the only possible difficulty I can see is that I would have to go slow at first, at least until I got a little more familiar with the exact way you people operate.
INTERVIEWER: [*Restating*] You tend to start off slowly and then pick up speed as you get more familiar with the work.

APPLICANT: Yes, I guess that's right. I like to be pretty sure of myself before I really take over the full operation of a machine. Besides, the kind of equipment we had at the other company isn't exactly the same type you have here. I guess I'm not as familiar with your kind of process as I should be.

Here is another example of restating.

INTERVIEWER: What would you say might be some of your shortcomings?
APPLICANT: I really can't think of any significant shortcomings I have. Whenever I felt I was weak in something, I worked hard to overcome it.
INTERVIEWER: [*Restating*] You feel then that there really aren't any things you could improve very much upon.
APPLICANT: Well, of course, I couldn't say that. I guess everybody can improve in some things.
INTERVIEWER: [*Restating*] There might be some things you could possibly do better in.
APPLICANT: Well, as I said, yes. I guess everybody can improve somewhat. The only thing that I can really point to is that fact that I. . . .

The restating promotes meaningful discussion because the interviewer is attempting to understand what the applicant is saying. In most cases, restatements should not prove threatening to the applicant who has already said whatever is being rephrased. Restating, in effect, says, "I'm interested; I'm trying to understand; the door's open for you to tell me more if you want to." Usually, others accept the invitation to expand on the point they have just made.

A more sophisticated version of restating is to reflect back not the content (words) of what is being said but, instead, the feelings being conveyed. This action is most appropriate when the other person is experiencing strong feelings or when objective discussion is hampered by emotions (even though mild). Here's an example from an employment interview:

APPLICANT: [*Angrily*] In XYZ Company, they just let people go without any reason or cause.

INTERVIEWER: [*Reflecting feeling*] It makes you angry even to think about it.

APPLICANT: You bet it does! There was only one time when I ever got out of line in that company and that was when. . . .

Here's another example from a job-coaching situation:

MANAGER: . . . and it seems to me that you really let down the rest of the group.

SUBORDINATE: [*Obviously emotional*] That's so unfair! I wasn't the only one responsible for getting that project done, and now you're blaming it all on me.

MANAGER: [*Reflecting feeling*] This discussion is really getting you upset.

SUBORDINATE: Well, I guess I am. I hadn't realized how much your accusation bothered me. I'm sorry I sounded off and I realize that I had some responsibility for this problem, but. . . .

Occasions for Using Restatement   Restating is most helpful when:

- The interviewee's comments become emotional.
- The topic being discussed is touchy or sensitive.
- There is conflict.
- What is being said is obscure.
- The interviewer feels on the spot and doesn't know what to say.

When these conditions are present, asking a question is very likely to put the other person on the defensive. This is particularly true during employment interviews or job-coaching sessions. For instance:

INTERVIEWER: Tell me something about the job you had at the Smith Company.

APPLICANT: Well, to be quite frank, my boss and I had a personality conflict and . . . well, I was let go.

INTERVIEWER: [*Restating content*] You and your boss didn't get
on that well. [*Reflecting feelings*] You feel a little uncomfortable talking about it.

APPLICANT: Well, yes. . . . You see what happened was. . . .

The reader can imagine the kind of response that might
have been given if the interviewer had asked directly: "What
happened between the two of you?" The interviewer would
have received an answer all right, but quite likely it would have
been carefully phrased to show up the boss as unreasonable. In
essence, the use of questions at these times usually puts the
other person on the defensive; it virtually requires the interviewee to justify his position. A restatement, on the other hand,
does not imply that anything is wrong or needs to be justified.
Restatement or reflection of feelings shows neither approval
nor disapproval; rather, it provides tangible evidence of listening and, above all, if reflected accurately, conveys understanding.

Problems With the Use of Restatement   Sometimes interviewers will intentionally misstate another's remark in order to
check out an assumption that they have made regarding something an interviewee has said. For example:

APPLICANT: I always look at things pretty carefully and weigh
the long-term consequences of each decision.

INTERVIEWER: Sometimes you procrastinate until you feel
you've got the correct solution.

Deliberate misstating is not recommended, however. If the
interviewer misstates with any frequency, the other person will
feel he is being manipulated; sometimes the interviewer will
come across as inattentive or, worse, appear stupid.

It is generally more rewarding to restate key remarks as
accurately as possible on the assumption that as the other person responds to a sincere restatement, he will reveal enough to

confirm or reject one's original speculation. Using the same example just shown, let's see how this might work:

APPLICANT: I always look at things pretty carefully and weigh the long-term consequences of each decision.

INTERVIEWER: You're cautious in the way you go about making decisions.

APPLICANT: Yes, that's right. I find that the time invested in making the right decision really has a payoff when you compare it with the wasted effort that is required to undo a wrong decision. Of course, some people might call it procrastination, but I believe it's just good management.

When managers first learn about restating, they have a tendency to overuse the technique or to apply it in situations where it is inappropriate. In most discussions, restatements should be used sparingly. There is always the danger that they may come across as gimmicky, especially if the interviewer's intention is not a true desire to better understand what is being said.

Despite the interviewer's sincere desire to listen and to understand, there will be occasions when the restatement just doesn't work, when it begets little more than a monosyllabic and unhelpful "yeah" or "no." When this happens, the interviewer is no worse off than before restating, and can always come back to the topic by asking: "Why do you feel that way?"

There are, however, two simple rules of thumb that, when followed, usually preclude getting a "yeah" or "no" response.

1. *Don't restate the obvious.* For example, when an interviewee comments, "It sure is warm out there today," don't respond with the inanity, "You feel it's quite hot." But if you do, don't be surprised to hear him say, "Yeah, that's what I said!"

2. *Don't phrase your restatement as a question.* A restatement should not have the inflection on the end of the sentence that turns it into an interrogative. Rather, correct restatements are best made in a flat, declarative manner.

To sum up, restatement and reflection have their greatest value when the topic being discussed is touchy, sensitive, obscure, or conflict-ridden.

Pausing or Being Silent

One of the most powerful tools in an interviewer's repertoire is the use of a pause or of silence. Whenever two or more people are engaged in discussion and an extended pause occurs, tremendous psychological pressure builds up to fill the conversational gap. Silence asks, without use of words, "Well, what else can you add?" It suggests to the other person that more is expected.

The use of silence, however, carries with it the inherent problem of threat. As was discussed earlier, threat is more likely to discourage free-flowing conversation than to encourage it. Thus silence can be misused and abused. There are, however, two occasions in which silence can be used effectively without accompanying threat or discomfort.

Silence After a Question   First, a pause is most effective after the interviewer has asked a question. When a question is addressed to anyone, it is clearly understood that it is the other person's turn to speak. However, whenever an applicant does not immediately answer the question asked, most interviewers will jump into the discussion and answer the question themselves. Sometimes interviewers clarify their questions with additional statements.

There is little justification for the interviewer to continue speaking once a question has been asked. It cannot be assumed just because there is silence that nothing is going on. The other person may be thinking through what to say or how to phrase the answer. It is almost always true that *comments made after long pauses are the most meaningful.*

In psychotherapy, for example, the most valuable insights on the patient's part come after a period of silence, not in the ongoing dialogue with the therapist. Let's look at what typically happens: The patient is talking freely, but then is stopped by a thought that he cannot decide whether to share with the therapist, or perhaps cannot even face himself. There then occurs a long pause, and after awhile, the patient speaks. What is said then is almost always more significant than what was expressed in the earlier phase of the conversation. The same is true during interviewing. In fact, the longer the interviewee's silence lasts, the more significant the next statement is likely to be. A sound principle of interviewing is, *when you ask a question, do not speak next.*

At this point, an interviewer might be wondering what would happen if the silence persisted for an extended period. He is perhaps concerned about the stress or discomfort the interviewee might experience. This should not be a concern, however, because it is not the interviewer who is creating the silence but the interviewee.

If the interviewer has asked a question and the other person has not responded, it is very clear whose turn it is now to speak. The fact that the interviewee permits the silence to continue suggests that it is not bothering him as much as the interviewer believes it is. And even if the silence were causing stress, that individual could break the awkward silence simply by saying: "Would you mind repeating your question? I'm not exactly sure what you meant by it."

If an interviewer feels compelled to say something (rather than maintain absolute silence), he can always say, "Take your time, I know you're thinking about it." But whatever else he may do at this point, he should not ask another question.

Pausing After an Answer   A second occasion in which the pause can be helpful and yet nonthreatening is when the pause is of relatively short duration. These pauses are best used once the person has completed a thought or answered a question. For example:

INTERVIEWER: How did things go with you over at ABC Company?

APPLICANT: OK, we had our ups and downs, but generally, I'd say OK.

INTERVIEWER: [*Pauses for five or six seconds*]

APPLICANT: Well, actually my boss wasn't the kind of person I liked working for. . . . He. . . .

Tape recordings reveal that when a pause is used after the applicant has made a statement, the applicant often adds something. He says, for example, "And another thing. . . ." Or he will say, "I'll tell you something else. . . ."

If this process is examined, it is easy to understand why interviewees add meaningful comments after a pause even though it appears that they have finished. While responding to a question, the other person is simultaneously filtering, censoring, and organizing his thoughts and pondering whether or not to reveal them. When the pause occurs at this point, there is a strong likelihood that the interviewee will decide to share the thought with the interviewer. He feels almost compelled to go on and then says, "The other thing about that is. . . ."

The interviewer who jumps in as soon as the other person has finished a statement will be cutting off all chance of hearing any addendum. Thus good interviewing, like good listening, is typically slow-paced. There is no need for the interviewer to worry about having a probing question to ask next or responding in a witty or highly intelligent manner. The interviewer should relax and lead the discussion at a comfortable pace. Pauses of short duration during the interview are not going to create problems and may even help the interviewer learn many useful things that otherwise would have escaped him.

Using Nonverbals

Another important tool that helps keep the interviewee talking is the appropriate use of nonverbal cues. Often, more information is communicated through nonverbals than by words. An interviewer may say, "I'm very interested in what happened on that job," but, at the same time, his gestures, frowns, or body postures might clearly indicate boredom or distraction. It is important, therefore, that interviewers pay attention to the nonverbal cues they transmit.

A helpful nonverbal is to nod understandingly at the completion of a statement by the applicant. Interviewers can also lean forward, show attention, and use appropriate hand gestures. All these cues indicate the interviewer's interest and encourage the applicant to continue talking.

A question often arises concerning the use of eye contact. If the interviewer continually focuses his attention out the window, or on the wall, or on a notepad, it will be distracting and is likely to be interpreted as indifference. On the other hand, constant eye contact can become quite uncomfortable; the interviewer should not try to engage in a staring contest. Instead, occasional eye contact is recommended. It helps build rapport and shows the others that they have the attention of the interviewer.

Interviewers would also be well advised to avoid distracting nonverbal gestures, such as toying with pencils, slouching in chairs, rattling papers, or picking lint off their clothes. All these actions say to interviewees that the interviewer's attention is elsewhere and not focused on them.

Nonverbals show others how they are "coming across." The occasional smile, the hand gesture, the nod of the head all say, in effect, "Hey, I'm interested, I'm with you, and I'm listening." In contrast, when the interviewer engages in no overt nonverbal behavior, but instead remains immobile, it is difficult for people to understand the impact of their statements upon the interviewer. This unknown makes interviewees uncomfortable and will make it difficult for the interviewer to establish an easy rapport.

Another aspect of nonverbals has to do with the proximity of the interviewer to the applicant. Generally, the physical distance between the interviewer and interviewee should be not more than five feet and not less than two feet. It is usually desirable to provide some safe territory for the other person and not to suggest too much familiarity.

Summary

Five basic techniques—questions, accepting, restating, pausing, and nonverbals—have been outlined as tools for listening and for keeping the interview moving on a conversational plane. The question usually serves as the interviewer's control device. It determines the topic to be discussed. The five techniques are then used together to draw out the interviewee on the topic at hand until sufficient information has been gathered.

It is not good interview technique to rely on any one of the five devices to the exclusion of the others. This is particularly true with questions. Restating is best used when discussing topics that are sensitive or threatening.

The listening techniques described in this chapter are the tools of interviewing. Their effectiveness, however, depends, above all, upon a true desire to hear and to understand.

Chapter 2

Sources of Candidates

Effective assessment techniques are most helpful when there is a pool of good talent from which the most qualified can be selected. This chapter provides a description of some of the usual, major sources of talent, as well as of a few that are often overlooked. Some pointers are also provided for making optimal use of these sources. Campus recruiting is not discussed here. It will be explored in detail in Chapter 5.

Employment Agencies

Employment agencies are licensed and regulated by state laws and normally represent the job seeker. Because they require employment opportunities for their candidates in order to earn their fees, agencies aggressively pursue potential employers to learn about their present and future personnel needs. Employers also may list job openings with agencies. In large cities, many agencies specialize in certain occupations such as sales, personnel, computer programming, bookkeeping, or nursing.

Agencies work on a contingency basis. That is, a fee or charge is not incurred until a candidate referred by the agency is actually hired. Agency fees vary greatly, from one percent per $1,000 of salary up to 25 percent of total compensation. The maximum fees are usually controlled by the state in which the agency operates. With some agencies, the employer pays no fee; the cost is met by the individual seeking employment.

When many jobs must be filled, or when an organization makes extensive or exclusive use of the agency, it is often possible to negotiate lower fees or to make other arrangements to improve the cost effectiveness of this recruiting source.

Most employment agencies operate according to a percentage philosophy, that is, in the belief that "if we send enough résumés to the client, eventually a match will be found and we'll place somebody." This often means that company personnel departments and employers rather than the employment agency are doing the actual screening. For the fees being paid, employers deserve more. The employment agency should refer only qualified applicants to be interviewed. This will not occur, however, unless it is demanded. In working with employment agencies, the word "demand" is well taken. Managers must be absolutely firm in pointing out to agency personnel that they want to see only those individuals who meet specified criteria and if nonqualified candidates are referred, use of their services will be terminated. The impact of this threat, of course, depends somewhat on the volume of business done with the agency and the availability of other options in the community.

It is recommended that managers develop behavioral specifications for each of the jobs to be filled and that they communicate these specifications to the agency, at the same time indicating which items are absolutely critical. The agency should be informed that unless the essential background and required job behaviors are clearly evident in applicants, forwarding their résumés will be a waste of time. On the other hand, managers must be realistic and also certain that their demands are in compliance with equal employment opportunity regulations.

When working with agencies, it is also important to be aware that unless proper precautions are taken, the company could be saddled with paying a fee for candidates it has discovered through other means. The situation can arise, for example, when someone sends in an unsolicited résumé, or perhaps when a company employee turns in a friend's completed application blank. The next day the employment agency forwards a résumé describing the same person. If that individual is then hired, the agency will claim the fee for "finding" the employee. It is important, therefore, to require the agency to list the names of all candidates before it forwards their résumés. At the same time, this list of names should be reviewed against all in-house applications or résumés currently in the company's possession.

Another step that can be taken to prevent that problem from arising is to make one person or group within the company responsible for dealing with employment agencies. Letting that person or group be the sole contact with agencies, with exclusive responsibility for the flow of candidates and for fee negotiations, makes for smoother relations and greater efficiency.

Advantages of Using Agencies

Speed. Agencies can often provide many applicants rather quickly—something that is especially helpful when there is an urgent need to fill an opening.

Privacy. Use of an agency allows a company to go into the job market and yet keep its name or job opening confidential (at least until the first candidate is interviewed).

Research. Study of candidates sent by agencies can often help determine the nature of the labor pool available to fill certain jobs as well as average salary demands and the like.

Disadvantages of Agencies

Aggressive "sell." Employment agencies are often criticized because of the unprofessional behavior of some of their employees. Many try to sell employers candidates who do not meet the job requirements.

Not for higher management. Employment agencies are not suitable as sources for top management assignments. Usually, employment agencies work on jobs at the lower salary levels, although many now actively place individuals at middle management and professional levels, such as engineers, personnel managers, computer experts, and sales managers.

Executive Search Firms

Most reputable executive search firms perceive themselves as consultants to the clients they serve. Unlike the employment agencies, search firms are engaged by the employer, not the job seeker. Thus, they are hired to seek out and present to their clients candidates who meet desired specifications. Most search firms are organized to find candidates at professional, upper-middle, and top management levels. Difficult-to-find candidates, such as those with special technological skills, also make up a portion of the business of most search firms.

Executive search companies charge 25 to 30 percent of the recruited person's first-year compensation; out-of-pocket travel and search costs can run between 10 and 25 percent of the search fee and are billed in addition to the basic fee. Unless it is on behalf of a long-term client, most executive search firms will not accept assignments for jobs paying less than $25,000 a year. However, some firms may take the assignment for relatively low-paying jobs for a negotiated fee that is not related to the incumbent's compensation level.

Working With a Recruiter

The first task, obviously, is to find a search firm that can do a professional job. This field is easy to enter, so it is filled with a large number of one- and two-man shops, some of which are highly competent, and others that disappear almost as quickly as they appear. Unless you personally know the background or reputation of the very small, independent search group, the safer course of action is to consult the Directory of the Association of Executive Recruiting Consultants, Inc.*

The executive search business is in many ways dominated by a Big Six. These firms account for approximately 30 percent of all searches, and it is estimated that they account for more than 50 percent of the searches involving positions paying at least $100,000 a year. While each of these Big Six (Russell

---

*Association of Executive Recruiting Consultants, Inc., 30 Rockefeller Plaza, New York, N.Y. 10020.

Reynolds Associates, Boyden Associates, Spencer Stuart & Associates, Heidrick & Struggles, Korn/Ferry, and Egon Zehnder International) claims to be unique, all use basically the same process. First, they determine a description or profile of the executive the client desires. They locate and present several individuals who closely fit the profile, assist in negotiations, and then aid the company in persuading the candidate to take the offer.

Other sources are some of the major public accounting firms and management consultants. If your company already employs one of these consulting organizations, it can often be effective in finding just the right candidate, since it is probably already knowledgeable about your company and its operations.

In selecting a search firm, it is advantageous to obtain the appraisals of business associates who have used various firms. Invite several search firms to make a presentation to you about their fees, approach, track record, experience in recruiting for the type of job you are trying to fill, and who will actually be in charge of the search. This last point is important. For the presentation, the larger firms are likely to send a top-level officer, who in most cases will be impressive. However, the actual search work and liaison between you and the search organization may be with a junior staff member who does not attend the presentation meeting. In working with a search organization, the kind of relationship (openness and ease of communication) you establish with the specific recruiter handling the search is extremely important and should not be underestimated.

Once the firm has been selected, the most important single step you can take is to be clear in your own mind about what kind of candidate is desired. All recruiters will interview you about the job requirements, but it is the preparation for these discussions that matters. Carefully thought-out behavioral specifications can be most helpful (see Chapter 15). If these are prepared in writing for the recruiter, there can be no question about your expectations. Explain to recruiters that as they present the background of a candidate, you will expect them to describe to you how the candidate does or does not fulfill the specifications. Such a procedure should help you decide whether you want to invest time in interviewing the candidate.

Sometimes, when recruiters use their own formats for presenting a candidate, a smooth presentation and highlighted
strengths may make the candidate appear extremely attractive;
yet, on critical analysis, the individual may not be able to do the
job you want accomplished.

Don't seek the impossible. Sometimes a company approaches recruiters with the attitude that because these people
are professionals, and because it is paying them a lot of money,
recruiters should therefore "shoot for the stars" and come up
with the perfect candidate. While the goal is admirable, it is
usually self-defeating. Of course, there is no perfect candidate.
As in purchasing a new sailboat, it is often a matter of finding
the best compromise—trading off one feature against another.
The essential question must always be, "Can the candidate do
the job?" All kinds of people can succeed, depending on the
unique blend of qualifications they bring to the job, just so long
as they function as the behavioral specifications demand.

Be realistic about compensation. Most recruiters have an
excellent feel for what it will take to recruit top personnel for
the job you are trying to fill. Demanding top people but then
being unwilling to pay adequately will usually result in disappointing candidates and/or your own frustration.

It is also important to allow adequate time. Finding the
best candidates is often a time-consuming process. Even if the
recruiter personally knows of a good potential candidate, arranging a meeting, reviewing qualifications, and making com-
parisons with other candidates takes considerable time. The
average time to complete a successful search is ninety days. If
possible, don't wait to initiate the search until the need is des-
perate. A last-minute crisis approach often occurs after a company has exhausted all possibilities itself, has not developed the
caliber of candidate wanted, and then calls in the professional
recruiter.

Be frank and open with the recruiter. No consultant can
do the best possible job for you unless he really understands
the job, compensation, and environment in which the successful candidate will be placed. For example, give the recruiter an
opportunity to review the key personnel to whom the incumbent will report (unless, of course, disclosure of the search will

create internal organizational problems). It is helpful for the recruiter to know, for example, whether the organizational climate is formal or informal, structured or relatively loose and free-flowing.

An interesting and creative approach to the use of search firms is to allow the subordinates of the potential incumbent to work closely with the executive recruiter in determining behavioral requirements. In this approach, the employees help select the individual who will be their boss.

Advantages of Using Search Firms

Experience. Most professional recruiters have an extensive range of contacts that are personally known to them. Even more important, they know where the sought-after talent can be located. Each good search firm has developed its own system of identifying and tracking down desired candidates. In brief, these firms are in the business, searching every day, and know where and how to find people.

Confidentiality. Very often a company may wish to keep from its own employees or competitors that it is seeking to fill a key position. Frequently, too, it may wish to put out "feelers" to a particular person before making a direct approach. In such cases, the recruiters can meet the candidate and discuss job opportunities without identifying the company or committing it.

Time. Recruiting top people is usually difficult. Most of them are already engaged in jobs and careers that are rewarding. Therefore, it is a matter not only of locating such people but, equally critical, of selling them on the job to be filled. Even getting potential candidates to listen to the basic facts about a new job opportunity over lunch is often difficult. The recruiter's greatest assistance lies in his ability to save the client time by presenting for interview only qualified and interested candidates.

Disadvantages of Using Search Firms

There is an up-front risk in using search firms in terms of expense. Most recruiters work on a one-third, one-third, and one-third basis. That is, they are paid one-third at the time you engage their service; one-third after one month; and the remaining third on completion of the assignment. If, for some reason, the search firm cannot find your person, the investment is lost. Frequently, too, changes in the company result in a decision not to fill the vacancy. In these instances also, the fee is lost.

Advertising

Placing classified ads in newspapers or block space advertisements in trade journals and/or newspapers is another way of flushing out candidates. Advertising is difficult to evaluate because its effectiveness depends so much on the level of job and the impact of the advertisement. Media costs can run from as little as $100 to more than $10,000, depending on the size of the ad, the frequency with which it is run, and the circulation of the publication. Considering the potential number of applicants an advertisement can raise, advertising is usually a cost-effective way to identify candidates. TV commercials are also being used successfully—especially when a large number of vacancies must be filled in a short period of time (staffing a new shift, for example).

Generally, advertising will provide a large number of résumés from candidates who will not meet the company's needs. For example, one consulting firm ran a block advertisement in the Sunday issue of the Los Angeles *Times*. Within a week it received 248 replies. Of these, only five respondents were deemed sufficiently qualified to invite for an interview; however, one of those interviewed was hired.

Working With Advertisements

Most companies find that advertisements are most useful in producing good candidates when one or more of these conditions exist: (1) a large number of people must be hired (for example, because a new plant is being put into operation); (2)

the skill or job requirements are not stringent (that is, a wide range of individuals could perform the job); and (3) a specific, easily ascertainable skill or knowledge is required (that is, the advertisement performs much of the screening, such as advertising for an aircraft flight test engineer).

Most large organizations will find it productive to engage an advertising agency to develop and place their advertisements. Many of the larger advertising agencies have subsidiaries whose primary thrust is the development of effective recruiting ads. These specialized agencies can save much time and effort by determining the best media for the ad (newspaper, radio/TV, trade journal), developing the copy, and handling the placement, scheduling, and payment for the ads. If you employ an advertising agency to assist you, be certain that the final ad is always submitted to you for approval. In this way, any errors can be picked up; even more important, you can check it for discriminatory statements. Your legal responsibility does not end simply because an outside agency developed the copy.

Advantages of Advertising

Speed. Advertising can often yield a wide range of applicants rather quickly. If a large hiring is to take place, with many jobs to fill, advertising may be the most efficient approach.

"Feel" of the market. Employers may want to know what is out there in the marketplace. The company may be considering expansion into a new product area, for example, and wants to ascertain the availability of individuals possessing special technical skills. Thus, advertising a job opening can serve as a form of market research.

Public relations. Frequent advertisements in which the company name is prominent can have a positive impact on future recruiting. Quality advertisements suggest that the company is growing and "on the move." The image of a company that is expanding and has growth opportunities often results in top people in competitive organizations coming forward without solicitation.

Disadvantages of Advertising

Attracts the disgruntled. One reason advertisements are frequently not productive is that the better candidates do not respond to them. Either they are happily employed elsewhere and therefore not likely to read the ad or, if they do observe it, they may be reluctant to expose themselves by responding to the advertisement (unless the ad reveals the company name and location). The business community abounds with tales of employees who revealed their discontent by responding to a blind ad (box number) only to discover that the ad had been placed by their own company—occasionally for their own job.

Creates a screening problem. As suggested, the number of well-qualified applicants per hundred replies is likely to be low. Depending on the resources available to review the mail or answer telephone calls, sifting through the responses can be burdensome, particularly if the company name is displayed. In such cases, good public relations would dictate that applicants deserve some acknowledgment of receipt of their résumés. If a box number only is provided, then, of course, there is no need to reply.

Unsolicited Applications or Résumés

Without question, the most cost-effective way of recruiting personnel is through self-referrals or referrals by customers, employees, or friends of the company. Such applicants have two good qualifications: They want a job and they are interested in the company. Unfortunately, this potential pool of talent is often not capitalized on. The persons who visit the company or send in résumés often get lost in the shuffle, because at the time of their availability there is no appropriate vacancy. It is not uncommon for an executive who has been hired after a lengthy and costly search to indicate that he had filed an application with the company a few months earlier, but had never heard from anyone at that time.

With easy access to computers in most organizations, there is little reason not to capitalize on this self-referral source of talent. It is relatively easy to keypunch essential data from résumés, which can then be matched against an in-house personnel requisition format. In this way, whenever a vacancy occurs, a readymade pool of talent can be quickly scanned for potential candidates.

Many companies find that referrals from current employees make for an excellent source of candidates. Because these individuals already work for the company, they can often be effective recruiters in enticing others to join. Also because they go "on the line" when they make a recommendation to the company, they are likely to solicit only those individuals who will perform well or at the least not embarrass them by failing. In fact, a recent study of quit rates found that employee referrals had significantly greater job tenure (stayed with the job for much longer periods) than referrals from employment agencies or newspaper advertisements.

To make good use of in-house company referrals, it is, of course, necessary to post job openings through company bulletin boards and house organs. Some companies offer employees recruiting awards or financial bonuses for individuals they recommend who are subsequently hired.

The advantage of this approach is that high-quality candidates may be found at low cost. The disadvantages are the possibility of ill will if an employee-recommended applicant is rejected, particularly if that person is a close friend of the employee, and the company's sacrifice of confidentiality if it posts the job opening.

Job Posting

Many organizations routinely post job descriptions and job requirements for employment opportunities within the company. Even if an organization does not routinely follow this practice, posting should be considered when trying to fill certain personnel needs.

Most companies find it impractical to list jobs at upper management levels because they want the latitude to bring in outside talent when necessary. Also, there is often reluctance to publicize management openings, especially if significant organizational changes are planned. The cutoff point for job posting in many organizations is at the level of lower-middle management. The exact level is usually defined in terms of salary grade.

The success of job posting in any organization depends largely on the personnel department's ability to constructively manage the volume of candidates the posting system may generate. The problem can become acute because everyone who responds to the job opening should be talked with. Even those applicants who are obviously unqualified will need an explanation as to why they were not selected. If personnel is not staffed to conduct these turndown interviews, there is a high probability of engendering hostile feelings toward the posting system and/or the company. For a job posting program to be effective, it is essential at the outset to establish efficient procedures for evaluating employees who apply as well as for constructively informing those who are not selected.

Organizations considering implementation of job posting ought to make it clear that all jobs beneath a certain defined level must be posted when a vacancy occurs. This principle of all jobs being posted is critical to the success and integrity of any such effort and must be clearly understood at all levels in the organization. Failure to post all jobs results in a collapse of the system, because disillusioned employees will then pay little attention to it. When posted vacancies are filled by the most qualified individuals, regardless of what segment of the company they have worked in, employees feel good about job posting; it means that advancement possibilities are multiplied many times beyond those in their own work areas. However, when the policy is not firmly and consistently followed, employees will assume that most jobs go to certain favored insiders.

Circumventing the posting program is often abetted by managers who wish to promote their own staff to vacancies in their respective departments. Managers are sometimes reluctant to open the door to unknowns from other areas within the company. This is the primary reason that clear and firm policies about posting are important and that it is essential to have a strong personnel department to implement the system.

Advantages of Job Posting

Builds morale. Managed properly, a job posting system clearly supports organization efforts to promote from within. It also offers promotional opportunities to the best employees (and helps retain them), even for those working in segments of the company in which there is little turnover or growth.

Uncovers talent. Because job posting requires that all who apply must at least be considered, the system often uncovers employees who are well qualified but who might otherwise have been overlooked. It facilitates employees' career path changes.

Disadvantages of Job Posting

Demotivates. Unless employees who have applied but who are not selected are made fully aware of how they were lacking in comparison to the chosen candidate, the company will have one happy and five or six disgruntled employees on its hands.

Demanding. Job posting requires a well-staffed personnel department to effectively administer the system.

Usually, the system is not appropriate for uncovering talent qualified to fill upper-level management positions.

Summary

Five sources of job candidates are considered here: employment agencies, executive search firms, advertising, self-referrals, and job posting. College recruiting will be discussed in depth in Chapter 5.

The method that a manager uses to find candidates depends upon the nature of the job to be filled (salary grade level and special requirements of the job) and the number of candidates needed. Often a combination of several recruitment sources is appropriate.

The most cost-effective methods of finding candidates are self-referrals or referrals from current employees.

Chapter 3

Legal Risks in Recruiting and Employment Interviewing

This is an important chapter. Interviewers must be concerned with more than job qualifications, finding the right candidates, and mastering interview techniques. There are also important legal ramifications to the conduct of the interviewer's job.

Three potentially dangerous aspects of interviewing are presented in this chapter. The risks involved stem from the potential liability of lawsuits that can be costly, both from the standpoint of money and bad publicity. They are:

1. *Risks of wrongful dismissal.* Recent trends in the courts clearly demonstrate the danger of making statements during an interview that imply an employment contract. Such statements can lead to expensive litigation if it is later decided to discharge the employee.
2. *Risks of discrimination in hiring.* Violations of equal employment opportunity (EEO) regulations make the employer liable to charges of discriminating on the basis of race, color, religion, sex, age, or physical condition unrelated to the job qualifications.
3. *Risks of negligent hiring.* Failure to conduct an adequate background check on an employee may result in significant damages being assessed against a company if the employee steals or hurts others.

Wrongful Dismissal Risks

Today there is a growing tendency for courts to erode the traditional "employment-at-will" rule, and this trend is likely to become stronger in the years ahead. The employment-at-will doctrine states that every employment, except those involving specific contractual agreements such as union contracts or employment agreements, is "employment-at-will." In other words, the employer is free to terminate employment for whatever reason (or no reason) the employer sees fit. This traditional right is now being restricted by landmark court decisions. Unlike the past, employees who believe they have been unfairly treated (that is, fired) by their employers are taking their grievances to court and frequently winning.

The implications of these court decisions are quite clear: Your decision to terminate an employee may end up being second-guessed by a jury. The *Wall Street Journal* (March 1, 1988) revealed that in California the average award was in the $400,000 range; another report indicated that employees were winning in 91 percent of the cases brought! These trends suggest that there is an urgent need for employers to take corrective or preventative measures to protect themselves against "wrongful discharge" litigation.

Principles Operating in Court Decisions

First of all, it may be helpful to examine the principles that are currently operating against the employment-at-will rule. In almost every instance, they involve a question of the fairness of the discharge. Four specific concepts are most often cited:

1. *Breach of implied promise of job security, written or oral.* Any statement that alludes to job security can be interpreted by a court as a promise of job security. For example, in one case, statements that designated employees as "permanent" in contrast to those designated "probationary" were deemed to constitute a "contract" for long-term employment, one that guaranteed job security.

2. *Discharges that are contrary to public policy.* If an employer terminates an employee because that individual has taken some action that is clearly within that person's rights as a citizen, the courts have been leaning in favor of the employee. One example is the terminating of an individual because of time taken off to fulfill jury duty or to honor a lawful subpoena.

3. *Breach of implied agreement of good faith and fair dealing.* Even though there may be no written contract about what constitutes "good faith or fair dealing," courts are allowing wrongful discharge suits when it appears that the circumstances surrounding the termination were unfair.

4. *Failure to honor a promise of employment.* In one case, a employee was hired, subject to satisfactory reference checks. The plaintiff resigned from his current job, giving two weeks' notice. Meanwhile, the employer was unable to obtain satisfactory references and withdrew his offer of employment. The court ruled that the individual had resigned from his current job in good faith and turned down other opportunities, and that, in fairness, the new employer had to live up to his "promise."

Protecting Against Exceptions to the Doctrine of Employment-at-Will

There are a number of practical steps an employer can take to minimize exposure to wrongful discharge litigation. In this chapter, attention will be focused on the courses of action that can be taken during the recruitment and job interview processes.

Recruitment   Examine all recruiting advertisements and literature for statements that could be construed even remotely as a promise or contract of employment. As an example of the dangers involved, consider the following example. One company whose employees were on strike placed advertisements in a local newspaper soliciting applicants for employment as "permanent replacements." After these individuals were hired, the strike was settled. To enable the strikers to return to their jobs, the company terminated the replacements. The Supreme

Court held that the strike replacements had a valid cause of action against their former employer.

Each organization should carefully review its company recruiting literature, brochures, and advertisements to be certain that they do not contain any words that could be construed to imply a fixed duration of employment. Employee handbooks, for example, often contain statements about "our company family" and related statements about job security or lack of lay-offs within the company.

An area of particular concern is the *employment application blank*. Words implying that the company terminates employees only for specific reasons could be used against the company. In one case, words on the application blank stated that the employment was subject to the employer's "handbook on personnel policies and procedures." Eight years later, that wording on the application form helped the employee to win his case against the company; the handbook indicated that terminations were made only on the basis of "just cause."

One way to ensure written documentation of the employer's intention to maintain employment-at-will rights is to include, on the application blank, a phrase that explicitly states this posture. Here is an example of such a statement:

> In signing this employment application, I understand that this document, as well as other company documents, are not contracts of employment. I acknowledge that I may voluntarily leave the company upon proper notice, and that the company has the right to terminate my employment, at any time, for any reason. I also understand that any oral or written statements made to the contrary are expressly disavowed.

While such a paragraph offers some protection, a lawyer acquaintance warns that under certain circumstances the signed statement might be judged invalid. It is possible that a court would view the employee's acceptance of the terms of employment as an "adhesion contract," that is, one in which both parties did not have reasonably equal bargaining power.

The safest course of action is to explicitly state in handbooks and elsewhere that "there are no contracts" and/or to make some reference to the company's and the employee's right to terminate at will. The downside of such explicit statements, of course, is the danger that they will have a negative impact on employee morale. Unions might also use them as a rallying point in organizing nonunion employees. Each company will have to weigh such risks versus the obvious need for protection against suits for wrongful discharge.

Job Interviewing   Interviewers must be careful to conduct their employment interviews without implying that prospective employees have any contractual rights. It is quite easy, during employment interviews, to slip up and make statements that could imply promises of employment or longevity of employment. This is especially likely when interviewers are attempting to recruit hard-to-find candidates. Interviewer's will have to guard against making such statements as:

"You'll be with us as long as you can do your job."
"You will not be terminated without 'just cause.'"
"If you are 'doing the job,' you will not be fired."
"This is a company in which you can 'stay and grow.'"

Concerning the last example given, the Federal Court for the Eastern District of Pennsylvania ruled that a "stay and grow" comment constituted an oral employment contract. In this case, a copywriter was hired and moved to a city some distance from her home. Six months later she was fired. She claimed that she had relied on the interviewer's statement and given up certain opportunities in the area where she had lived before taking the job.

All individuals involved in the organization's hiring process ought to be appraised that their oral statements may constitute enforceable contracts of employment. A list of "do's" and "don'ts" circulated to all interviewers represents a good first step in training on this issue. An example of such a handout is provided in Appendix F.

Discrimination Risks

What constitutes fair employment practices is an important subject for interviewers because about 70 percent of the discrimination complaints arising out of compliance legislation have occurred as a result of the interviewing process. For this reason, interviewers need to be clear about the requirements of equal employment opportunity regulations. Let's first look at who is affected by the EEO regulations and then examine ways of proceeding when interviewing these protected groups of job candidates.

Groups affected by EEO regulations include:

■ Women
■ Vietnam-era veterans (separated after August 5, 1964)
■ Forty- to sixty-five-year-olds
■ Minorities (blacks, Asians, American Indians, or Spanish-surnamed Americans)
■ The handicapped

The EEO Regulations

The interviewer should understand that no question, per se, is really illegal. The problem in interviewing is that asking certain questions could make the interviewer vulnerable to the charge of discrimination. If the interviewer inquires about age, for example, and subsequently a fifty-five-year-old male applicant does not receive a job offer, the candidate could claim that the interviewer had failed to hire him because of his age. It would then be incumbent upon the interviewer to prove that age was not a factor in making the no-hire decision.

Basically, federal laws state that decisions about employment cannot be made on the basis of sex, race, color, age, religion, national origin, or handicap. There are, of course, exceptions to these rules in situations where bona fide occupational qualifications (BFOQ) are called for. If you were hiring a fashion model, for example, you could set age and sex requirements and reject those not meeting your criteria.

It should also be noted that unintentional discrimination is just as illegal as intentional discrimination. It is no protection in a suit against your company to say that you "didn't know" that the information you solicited was discriminatory. The burden of proof of innocence is the one doing the hiring. Even apparently innocent questions, asked in good faith, can leave the company open to costly and time-consuming litigation.

It should be recognized, too, that each state has its own laws on discrimination, so organizations should obtain copies of these regulations from their state Human Rights Commission.

Volunteered Information Sometimes, without prompting from the interviewer, applicants volunteer information that could provide the basis for a charge of discrimination in hiring. A woman applicant, for example, may reveal that she is planning to be married next month. In such a case, the interviewer should refrain from asking anything about her plans for a family or relocation plans and, instead, stop the applicant from volunteering additional information on the topic. The interviewer at this point can say, "I would appreciate your not saying anything further about your marriage status. It is our policy to hire only on the basis of your ability to do the job. We really don't need to know this information to judge your qualifications, so while I thank you for your openness, let's go on now to another topic."

Once illegal information is "out on the table" and you have attempted to stop the flow of such information, it would be wise to indicate in your notes that the candidate volunteered data about some particular point but was asked to refrain from further discussion on the topic. The specific information should be kept with your records and not forwarded to the next interviewers.

Interviewers should recognize that attempts to be nondiscriminatory will not be lost on applicants. Most will appreciate your effort to comply with the law. In fact, your statements could have a positive impact in making the company attractive to candidates.

What You Can and Cannot Ask

Many seemingly appropriate questions can get an interviewer in trouble with the EEOC. Major areas to be alert to, along with specific questions that should be avoided, are given below.

Sex   You cannot use sex as a basis for hiring, unless sex is a bona fide occupational requirement. Few companies have such jobs. Here are some often-used sex-based reasons for not hiring a candidate—all of which could be the basis for a claim against the company of discriminatory hiring practices:

1. The job was traditionally restricted to members of the opposite sex.
2. The job involved travel or travel with members of the opposite sex.
3. The assumption that, because some members of one sex are unable or unwilling to do the job, other candidates of that sex are inappropriate choices. Examples are assuming that a woman candidate is not suitable for a job as a miner or firefighter, or that a male candidate is not appropriate for a secretarial position.
4. The job involves heavy physical labor, unpleasant work surroundings, overtime, isolated working conditions, or late hours.
5. Preferences of customers, clients, co-workers, or employers.
6. Stereotyped characterizations of the sexes, for example, that men are less capable of assembling intricate equipment, or that women are less capable of aggressive selling. The principle of nondiscrimination requires that individuals be considered on the basis of individual capabilities, not on the basis of any characteristics generally attributed to the group.
7. Unavailability of physical facilities, such as rest rooms for both sexes.

Because the potential for engaging in discriminatory practices against women is so great, the focus here is on topics to avoid when interviewing women candidates. These are:

- Marital plans or status
- Plans for raising a family
- Number and/or ages of dependents
- Babysitting arrangements
- Occupation of husband
- Training or experience not expected of a male in a similar job, for example, typing ability for a chemist's job
- Husband's reaction to travel away from home

A more comprehensive view of the possibilities for even inadvertent discrimination can be gleaned from the items listed in Figure 1. This is a brochure put out by the National Organization for Women (NOW). The reader should particularly note its last sentence.

Race or Color   Race is such an obvious area in which discrimination must be avoided that the subject will not be belabored here. The law states that you cannot discriminate against blacks, Hispanics, Asians, Pacific Islanders, American Indians, or Alaskan natives. Don't ask questions with racial implications, for example, "Did you ever receive public assistance?"

Age   Age discrimination legislation protects people who are between forty and sixty-five. Any questions, therefore, that could easily lead to a determination of age should be avoided. For instance, do not ask, "How old were you at the time of graduation?" It is the more subtle questions, those that imply concern about age, however, that could provide the basis for a suit. Don't ask about:

- Ability to "keep pace." For example, avoid such questions as, "Do you think you can keep up with the hectic atmosphere here?"

Figure 1. NOW brochure identifying sex discrimination.

Have You Met With Sex Discrimination?

While Looking for a Job

Was the job advertised under a Help-Wanted column titled "male" or "female"?

Did the ad state or imply that a member of one sex was wanted for the position?

Were there different application forms for men and for women?

Did the employment agency/personnel office refer you to stereotyped "female" jobs if you were not seeking that type of Job?

If a test was administered, was it related to the type of position you were seeking?

During a Job Interview

Did the interviewer ask you questions that would not ordinarily be asked of a man seeking a similar job?

Did the interviewer inquire about your children, marital status, marriage plans, plans to have children, birth control practices?

Did the interviewer state or imply any stereotyped myths about women employees, such as "they never stick with a job," "they are too emotional," "they can't get along with the men in a business-like fashion"?

When Negotiating a Position

Did the employer offer you a lower salary than was advertised?

Are other positions still unfilled more commensurate with your education and experience?

Has the position been "downgraded" since the initial interview through changes in the number of employees to be supervised, changes in the person to whom you would report?

(continued)

(Figure 1 continued)

Did They Fail to Hire You

Because the job involved travel, or travel with members of the opposite sex?

Because of unusual working hours, lack of rest room facilities, or weight lifting requirements?

Because you are pregnant, have small children?

Because the job has always been held by a man, or because the other employees indicated they would not work for a woman or with a woman?

Because a man applied who was almost as qualified?

In Your Present Job

Are there different seniority lines for men and women?

Do you receive less pay than a man doing a similar job?

Are raise and promotion policies different for men and women?

Are training programs, educational leaves restricted to men?

Are fringe benefits different for men and women—different pension plans, life insurance plans, health insurance plans, dates of optional or mandatory retirement?

Are the employee rules and regulations different for men and women?

Are there general patterns of discrimination in your place of employment, such as all-female departments, all women in certain types of jobs, no women in others?

Are disabilities caused or contributed to by pregnancy, miscarriage, or abortion exempted from disability benefits?

Are benefits conditioned on whether or not the employee is the "head of household" or "principal wage earner"?

IF YOU ANSWERED YES TO ANY OF THE ABOVE QUESTIONS, THEN YOU HAVE A BONA FIDE COMPLAINT AND MAY FILE A CHARGE AGAINST THE EMPLOYER.

- Age-related relationship. For instance, avoid asking "How do you feel about working for a person younger than you?" Or, "How do you think you'll get along with the younger people here?"

Religion It is illegal to discriminate on the basis of religion. Any questions, therefore, that inquire about religion or religious practices should be avoided. Examples of questions to steer clear of are:

- Do you attend church or synagogue regularly?
- Do you miss work in order to attend services on religious holidays?
- Are you active in any church groups?

National Origin It is discriminatory to ask about an applicant's lineage, ancestry, national origin, descent, parentage, or nationality. Any questions from which national origin can be deduced are inappropriate.

Do not ask for the applicant's birth certificate, baptismal record, or naturalization papers. You can ask for proof of age if there is concern that the applicant is a minor or over 65. Unless needed, avoid asking the maiden name of a married woman applicant. Here are examples of types of questions to be avoided:

- Inquiry into how an applicant acquired the ability to read, write, or speak a foreign language
- Inquiry into the nationality of an applicant's parents or spouse
- Inquiry into the clubs, societies, or lodges to which the applicant belongs
- Inquiry about the name and address of the nearest relative to be notified in case of accident or emergency (Interviewers can ask the name of a person to be notified, but should not specify a relative.)

You can ask:

- What languages the applicant writes or speaks fluently
- Whether the applicant is a citizen of the United States
- Whether the applicant is on a visa that will not permit work in the United States

Handicaps   The Rehabilitation Act of 1973 states that discrimination against handicapped applicants on the basis of nonjob-related criteria is illegal. In effect, you cannot discriminate against a "qualified handicapped" individual, that is, an individual capable of performing a particular job with reasonable accommodation to the handicap at the minimum acceptable level of productivity applicable to a nonhandicapped incumbent. Moreover, this same act requires that government contractors, subcontractors, and agencies take affirmative action in the employment of qualified handicapped persons. Thus, contractors must make an effort to ensure that handicapped persons know about the open positions. Interviewers may find it helpful to obtain a list of national organizations serving the handicapped. They can be found in the *Directory of Organizations Interested in the Handicapped,* published by the People to People Committee on the Handicapped, 1146 Sixteenth Street, N.W., Washington, D.C. 20036.

Interviewers should avoid asking questions about the handicapped candidate's height, weight, previous illnesses, or physical ability to handle the job. On the other hand, they are permitted to describe the nature of the job tasks to be accomplished, and then to ask if the applicant believes he is capable of performing those tasks.

A helpful summary of key points is shown in Figure 2.

Retention of Interview Notes   The interviewer's primary defense against claims of discrimination are the interview notes he has kept. This is another good reason to take careful notes during the interview. The various acts and laws concerning discrimination in hiring specify the duration of time that records must be kept. For example, the Age Discrimination in Employ-

Figure 2. Summary of interview guidelines.

Legal Guidelines
(All applicants)

In accordance with the latest EEOC legal requirements, organizations should consider revising their application forms so as to eliminate the following items:

- Race
- Age (date of birth)
- Names and number of dependents
- Name and/or address of any relatives
- Job title and occupation of spouse
- Height
- Sex
- Marital status
- Weight

In addition to these, it is illegal to discriminate against applicants because of physical handicap or liability to military service. Questions in these categories should not be asked either on the application form or during the interview.

Following are some examples of both discriminatory and acceptable inquiries:

Birthplace and Residence

It is potentially discriminatory to ask for:

It is acceptable to ask:

- Birthplace of applicant
- Birthplace of applicant's parents
- Birth certificate, naturalization papers, or baptismal record

- Applicant's place of residence

Creed and Religion

It is potentially discriminatory to ask:

- Applicant's religious affiliation
- Applicant's church or synogogue or the religious holidays observed

---

(continued)

(Figure 2 continued)

Race or Color

It is potentially discriminatory to ask:

• Applicant's race

Age

It is potentially discriminatory to ask:

• Applicant's date of birth or age except when such information is needed to:

—Maintain apprenticeship requirements based upon a reasonable minimum age

—Satisfy the provision of either state or federal minimum age statutes

—Avoid interference with the operation of the terms and conditions and administration of any bona fide retirement, pension, or employee benefit program

—Satisfy insurance requirements

Citizenship

It is potentially discriminatory to ask:

• Whether the applicant is now or intends to become a citizen of the United States

It is acceptable to ask:

• Whether the applicant is in the United States on a visa that would not permit work here

National Origin and Ancestry

It is potentially discriminatory to ask:

• Applicant's lineage, ancestry, national origin, descent, parentage, or nationality

• Nationality of applicant's parents or spouse

Language

It is potentially discriminatory to ask:

It is acceptable to ask:

• Applicant's mother tongue

• Language commonly used by applicant at home

• How applicant acquired ability to read, write, or speak a foreign language

• Language applicant speaks and/or writes fluently

Relatives

It is potentially discriminatory to ask:

It is acceptable to ask:

• Name and/or address of any relative of applicant

• Names of relatives already employed by the company

• Name and address of person to be notified in case of accident or emergency

Legal Guidelines
(women applicants)

EEOC and the courts have declared that women must not be considered on the basis of any assumed characteristics generally attributed to females, nor may job opportunities be denied women on the basis of the physical requirements of a job, such as heavy labor or late hours.

Women applicants should not be asked questions about the following:

• Plans for raising a family
• Type of birth control used in family
• Number and ages of dependents
• Babysitting arrangements
• Occupation of husband
• Training or experience not expected of a male in a similar job, for example, typing ability for a chemist

ment Act of 1967 requires that employers keep records for one year on applications, test papers, physical examinations, and advertisements. Even for temporary jobs, applications must be kept for ninety days. The notes developed by the Hypothesis Method (an interview procedure described in Chapter 11) represent an ideal form of documentation.

Applications and employment data for apprenticeship programs must be kept for two years or the period of the successful applicant's apprenticeship.

How the Law Works

The agencies that enforce antidiscrimination laws are empowered to initiate investigations of companies' employment practices. However, most often they respond to specific employee complaints of discrimination. When an investigation reveals that discrimination may have occurred, the agency will attempt to work out a voluntary solution with the employer. If these efforts fail, public hearings may be required.

If a hearing reveals that discrimination has in fact occurred, the company involved may be required to provide redress to the aggrieved party or parties. Redress may take the form of rehiring, back pay, early promotion, or whatever is relevant to the case.

In some cases, enforcement agencies may impose special rules for remedial action when companies are found to be lagging in their antidiscrimination efforts. In cases under the Executive Orders, a company may lose its government contract.

The Hypothesis Method Can Keep You "Legal"

The Hypothesis Method (Chapter 11) is designed to help the interviewer to understand how the applicant behaves and functions and to predict job behavior from past achievements. Because the goal of almost all employment assessments is to determine whether the individual can carry out the tasks and behaviors needed to successfully perform the job in question, historical data (except for knowledge and experience) in and of themselves are of no particular significance. The past is relevant only in the sense that it provides a means of predicting the future.

This point can be illustrated by examining a classroom discussion. Imagine an interview demonstration in front of a class. Suppose that the demonstration includes an interview of a fifty-year-old man and that the life area being explored is "years before high school." During the interview, the class is asked to write down hypotheses that emerge. Once the demonstration is over, hypotheses are solicited from class members and are written on the blackboard. Now the "applicant" is asked the extent to which these hypotheses describe him *today*. Almost invariably, the applicant will indicate that about "80 percent describe me." If I ask those in the class who personally know the applicant if the recorded hypotheses are correct, they almost always say that the hypotheses correspond exactly to how the person really behaves.

Notice what has happened here. The applicant is talking about episodes in his life that took place thirty to forty years before the time of the interview, and yet the candidate, as well as those in the class who know him, indicate that the generated hypotheses describe the person *today*. How is that possible? One explanation, of course, is that many behavior patterns are set early in life and don't change much. But another more significant reason for this phenomenon is that the person is interpreting past events through current perceptions. When the applicant is asked, for example, what he has learned from an early school experience, he is not answering this as a ten-year-old child but from the viewpoint of an adult today. In other words, the factual background that is being explored is the remote past; the hypotheses that develop from that past (in response to the self-appraisal question) explain how the individual functions right now.

It is not necessary, therefore, to explore an applicant's personal life or probe areas that are illegal to learn what a person is like and how that person functions. What interviewers are really trying to learn from the interview is whether the person thinks, deals with people, is motivated, or is knowledgeable in ways that will enable him to perform the job in question.

A person's history is simply an admission card to the interview. If the candidate's educational background or work history were not reasonably appropriate, the odds are small that the applicant would be in the interview situation. Once the applicant passes that initial screening and is deemed qualified by virtue of knowledge and experience, it is less important to elicit new facts than it is to understand *how* and *why* the facts already presented came about. Self-appraisal questions and observations during discussion of legitimate topics allow the interviewer to describe how the person currently functions and performs. This should be the real test as to whether or not an applicant is suitable for the job. There is no reason for interviewers to feel handicapped in assessing candidates because of current laws and regulations about hiring practices.

Negligent Hiring Risks

It used to be that if an employee committed a harmful act within the scope of his job duties, his employer could be held liable for the negligence or wrongs. This liability stems from the long-standing legal doctrine of "respondent superior." An example of this kind of liability is when relatives of a plane crash victim sue the airline once it has been determined that the crash was caused by "pilot error."

Under today's negligent hiring theory, however, *an employer may be liable for an employee's behavior even when the employee is acting outside the scope of his job and even when the employee is acting outside the normal hours of employment.* Recent court cases have held employers liable for the negligent hiring or retention of employees who engage in criminal or violent acts. In these instances, the employers have had to pay substantial monetary damages. Some cases that have been settled before the courts involve situations in which an employee raped, killed, assaulted, stole, or committed fraud. Here is a typical example:

A manufacturer of gold sunglass frames recovered more than $300,000 from a security firm. In this case, a guard for the security firm who worked at the manufacturer's was involved in thefts of gold used to make the frames. The security firm was found liable for negligent hiring because it did not contact the character references listed by the employee and did not specifically make inquiry of former employers concerning the employee's honesty and trustworthiness.

A legal writer explains the thinking behind this case:

> In upholding the jury verdict, the court stated that when an employee is being hired for a sensitive occupation, mere lack of negative evidence may not be sufficient to discharge the employer's obligation of reasonable care The court also stated that an employer's duty to guard against negligent hiring does not terminate once an applicant is selected for hire. Rather, the court said, an employer has a continuing duty to retain in its service only those employees who are fit and competent.*

The concepts involved here are quite straightforward. Whether or not an employer is liable for damages under the theory of negligent hiring depends on the reasonableness of the effort made to check into the employee's background considering (1) the nature of the job for which the person was hired, and (2) the risk of harm to third parties—co-workers or customers.

Taking Steps to Avoid Liability for Negligent Hiring

With due caution and forethought, you can minimize liability by taking certain steps:

1. *Don't hire applicants with criminal records.* One way to minimize liability risk is to screen out anyone with a criminal back-

*Ronald M. Green, "Negligent Hiring: An Emerging Theory of Employer Liability for Employee Misconduct," Epstein Becker & Green, Ninth Annual Client Briefing Conference, New York, 1987.

ground. Whether this is legal or not, however, depends upon the state in which the employer is located. Many states as well as recent amendments to the Civil Rights Act of 1964—Title VII encourage hiring of such individuals. In New York State, for example, it is unlawful to deny employment to someone who has been convicted, even several times, unless it can be demonstrated that there is a direct relationship between the conviction and the job and that an unreasonable risk would be incurred. For example, if an applicant had been convicted of bank robbery and later applied for a position as bank guard, an employer who rejected his application would not be judged to be in violation of the law. Because states vary in these regulations, employers will have to determine how the law applies in their respective locations.

It must be of particular concern to employers if the convicted person is also a member of classes protected by Title VII of the Civil Rights Act of 1964. If the employer chooses not to hire, or terminates, someone with a conviction record, then it is incumbent upon the employer to show that the decision was made only after consideration of three factors: (1) the nature and gravity of the offense; (2) the amount of time that had elapsed since the conviction; and (3) the nature of the job.

So, the "bottom line" on hiring persons who have been convicted is that good judgment must be used; no categorical employment policy is justifiable. The three factors cited make good sense in most instances. There is no point in putting customers or fellow employees in jeopardy, but, on the other hand, there is a need to reintegrate convicted persons into society so that they can play a productive role. In short, there are both moral and legal issues at stake here.

2. *Check out all references and past employers.* Although it is difficult to get more than "name, rank, and serial number" on most reference checks, for the purpose of avoiding liability it is nevertheless important to demonstrate that a "reasonable effort" was made to learn about the applicant's past. In cases in which large sums have been awarded to plaintiffs, the decision has often turned on the employer being found "negligent" in checking out background information for sensitive jobs.

3. *Consider employing an investigation firm.* In view of the negligent hiring awards, a number of investigative firms now offer services that include interviewing former employers and checking out criminal records, credit files, and educational credentials.

4. *Purchase credit information.* In every major city, credit bureaus, for a fee, will sell information about an individual's bank accounts, bankruptcies, tax liens, and other financial factors.

5. *When interviewing, make sure that all time is accounted for.* Working through a person's background in chronological order can make this effort easier. If you are the least bit uncertain about the chain of events or if time gaps are evident, don't be afraid to probe. Questions such as "Are you saying that *immediately* after you left the Jones Company you went to New York?" are necessary and quite in order.

6. *Inquire directly about the likelihood of recidivism.* As interviewer, you might as well deal directly with the issue. Here's an example:

> "Billy, you have twice been convicted of assault. You have hurt people. What can you say to convince me that it won't happen again—that it won't happen when you run into someone who gives you a hard time?"

Listen carefully to the response and challenge the answer. Most important of all, *make careful notes* about what the applicant says. This action will demonstrate that something more than reasonable care has been taken to hire or keep in employment those who are likely to cause harm to others.

Inquiring About a Person's Possible Criminal Record

For most businesses, there appears to be no need to look into the possible criminal record of every applicant or employee. The courts, thus far, have taken the position that even if the employee has to deal with the public, all the employer must do is to conduct a good interview and make adequate inquiry into the employee's capability and fitness for the job. Assuming that the checking was adequate and that no evidence was uncovered to suggest possible future difficulty, the risk of liability claims is fairly minimal. However, if the applicant indicates on the application blank or mentions in the interview a criminal conviction, or if there are gaps in the employment history, it would be most prudent at this point to delve further into the candidate's record.

A Word of Caution

Information provided in this chapter should help the interviewer gain an understanding of the current rules and regulations governing employment practices. However, the field is in flux. New court decisions add new interpretations to the law, and the law is frequently changed, particularly at the state level. Therefore, while this book can assist you in avoiding major discriminatory practices, it is advisable that you consult your company's legal staff to keep you current on the new laws and court interpretations of them. Questions can also be directed to the local department of labor or civil rights commission.

Summary

This chapter has described three significant aspects of the interview/hiring process that pose risks of legal action being taken against the employer. One risk has to do with current judicial trends that have led to an erosion of the traditional employment-at-will concept. To avoid litigation, organizations ought to review carefully all printed literature such as company handbooks, application blanks, and recruitment advertising for statements that could imply, even remotely, a contract of employment.

To help retain the rights of employment-at-will, company interviewers should also take care to avoid any oral statements that could imply conditions of termination or job longevity.

Promises, or even hints, of "job security" have resulted in judgments against employers.

Employers also face legal risks when they knowingly or unknowingly act in violation of EEO regulations forbidding discrimination. Questions that inquire about race, sex, age, marital status, religion, national origin, and physical handicaps, although not illegal per se, could provide the grounds for a legal action claiming discrimination.

The Hypothesis Method is a technique that can help the interviewer understand how the applicant functions *now*, today. It is this information, rather than data that are risky to inquire about, that should be the basis of the hiring decision. Interviewers need not delve into illegal areas to make an effective assessment of a candidate's qualifications.

Interviewers are cautioned to check with local human rights commissions, because laws are changing and also vary from state to state.

The risk of negligent hiring refers to the danger of being sued if an employee commits a hurtful act such as assault, robbery, or fraud. Large awards have been granted in cases in which the court ruled that the employer did not take adequate measures to check the background of an employee who had dealings with customers and/or the public. Five investigative measures are suggested for minimizing these risks.

Employers must also check state and federal regulations concerning the legality of denying employment to persons with prior convictions.

Chapter 4

A College Recruiting Game Plan

This chapter provides a detailed outline and guide for establishing and conducting an effective college recruiting effort. It is based on my personal experiences and those of countless client organizations. Despite the costs, college recruiting represents a major source of talent for many organizations, especially those that are expanding or in need of a constant source of new professional or managerial talent.

Successful college recruiting depends upon careful preparation before the campus interview and astute management of the follow-up. This means that responsibility and authority must be clearly defined to achieve maximum results from the recruiting effort. A step-by-step game plan, including timing and accountability, follows.

The Recruiting Manager's Responsibility

Whenever the company will be recruiting at more than a few campuses, it is essential that someone be responsible for the planning, organization, and coordination of the recruiting effort. At least ten crucial steps have to be managed. This responsibility should be assigned to a recruiting manager, who must be at a level in the organization that allows for control of a substantial budget and permits identification and selection of other company persons to be involved in the recruiting effort.

In the broadest sense, the recruiting manager is responsible for the following:

- Development of strong working relationships with campuses at which the company recruits.
- Determination of personnel needs for recent college graduates or graduate-level students and the best ways to obtain them.
- Development of an organization to carry out the recruiting function. This structure most often will include a steering committee and a group of executives, referred to as visit coordinators, responsible for specific recruiting activities at each school.

The Steering Committee

The steering committee should be composed of management representatives from the major operating units of the organization. Their primary responsibility is to determine the number and type of individuals, companywide, that must be obtained from college sources. In addition, they often determine the salary ranges to be offered, concern themselves with fulfilling equal employment opportunity objectives, select the target schools for recruiting, and evaluate the accomplishments of the recruiting effort. In some organizations the steering committee also organizes the structure of the jobs in which the recruits will be placed initially as well as the design of development activities for the new college hires.

Visit Coordinators

Visit coordinators are responsible for relations with the college and for the recruiting effort at a specific school. For the recruiting aspect of their job, they report directly to a member of the steering committee or to the recruiting manager. Visit coordinators should be selected on the basis of their ability to cultivate faculty and students; often they are graduates of the school in question. These coordinators should be willing to devote at least two or three years to cultivating the school and its related organizations. Success in recruiting is not likely from a series of one-shot efforts. It requires a consistent, continuous effort that leads to a personal relationship between college placement officials, faculty, and the company's representatives.

Prerecruiting Preparations

Some factors to be considered in making the initial list of target schools are as follows:

1. Relevance of the course curricula to company needs. For example, not all engineering schools are equally capable of developing good chemical engineers; some specialize more in electrical or mechanical engineering. Of pertinent concern is the number of graduates turned out each year in the company's area of interest.
2. Closeness of the college to the hiring location(s). The majority of college students attend schools within a 500-mile radius of their homes. The same reason that the student selected the college—preference for that geographic area and proximity of family or friends—may also be instrumental in the choice of employment location.
3. Extent to which the faculty and others on campus think well of the company. What are the attitudes about your organization on campus? Faculty and administrators are affected by news events, and sociological trends, just as students are. For example, if one of the company's plants has recently been cited for an environmental violation such as water pollution, the faculty and students in that locality may have spoken out in negative terms about your organization. Recruiting visits to that campus might be an excellent beginning toward changing a negative image, but attitudes on campus sometimes determine what campuses to visit.

Obviously, once an organization has had recruiting experience at a particular school, the productiveness of those recruiting efforts should be a major factor in the decision to continue or not to continue recruiting on that campus.

The Key Elements in Planning

The following time frames are recommended for pre-recruitment planning elements.

Selection of schools. Unless manpower needs dictate an extremely wide coverage of campuses, companies should carefully evaluate the schools to be visited and target only those that are likely to be highly productive. This evaluation ought to be ongoing and revised from year to year, predicated on organization needs and experiences with the school.

Scheduling campus interview dates. Scheduling should be completed approximately twelve months before the actual visit. Many companies schedule the following year's visit dates while on campus for the current year's recruiting. Organizations seeking the most desired recruiting date, late fall or January– February may be relegated to late spring on the more popular campuses unless dates are confirmed well in advance.

Forecasting requirements. Approximately six months before the visits begin and recruiting plans are established, manpower needs should be determined. In smaller organizations, this is not often much of a problem, but in large companies, the task is complex, involving correlation of needs with budget constraints and long-range corporate plans. Care should be taken, too, that personnel needs are not automatically allocated to college recruiting when in-house personnel (for instance, current employees who are completing evening undergraduate or graduate degree programs) might well meet some of the requirements.

A final review of personnel requirements should be made six months later. Manpower needs determined in the spring or early June have a way of changing by September. Therefore, at the outset of the recruiting cycle in September, the requirements for college-recruited personnel should be reviewed and the original recruiting objectives adjusted accordingly.

Development of recruiting materials. Three months before the first scheduled visit is about when the drafts of recruiting materials should be ready. These include brochures describing the company and its operations, interview report formats for campus interviewers, formats of job offer and rejection letters, and an information packet for recruiters. This packet should contain organization charts, showing traditional lines of advancement in major areas of the company's operations; data about starting salaries and reasonable expectations for new employees after six months or a year of employment; and an outline of the specifics of the various benefits the company offers, such as health plans, insurance policies, and vacation policies.

Development of plans for each campus. Two to four months in advance of the fall or spring recruiting dates, prerecruiting efforts should be planned and initiated. One aspect of this plan includes the determination of who will visit each campus. A number of different strategies have been found effective. Consider sending to the campus an employee who is a recent graduate of that college. Such a person might have much credibility with the students and could relate in a meaningful way his satisfaction with the company and its opportunities. A recent graduate may also know faculty members and thus be in a position to establish or reinforce a positive image of the company. A risk is that relatively new employees may not be sufficiently knowledgeable about operations in the company other than their own, but this shortcoming can be corrected rather easily.

Another approach that has been quite effective on some campuses is to send as a recruiter someone who is competent and experienced, or who has progressed rapidly in the organization. This approach is especially suitable when recruiting candidates for high-technology areas. Such an interviewer is readily able to answer technical questions that may arise. Moreover, such a person may be a successful salesman for the company through an ability to excite or challenge students by describing the technological problems in which they may become involved by joining the company.

Another effective way to recruit is to send a team of two or more persons. In this way, it is possible to combine the advantages of a young recent graduate with the knowledge and experience of a longer-term employee. Another excellent combination is a line manager paired with an experienced or professional interviewer, such as someone from the company's personnel department. This approach is discussed in more detail in Chapter 5.

Many organizations send professional interviewers to conduct the campus interview. These individuals are usually more effective than amateurs in screening candidates and, possibly because of their interview experience and human relations skills, are able to sell the company quite well. If many campuses are to be visited, however, this approach is not always practical.

If sufficient manpower is available, a team of three or more can be effective on campus. It is not recommended that three or more be present for the actual interview, but activities of the larger team, both before and after the interview schedule, have been productive for many companies. Some of these activities are described in the following paragraphs.

A key element in developing a recruiting plan for each campus is the character of the overall relationship with the college. The single most important factor in successful college recruiting is the care devoted to developing a year-round college relations program. It must be recognized that attitudes toward the recruiting organization make or break recruiting efforts for that company on the campus. One negative comment about an organization from a respected professor can easily result in none of the better students signing up. Positive attitudes, on the other hand, can do wonders in increasing the number of top applicants that sign up for interviews. Following are some approaches that companies have used on an ongoing basis to stimulate positive interest in the company.

- Advertising throughout the year in the college newspaper
- Visits to faculty members during the year, informing them of new industry developments and sharing with

them new technological publications and copies of books by company staff members or alumni
- Company offers of financial assistance to needy students
- Contributions to endowment funds
- Offering faculty members employment during the summer months
- Inviting faculty members to new plants or research centers for a firsthand look
- Making obsolete technical or office equipment available to the university

For a college relations program to be effective, the kinds of activities listed here cannot be sporadic; plans should be drawn so that these efforts remain reasonably frequent and ongoing. This means that someone must be held responsible for the relations program on selected campuses. It is not surprising that companies that seem to get the cream of the crop usually have established excellent relationships with the faculty. Such companies typically designate someone to serve as college coordinator, and this individual initiates, coordinates, and directs all company contacts with the college.

Another aspect of the recruiting plan for each campus is the effort made to ensure that the most capable candidates sign up for the recruiting interviews. Such steps are geared to educating the students and faculty about the company and to creating interest in the opportunities the organization offers. Several weeks before the scheduled recruiting visit, a company may sponsor an open house, during which representatives give a presentation about the organization and industry and conduct an open question-and-answer period. The open house may feature coffee and doughnuts or an elaborate cocktail party. Some attraction is usually needed to induce students to turn out in large numbers. Such a social meeting provides an opportunity to promote the company in ways that are impractical during the regular interview procedure. Movies or slides can be shown, and faculty members should also be invited.

Another prerecruiting effort is to send letters or make phone calls to promising members of the graduating class, in-

Figure 3. Sample letter inviting candidates to sign-on schedules.

Dear_____:

We have had an opportunity to review a résumé of your background and interests. Congratulations on your fine record.

Your interests seem to match with the opportunities available here at [name of company]. This year, as in the past, we are looking for a number of outstanding individuals to join our company. We believe you might have those excellent characteristics we seek. I am enclosing a copy of our literature, which describes our company and the career opportunities it offers.

We would like to invite you to our interview session scheduled for [date]at the [location]Placement Office. Your Placement Office will be able to supply you with additional details regarding our visit.

I look forward to seeing you at that time and extend my best wishes for a successful final semester.

Cordially yours,

viting them to sign up for an interview. Similarly, letters may be directed to faculty members, telling them of the visit and of any specific or unusual opportunities the company may be offering. An example of such a letter (for students) is shown in Figure 3.

Training Recruiters

An essential ingredient in any successful college recruiting effort is the ability of the interviewers not only to assess the best prospects but also to interest them in further contacts with the company through second interviews or meetings. It is folly to send to the campus managers who are not adequately prepared. Most organizations devote a full day or two days to this training, which should be scheduled a few weeks before the visits are to commence. Here are some topics that should be covered:

- Overall scope of the recruiting effort (manpower needs for the organization)
- Procedures for reporting interview appraisals, invitations to second interviews, and offering letters
- Equal employment opportunity policies and company's compliance instructions
- Techniques for conducting the interview, along with ample opportunity to practice in class the techniques being taught
- Corporate promotional material that has already been distributed to campuses as well as that available for use during the visit
- Data about the progress and career paths of typical young graduates hired during the past two or three years (Unless the recruiter is interviewing for only one or two job categories, it is helpful to have these profiles for a wide range of job entry points in the company.)
- A list of typical questions asked by students along with suggested interviewer responses
- Key facts about the company
- A "walk through" of the annual report or other company literature, indicating highlights and/or areas that are likely to be questioned
- Salary schedules and information on when and how deviations can be made from agreed-upon offered rates
- Review of all company benefits, particularly those of interest to young employees such as tuition refunds and compensation incentives

During the training of campus interviewers, it is helpful to give them an opportunity to try out their interview procedures through role playing or practice classroom interviews. Use of videotapes or, at the least, audio cassette tapes for feedback on the interview can be most helpful. Interviewers need to learn how to structure the twenty-five or so minutes of time available to them for the on-campus interview. The day the interviewers arrive on campus is not time to start this practice.

The Recruitment Interviews

Most of the campus interviews will be scheduled in October and November and again in January and February. With many colleges now revising their academic calendars to permit completion of the first semester by Christmas, December is fast replacing January as an important recruiting month.

The recruiting manager should be certain that dates are firm and that those persons scheduled to make the campus visit will be there at the time assigned to them. It is bad public relations when company representatives do not show up for a scheduled interview day, unless ample notice has been given to the college placement office. For this reason, most organizations involved in college recruiting have a reserve of trained backup interviewers who can be called upon at the last minute to make the visit. Techniques for conducting the campus interview are described in Chapters 5 and 6.

Secondary Interviews at the Company

The secondary interview is the one in which the hire/not-hire decision is made, and the Evaluation Model is employed at that time.

Within two weeks of the campus interview, a letter should be sent to all students interviewed containing either an invitation to the secondary interview or a turndown. Sample letters for this step in the recruiting process are shown in Figure 4. The period between the campus interview and the secondary interview is critical. In fact, most recruiting efforts rise or fall on how the company manages the period of time before and after the secondary interview. It is crucial, therefore, that all

Figure 4. Sample invitation and rejection letters (after campus interview).

Dear _____:

We are pleased to invite you to come to [name of company] in [town and state] on [date]. This will give us an opportunity to get to know each other better and to explore our mutual interests in a career for you at [abbreviated name of company].

Please call [name of visit coordinator] collect at this phone number [phone number] to confirm the above date.

He will prove additional details concerning travel and hotel arrangements at that time. Your visit will be at our expense.

I very much enjoyed meeting with you on my recent campus visit and am looking forward to seeing you again.

Sincerely yours,

Dear _____:

Thank you for your interest in [name of company]. We truly appreciate the time you have given to discussing career opportunities with us.

It has been a difficult task to select the relatively few candidates from the large number of outstanding people interviewed. We have carefully reviewed your qualifications in order to explore a possible match between your talents and our needs. Unfortunately, we do not feel there is anything appropriate at this time.

We certainly enjoyed meeting and talking with you and wish you much success in your employment efforts.

Sincerely yours,

visits to any location be clearly the responsibility of a visit coordinator. This person should be accountable for the schedule of visits, all communications with the students, and the management of the applicant's time while at the company location.

If there is to be a significant delay (four weeks or more) between the time of the invitation and the visit for the secondary interview, an effort should be made to maintain contact with desired students. This contact can be achieved by follow-up letters, phone calls, or additional printed materials about the company, such as a just-issued annual report.

Once the student confirms his intention to visit for the secondary interview, the visit coordinator should send a letter to the student giving information about hotel accommodations, hotel bills, transportation, the company contact person on the day of interview, and the time required for the interview. A sample letter containing this type of information is shown in Figure 5.

It is usually effective to designate a sponsor or contact person who will serve as the applicant's companion on the day of secondary interviews. In most organizations, the sponsors are individuals selected for their ability to relate well with recent graduates. Often, sponsors are graduates who were hired through the company's recruiting process in the previous year or two. The role of the sponsor is to establish an informal, personal relationship with candidates and to share with them enthusiasm for the job and the company. Sponsors frequently are called upon to meet candidates for breakfast at the hotel, drive candidates to the company facility, introduce candidates to the visit coordinator or other company personnel, take candidates to lunch, take candidates on a brief tour of facilities, and return candidates to the airport, train station, or bus depot.

The secondary interviews should be scheduled so as to involve the fewest possible number of interviews. No data are available to demonstrate that a large number of interviewers produce more accurate predictions than fewer interviewers. When a candidate is being evaluated for several different departments or operations, three or four interviews of approximately forty-five minutes in length should be scheduled. More

Figure 5. Sample letter confirming secondary interview (after secondary visit is confirmed).

Dear _____ :

We look forward to talking with you about career opportunities at [name of company] on [date] in [location of interview].

Overnight reservations have been made for [day of week] evening, [date] at [name of hotel and city]. Transportation to the hotel can be arranged by _____.

[Name of sponsor] will meet you in the hotel lobby at 8 A.M. for breakfast and will bring you to headquarters to begin your day. During the course of your visit, we will make full reimbursement to you for all expenses associated with the trip.

We would appreciate it if you would complete the enclosed application and bring it with you at the time of your visit. If you have any further questions before your trip, please do not hesitate to call me collect at [telephone number]. Thank you again for the interest you have shown in [name of company]. I look forward to seeing you soon.

Sincerely yours,

than four interviews, in most cases, should be unnecessary. As an alternative to the "beauty parade" approach, multiple interviews are recommended. Specific details on this subject are provided in Chapter 6.

Management of the secondary interviews requires much attention and advance planning by the visit coordinator. It is important that the interviews be handled in such a way that the candidate leaves with a positive impression of the company, whether or not an offer is made. Most college placement officials ask students to provide feedback concerning their visit, and a favorable student report can contribute substantially to the company's image on campus.

Visit coordinators should take steps to ensure that interviewers will

- Be on time for scheduled interviews.
- Be familiar with the candidate's school, name of sponsor, and schedule for the day.
- Cut off telephone calls and other interruptions.
- Spend at least forty-five minutes in an interview, most of which should be evaluative.
- Project a positive and enthusiastic picture of their career with the company.

To accomplish all this usually means that the visit coordinator must provide specific training for interviewers. In addition, interviewers should learn how to conduct the Evaluation Model described in Chapter 8.

The interviewer who conducts the last interview escorts the candidate back to the visit coordinator. At this time, the coordinator should settle expenses, explain the next steps, and ask if the applicant has any further questions. When all questions and administrative matters are settled, the sponsor usually takes the applicant to a transportation facility.

Making the Offer

The offering decision should be made as quickly as possible once the interviews have been completed. Thus, offering letters are mailed throughout most of the recruiting period—January to April. A quick reaction from the company is a tangible way of showing interest in and commitment to the applicant. A strong, positive impact can be made, for example, if candidates leave the secondary interview with an offer in their pocket.

Usually, there is little advantage in delaying notification to unsuccessful candidates unless it is known that several applicants from a given school will be visiting in close time proximity.

Figure 6. Sample turndown letter (after secondary interview).

Dear _____:

We enjoyed having you visit [name of facility] to discuss career opportunities with some of our managers.

It has been a difficult task to select the relatively few candidates from the large number of outstanding people invited to our facilities for second interviews. Your qualifications were reviewed against our current needs and, unfortunately, we have decided to make offers to other individuals whose backgrounds and interests more closely match these needs.

We sincerely appreciate your interest in [name of company] and wish you much success in your career.

Sincerely yours,

Then, it may be diplomatic to wait until all have had their secondary interviews before sending out offering or turndown letters. A typical turndown letter is shown in Figure 6.

Obviously, each organization must tailor its offering letter to match its own style and to include the specific information it wishes to convey. However, most offering letters should include the following:

- A strong, positive opening that shows the organization was impressed by the candidate. It is particularly helpful if the letter can be tailored to mention a specific trait, skill, or quality of the candidate that impressed the interviewers.
- The position and title of the successful applicant's initial assignment.

- Mention of salary and benefits (and/or inclusion of a benefits brochure).
- A statement about contingencies, such as the requirement for taking a routine physical examination prior to the starting date (if applicable).
- Information regarding moving and relocation.
- An indication of who will next contact the candidate.
- An indication of when the company would like to have the candidate's decision.
- A closing statement reemphasizing the organization's strong interest in the applicant.

A sample offering letter is shown in Figure 7.

Once the offer is made, continued contact is critical until the time of acceptance or rejection. It is especially important to maintain contact with the better candidates, who may receive many attractive offers. Organizations have found that a show of personal concern and genuine desire for the candidate to become an employee is often the determining factor in an applicant's saying yes. Sometimes, a turndown of an offer could have been avoided if the hiring organization had only been aware of a problem facing the applicant. For example, the candidate may have thought well of an organization's offer, but was not pleased by the location of the initial job. For many companies, switching the initial job location may present no difficulty and would be worth doing in order to recruit the candidate. The recruiting manager must see that close contact is kept with the student and the placement office at the student's school.

Some important steps that should be taken once the offer is made are as follows:

1. Contact the student shortly after the offer has been made to offer congratulations, answer questions, and inquire if any additional information or help is needed.
2. Contact the college placement office about the offer.
3. Use mailings to maintain ongoing contact. Newsletters, house organs, speech reprints, telephone calls, and let-

Figure 7. Sample offering letter.

Dear _____:

This will confirm our conversation of yesterday. We are pleased to offer you a position as [job title] in the [name of department and branch of company] at a starting salary of $_____ per year. In addition to your base salary, you will immediately become eligible for [name of health plan] and a variety of other group insurance and benefit programs, which rank among the finest in the industry. I've enclosed some descriptive material on these programs.

The company will reimburse you for the cost of moving your household furnishings to your new location. Reimbursement will also be made for your personal costs, transportation, and meal and lodging expenses incurred en route. In addition, as a new employee, you are allowed up to thirty days' meal and lodging expenses at the new location while arranging for permanent quarters.

We understand that this is an important and difficult decision for you to make on the basis of your limited exposure to [name of company]. I can only reemphasize the exceptional growth opportunities and exposure this position offers you.

If there are any questions that you feel are unanswered, or if any arise, please feel free to call me collect. Further, if you believe another visit would help you to arrive at a decision please let me know and we will make arrangements.

I look forward to your accepting our offer.

Sincerely yours,

ters from the head of the department in which the applicant is likely to be assigned are all appropriate.

4. Encourage students to call collect for any reasons concerning their decisions.
5. Offer to arrange another visit if such appears necessary.
6. Determine approximately when the student will be making the final employment decision.

Approximately one week before it is expected that the candidate will make the yes or no decision, the student should be contacted to determine if anything can be done to help him in reaching a positive decision. At this time, it is usually not appropriate, especially from the public relations standpoint, to engage in high-pressure tactics. Expressions of a personal desire to see the student join the organization and of concern for clearing up any questions or issues troubling the student are most effective. One can also stress any truly unique aspects of an organization or job offer that the applicant is not likely to have received from competing companies.

Once an offer has been accepted, the recruiting manager should arrange for a congratulatory letter to be sent by the president or other high company official. In some organizations, this same executive indicates an interest in meeting the applicant once he is "on board." This letter also can reaffirm the starting employment date and location to which the candidate should report on the first day. A sample of such a letter is shown in Figure 8.

Follow-through after acceptance is also important. Students change their minds from time to time, but this can be minimized if regular contact is maintained.

Postrecruitment

Once the recruiting season is over, the recruiting manager should assume responsibility for a number of significant steps. He should make an analysis of the results (number of students

Figure 8. Sample welcome letter (after offer is accepted).

Dear _____:

[Name of recruiting manager] informed me that you have accepted our offer and plan to join us this [date]. I am very pleased with your decision and hope [name of company] fulfills your career expectations.

I look forward to working with you, and if either [name of recruiting manager] or I can do anything for you in the meantime, please let us know.

        Sincerely yours,

        [Name of executive]

recruited) for each of the schools visited. These figures, compared against the costs of recruiting at each school, should help determine the efficiency of recruiting at that institution. This analysis can also help pinpoint weak elements in the recruiting effort, such as inadequately trained or incompetent interviewers, paucity of students for the requirements sought (perhaps the school is not the right one for the kind of candidates needed), poor follow-through, or negative attitudes toward the company on the part of certain faculty members.

  Within three months of employment, some follow-through on the placement of new recruits and their degree of satisfaction with the company is recommended. In employment interviews, students often express career or location preferences, which the company tries to match, at least in the initial assignment. However, interests or life status (a marriage, for example) may change between the time of acceptance and employment. Also, the realities of the job or location may prove to be different from what the candidate expected. Given the high percentage of turnover among young college graduates and M.B.A.'s during the first two years of employment, early identification of problems among new recruits before they become entrenched in a significant, permanent job assignment could substantially reduce turnover. Adjustments in career path and/or location are often relatively easy to make during the first few months of employment, but become more difficult later on.

A timetable for taking key steps in an effective recruiting program is summarized in Table 1.

Advantages of College Recruiting

It is difficult to see many direct advantages to college recruiting. Many large corporations wish the practice would just go away but are forced into recruiting to get their share of bright young talent. It would appear, however, that recruiting is here to stay. Here are some advantages:

Corporate image. There are public relations benefits derived from the company being known to graduating students. Even if they are not recruited as young graduates, their positive attitudes toward the organization may predispose them to seek employment in the future or to accept an employment offer at a later date. Of course, these advantages could easily vanish if the college recruiter or the recruiting process is ineffective and leaves a bad impression on candidates.

"Big net" value. Campus recruiting may be the only viable way of hiring a pool of young college graduates. Many organizations have effective management development and training programs that prepare young employees for key responsibilities, and the college graduate represents the right mix of intelligence, age, and educational background for the company's development effort. A good example is seen in public accounting firms, especially the Big Eight. For these firms, a college education provide the foundation; they themselves teach the technical skills needed by educated recruits to perform as certified public accountants.

Table 1.   *Timetable for Key Steps in an Effective Recruiting Process.*

Activity	Date	Responsibility
Evaluate Sources	Continuing	Recruiting manager
Schedule recruitment dates	Approximately 12 months in advance	Recruiting manager Steering committee
Identify needs for following year	July	Recruiting manager Steering committee
Review/develop recruitment materials	August	Recruiting manager
Develop college relations activity plan	September	Visit coordinators
Implement college relations activities	Ongoing	Recruiting manager Visit coordinators
Conduct college recruiting workshop	October/November	Recruiting manager
Conduct campus interviews	December/February	Recruiting manager Visit coordinators
Conduct second interviews	March/April	Recruiting manager; branch and home office management
Make offers	April/May	Recruiting manager
Evaluate program	August	Recruiting manager

Disadvantages of College Recruiting

Cost. Cost per employee obtained is high. It is not difficult to see why the costs of campus recruiting become so high. From a recent informal survey of several major corporations, it was found that approximately twenty-five applicants were interviewed for each person actually hired. These interviews included the campus interviews as well as the secondary interviews in the home office or plant location. When you consider the management time spent in preparing schedules, training interviewers, visiting campuses, conducting secondary interviews, and writing letters, together with the travel costs, hotel bills, and administrative expenses, it is not difficult to see how the cost of recruiting can easily total several thousand dollars per hire.

High salaries for inexperienced talent. Because of the competitive aspects of campus recruiting, starting salaries are quite unrealistic relative to the contribution these individuals can make, given their limited experience. So, in effect, hiring young graduates at competitive starting salaries is essentially an investment in the future. As it turns out for many organizations, it is an uneconomic investment because the turnover of these young hires after two or three years is quite high. According to a study recently conducted by the College Placement Council, one college recruit out of every three hired left within three years. Of course, the turnover varies greatly from one organization to another. Every organization should take a critical look at what happens to their campus recruits after a two-year period—at the time when most of them are finally becoming productive enough to warrant their earnings. This situation is particularly aggravated in the case of M.B.A.'s; their leave rate before three years is even higher, with many clients reporting a 40 percent loss. While hiring good M.B.A.'s represents a challenge, it's an even greater challenge keeping them.

Summary

This chapter provides a comprehensive, step-by-step procedure for carrying out an effective recruiting effort on college campuses. One of the essential points covered is the importance of designating people who will be responsible for coordinating the effort, for establishing good relations with the colleges where the recruiting is to take place, and for seeing that the recruiters who will do the interviewing are adequately trained.

A key element in the recruiting process is the management of procedures to be used when the recruited candidate arrives for the secondary interviews at the home office, regional office, or plant.

The importance of showing personal concern for and interest in the applicant is stressed. It is recommended that care be taken as to the nature of the evaluation forms used and that the paper process be kept minimal.

Chapter 5

The College Recruiting Interviews

When hiring college seniors, the manager is likely to engage in two types of interviews: the campus interview and the home office interview. The campus interview is essentially a recruiting effort at the candidate's school. The home office interview is a second interview in which the student visits a company location. It's primary purpose is to facilitate a final hire/not-hire decision and to sell a desirable candidate on coming to work for the company.

Each of these two types of interviews presents special problems from both the evaluation and procedural standpoints. Let's look first at the campus interview.

Uniqueness of the Campus Interview

There are significant differences between the campus interview and the traditional hire/not-hire interview (described in Chapter 13). These differences result in a unique interview situation because the campus interview involves:

1. The absolute need to sell the candidate on the company.
2. A strictly limited amount of time for conducting the interview.
3. Pressures of fatigue and boredom.

Because the campus situation places special demands on the interviewer, a specially designed interview approach must be used. Before describing this procedure, it may be worthwhile to examine the unique aspects of the interview in greater detail.

The absolute need to sell. Most interviews are conducted with the purpose of helping the executive to make a hire/not-hire decision. This is not true of the campus interview. The campus interview is fundamentally a selling situation accompanied by a weeding out of unsuitable candidates. It does little good to accurately assess a candidate, to determine that he is an excellent prospect for the company, if, at the same time, the interviewer fails to interest that individual. Clearly, the recruiting interview is one in which the interviewer must interest the desired student in coming to the company. On the other hand, the recruiter cannot indiscriminately make a job offer or issue an invitation to a company location. Thus the campus interview places unusual demands on the interviewer by the duality of its purpose. Many executives are effective in selling the firm and in assessing candidates, but few are good at performing both tasks simultaneously.

Time limits. A second problem posed by the campus interview is the time restriction placed on the interviewer. Most campus interviews are scheduled at twenty- or thirty-minute intervals, and of that time, only fifteen to twenty minutes are available for evaluating the student, the remaining time being required for the introduction, selling, and the like. In contrast, the Evaluation Model described in Chapter 13 requires forty-five minutes or more for the young college graduate. In view of the time limitation, the interviewer must set realistic expectations with regard to what he attempts to learn about each candidate.

Fatigue and boredom. The third feature of the campus interview that distinguishes it from the typical evaluation interview is the fatigue factor and the pressure placed upon the interviewer. It is not unusual for a campus interviewer to see fifteen or twenty students in one day. While there is a break for lunch, most campus interviewers feel completely knocked out, or punch drunk, after seeing seven or eight students. It is difficult for the interviewer to maintain interest, enthusiasm, and attentiveness for extended periods of time. Consequently, any approach to campus interviewing must take into account the numbness that will occur when many students are interviewed. The campus interview must be designed to permit the interviewer time to relax during the interview so that he can maintain alertness and perceptivity. Boredom also becomes a demotivating factor as the day proceeds.

The Campus Interview Model

The campus interview model, as shown in Figure 9, has been designed to take into account the issues already mentioned, namely, time pressure, fatigue and boredom, and the need to sell. It has been used extensively by a number of major corporations. The approach lends itself well to most campus interview situations and is recommended as a starting point for the formulation of each executive's method of interviewing on campus. Particular company needs may occasionally require modification of the model, but the basic approach works well for most situations and individual personality styles.

Part 1—Opening Comments

Because the time for the campus interview is limited, it is usually neither wise nor necessary to spend much time in attempting to establish rapport with the student. As is true for the evaluation interview, the most important factor in establishing rapport is for the interviewer to be natural; warmth, openness, and spontaneity also help. The interviewer should remember that the student may be more at ease than he is. It could be that the student has already completed twenty such interviews with other interviewers. Moreover, interviewers should recognize that the student is also interviewing them, so

Figure 9. Model for conducting a campus interview.

Interview Segment	Approximate Time Allotted
Part 1 Opening Comments Establish rapport	3 minutes
Part 2 Specific Facts	2 minutes

Part 3   Assessment Section
        Make-or-break questions
        Broad-brush/self-appraisal
        questions
	12 minutes

Part 4   Selling Section
        What is applicant
        looking for in com-
        pany?
        Questions student has
        about company
	12 minutes

Part 5 Closing Section Next steps	1 minute

the usual social remarks can be kept to a minimum. After a few opening comments, the interviewer should plunge directly into the interview.

In view of the pressure to cover a reasonable amount of ground in a short period, it is quite important that the interviewer maintain adequate control over the interview. Control, however, does not mean dominating the interview but rather having a firm hand on what is being discussed at specific points during the interview.

Students are often inclined to disrupt control by asking questions at a time when the interviewer is trying to obtain cer-

tain data. To discourage interruptions and to minimize the likelihood of losing control of the interview, the interviewer can
structure the discussion at the outset. Because of the added importance of control in this tightly scheduled situation, a somewhat modified structuring statement may be used.

INTERVIEWER: I know that in our meeting today we are both
    attempting to learn something about what we can offer one
    another. We certainly would like to learn about your back-
    ground and interests, and I know you are interested in
    learning about what our company has to offer. So let's di-
    vide up our time. I'd like to spend the first half of the in-
    terview getting acquainted with you, and then we'll turn it
    around and you can then ask me questions about us.

The time allotted to the opening portion of the interview
should be quite brief, no more than two or three minutes.

Part 2—Specific Facts

From each campus interview, it is important that the organization gather certain specific information. For at least two
reasons, this fact gathering should not be left to the end of the
interview.

If you wait until the end of the interview, the likelihood of
not recording the facts is great. It is often tempting to say to
yourself that you will write them down "at the end of the day."
However, fatigue and the inability to distinguish one student
from another at that point precludes this approach as an effective way of recalling data. Thus, critical factual data should be
obtained at the very outset of the interview and recorded immediately.

It is important to gather certain facts at the outset because
this information can dictate how the whole interview ought to
be conducted. You might find out, for example, that the student is not an applicant for full-time employment, but is merely
looking for summer work; or you could find that certain students are completely unqualified, in which case you may choose

to discontinue the interview, thus saving both the student's time and your own.

For most campus interviews, it is helpful to go over at least four items at the beginning of each interview. Each company may have its own list of such items and they, of course, should be added to the following.

1. Get a transcript request signed. A written request is usually required to obtain the student's transcript from the campus registrar. A sample form is shown in Appendix E. While the student is signing the form and filling out his address, several other questions can be asked.

2. Check to be certain that the address and telephone number given on the résumé are current. Students often move after they have worked up their résumés (which may well have been at the beginning of the school year), and if you do not have a current address, delays will occur in correspondence.

3. Check to see that the student is graduating when expected. Many students may be planning on graduating a semester later than originally scheduled and are therefore only in the market for summer employment at the time of the interview. Even if the student will not be graduating, however, it might be desirable to continue with the interview, assess the student, and try to sell him on the company. You can also suggest that the student talk with one of your company recruiters who may be visiting the campus closer to the time of that student's graduation.

4. Inquire whether the applicant has had any previous contact with personnel from your company—particularly if your company has several interviewers on campus. Such questioning can save your company's college placement office from sending out multiple letters to the same student—and also save the company from creating an impression of disorganization.

Part 3—Assessment Section

The assessment segment of the interview is designed to help the interviewer gain a better understanding of the applicant. Keeping in mind the problems of time and pressure, the interviewer must set realistic goals in terms of how comprehensive an assessment can actually be made. To try to make hire/not-hire decisions under the usual campus conditions is entirely unrealistic. What is realistic? The interviewer ought at least to try for an answer to this question: "If this candidate walked into my office, would he be the kind of person I would feel reasonably proud of having recruited?" In other words, in a campus interview, the interviewer should be able to determine the candidate's past record of performance, such as grades and achievements, and such easily observable characteristics as can be assessed in the face-to-face discussion. Some of these are:

- How the applicant communicates. Is he articulate or tongue-tied?
- The extent of the applicant's initiative or self-starting ability.
- How the applicant thinks. Are his thoughts organized or scattered? Does he focus too much on detail?
- The degree of the applicant's social perceptivity (which can often be gleaned from the student's perception of expectations regarding length of responses to questions, knowing when to talk and when to listen, and the appropriateness of his appearance and dress).
- The extent of the applicants poise and self-confidence. Does he fidget?
- The extent of the applicant's technical background.

To attempt to make assessments in these areas is to set a realistic goal. To obtain a more perceptive analysis in twenty minutes is not likely—at least not without the interviewer becoming a candidate for psychotherapy.

The assessment segment of the interview can be divided into two parts—a make-or-break portion and a self-appraisal section.

Make or Break Questions   Few things can be more frustrating to the campus interviewer than to spend up to thirty minutes with a student only to find out that he was really not interested in the company and is actually planning to go to graduate school; he only wanted to "hear about the opportunities in your industry." Immediately after the opening comments, the interviewer should introduce the make-or-break items about which there must be agreement if the candidate is to be considered further. For example, for most sales positions the candidate must have a valid driver's license. Lacking the license, the employee could not make customer calls. For some companies, willingness to relocate might be a crucial item, or willingness to travel, or a particular skill, such as knowledge of fusion physics. If such factors exist as fundamental requirements for hiring, it is prudent to talk about them at the outset. Most students will appreciate learning whether or not there is a "match," particularly if it saves them from needlessly investing their time. Of course, when recruiters are interviewing for many different departments or jobs, the make-or-break items may not have to be mentioned.

Here is one way of introducing make-or-break items.

INTERVIEWER: Before we get into the interview, there are a couple of matters we should touch on—just to make sure we're in the same ball park as far as your qualifications for the marketing position are concerned. First of all, the jobs that I'm interviewing for require considerable overnight travel. Is that any problem for you?

APPLICANT: I don't mind a little travel.

INTERVIEWER: Well, in this job you would be away, on the average, four and sometimes five nights a week. Is that excessive for you?

APPLICANT: Oh, I don't think I'd want that. I'm really not interested in having to be away that much. I'm interested in taking some evening graduate courses.

INTERVIEWER: As I say, this job would require fairly extensive travel; sometimes it could be less than I said, but often it could be quite prolonged, so I doubt very much that this is a job that's going to meet your needs.

APPLICANT: Well, thank you very much for telling me about the traveling, because I don't think I would be very interested.

If no make-or-break factors are connected with the job, the interviewer can skip this portion of the interview and go on to a more qualitative appraisal.

Broad-Brush and Self-Appraisal Questions   As stated earlier, there are certain inputs the interviewer can expect to glean from the campus interview—verbal ability, confidence level, poise, and appearance. But analysis of motivation patterns and assessment of personality strengths and limitations are difficult, if not impossible, in an initial interview. The interviewer should also recognize that as much of the needed factual data is already available to him through application blanks, college transcripts, or résumés, there is no point in again eliciting this information during the interview. Consequently, the interview should be focused on helping the manager to judge whether or not the applicant is the kind of person who can work effectively in the organization.

A second factor to be considered in the assessment portion is the interviewer's need for a little time to sit back, relax, and take notes on how the applicant behaves. To accomplish this and at the same time make some assessment of the candidate, the interviewer might ask the student a number of broad questions that force him to carry the burden of responsibility for the dialogue. These should be questions that require the applicant to think aloud, verbalize freely, and organize his thoughts, as a test of his communication skills. The ideal questions are those sufficiently broad in scope that they force applicants to analyze their own thoughts. Here are a few:

- "What long-term satisfactions do you expect to derive from a career in the business world?"
- "How do you evaluate your college career as a preparation for your future?"
- "What is it about [finance, accounting, history] that you think would sustain your interest and motivation in the years ahead?"

For each student, the interviewer should be prepared to ask two or three of these broad-brush questions. Once such a question is asked, the interviewer can sit back and observe the student. It is at this point that the interviewer can begin to make a judgment as to whether the student has some of the basic qualities the company is seeking. In this way the interviewer is also able to preserve his mental and physical well-being.

A problem that can occur if the interviewer asks the candidates the same questions is that the students will tell their friends the questions asked, and thus, as the day goes on, each applicant will appear more and more knowledgeable or fluent. To minimize this possibility, the interviewer should prepare a list of approximately twelve broad-brush questions. A long list of such questions is given in Appendix A. These questions can be written on a small card that is kept on the desk in front of the interviewer. For the first student interviewed, the interviewer will ask broad-brush questions 1 and 2; for the second student, questions 3 and 4; for the third student, questions 5 and 6. In this way, each of the first six students is asked different questions. The process then is repeated for the next six students. This procedure helps ensure that all students come equally unprepared for the questions.

While listening to the student's responses, the interviewer should be recording observations about their behavior and qualifications.

Part 4—Selling Section

Many campus interviewers have limited success in interesting students in their companies because the features they talk about do not adequately respond to the needs of the students. Interviewers are likely to recite a litany of the advantages of working for their company. But when students compare these with the advantages offered by other companies, the benefits and opportunities all begin to look alike. Thus much of the time spent trying to "sell" the student has little impact and, from the student's point of view, may even be completely irrelevant.

One approach that helps the campus interviewer relate the company to the needs of the student is simply to ask the student what he is looking for. Once an answer is given, the interviewer can point out how the company might fulfill that particular student's desires. Here is an example of how the selling section of the interview might be initiated.

INTERVIEWER: I am sure there are certain things you are looking for as you take these interviews with various companies—features that help you to evaluate prospective employers. What are some of the elements that would make a company or an employment situation particularly attractive to you?

APPLICANT: Well, I guess one thing I'm looking for is an opportunity to get my feet wet in a fairly responsible position quite soon. I feel I'm a little more mature than many of those graduating with me—having worked two years before starting school. I'd like a job where I can step in and really show what I can do. I don't think I'm interested in getting involved with a long training program, but I'd like a job where I could be given a little rope. And, I guess, the other major thing I'm looking for is that I would like to locate near a metropolitan area where I could continue my schooling in the evening. I want to work toward my M. B. A., so I wouldn't want to be in a situation where I had to travel a lot or where I wouldn't be near a graduate school.

INTERVIEWER: Well, the goals you've set for yourself certainly make a lot of sense and I think you'll be very excited and interested in the kind of responsibility you would be getting at XYZ Company. I think, too, I can assure you that going on to graduate school would present no problem in our organization. Let me tell you about. . . .

If, for some reason, the student is unable to delineate specific wants, it is helpful for the interviewer to be aware of some generalized findings about current job expectations as expressed by young college graduates. They seem to be saying that they are looking for a participative company climate or style, meaningful work, and a job that will provide a sense of achievement. A recruiter who can specifically describe how these objectives can be attained in his company will usually have little difficulty in stimulating student interest. A list of the most frequently asked questions, as shown in Figure 10, will help the interviewer better understand what is on the minds of most students.

Once the interviewer has ascertained the applicant's needs and has shown the applicant how these desires can be fulfilled within the organization, it is then appropriate to inquire about any question the applicant may have. The nature of the applicant's questions will provide clues for assessing the applicant's desires and motivations, as well as for how best to sell the company to that applicant.

A key point in responding to the applicant's questions is to be frank and honest. If the applicant raises a question to which you do not have an answer, do not bluff. The interviewer will come across as a much more effective company representative if he is seen as being straightforward and open. Instead of bluffing or making generalized comments, it is far better to say, "I don't know the exact answer to that, but I will be pleased to find out for you and let you know." This also provides a perfect opportunity for additional contact with the student.

Obviously, the more you know about the company, its op-

Figure 10. Questions most frequently asked by students.

1. What is involved in the training program?
2. How much travel is usually expected?
3. How frequently do you relocate professional employees?
4. What is the average age of top management?
5. How much visibility is there with top management?
6. What is the typical career progression?
7. How many trainees are you looking for?
8. Does the company promote solely from within?
9. How much decision-making authority is given?
10. How much input does a new person have on geographic location?
11. Is this position more analytical or more people-oriented?
12. What is your policy on tuition reimbursement?
13. Is graduate work encouraged during the training period?
14. How often are performance reviews made?
15. How soon after graduation would I be expected to report to work?
16. What is the average time it takes to become an officer?
17. What is the usual routine of a [job classification] like?
18. How much independence is allowed in dress and appearance?

erations, and opportunities, the better. On the other hand, no student can expect you to know in depth the answers to all the questions that may arise. In answering the questions you do know about, you have a great opportunity to show enthusiasm for the company and the advantages of working there.

It should also be mentioned that the selling portion provides additional opportunity for evaluation. Students are definitely revealing something about themselves as they talk about their interests and needs.

Part 5—Closing Section

The essential point in the closing section is to indicate to the student the next step in the employment procedure. The student should be told, for example, whether the next step will be an invitation to visit a company location, an offering letter, or whatever. The applicant also should be told the approximate length of time that will elapse between the interview and the next communication from the company.

Companies vary greatly in their procedures for postinterview visits or job offers, but it should be clear that speed and promptness are extremely important. One reason prompt action is so significant is that it represents a concrete way of showing that the company is interested in the applicant.

A survey was made of 130 chemical and mechanical engineers who were recruited by a major chemical company. Once the recruits were on board, they were interviewed to determine why they had accepted the company's job offer. The results are summarized here.

Reason Given	*Percent*
The company seemed personally interested in me	42
Advancement opportunities seemed good	27
The jobs seemed challenging or interesting	18
Reputation of the company	10
Miscellaneous	3

Placed under the heading of "The company seemed personally interested in me" were such statements as:

"I received my offering letter three days after my visit to the plant. It seemed that the company really wanted me."

"When I was at the plant, the plant personnel were interested in what I wanted to do and the kinds of jobs I wanted to get involved in—they didn't just try to sell me."

"The evening after the recruiter interviewed me on campus, he phoned the dormitory and extended me a verbal offer of employment. It seemed to me that I must have created a very positive impression and that he wanted to be sure that he got me."

In essence, these students seem to be saying that the prompt action by the company was a significant factor in their decision to accept the employment offer. Such action is interpreted by many students as a concrete measure of the company's true interest in them. It really is important, therefore, that the campus interviewer outline the next steps in the employment procedure and tell the applicants when they will take place. The sooner these next steps are taken, the better.

The Home Office Interview (Second Interview)

The home office interview usually takes place after an invitation has been extended during the campus visit or in a subsequent letter. Its purpose is twofold: to make a hire/not-hire decision about the candidate and to sell the candidate on the desirability of accepting a position with the company. The assessment procedures outlined in this book are ideally suited to this final interview. However, in most companies, special problems occur when the young candidates arrive at the doorstep. They are subject to the "beauty parade."

The approach used for the second interviews is the procedure described in Chapter 13 called the Evaluation Model, a comprehensive interview that requires at least forty-five to fifty minutes. However, the thoroughness of the interview makes it unnecessary to run candidates through more than two such interviews; more would amount to overkill. The thorough, in-depth evaluation interview also militates against the "beauty parade," a process in which the candidate is interviewed by five or six executives, each of whom is expected to evaluate the candidate and/or sell him on the company. The applicant is whisked from one manager to the next for a series of thirty-minute interviews, including, perhaps, a luncheon interview with one of the younger members of the staff. By the end of the day, the applicant feels like a limp ping-pong ball.

Problems of the Beauty Parade

Before discussing the positive steps that can be taken to make the secondary interview effective, it may be worthwhile to examine some of the problems inherent in the beauty parade approach. There is serious question whether thirty-minute interviews are capable of producing more than the most superficial observations. There isn't even thirty minutes for evaluation when one considers the time invested in introductions, small talk, and explanations of career opportunities in the interviewer's area of operation.

A second problem with the beauty parade approach is that it diminishes the ability of the company to make accurate predictions about job performance. An interviewing team may arrive at erroneous conclusions because its members disagree about superficial issues. This is because they do not all interview the same person; during the course of a day of interviewing, the applicant changes in several ways. The manager who interviews the candidate at 4:30 P.M. sees an individual quite different from the one with whom a breakfast interview was held at the airport.

One way in which applicants change is that they become sophisticated about the interview; that is, they begin to learn the right things to say. As students proceed from one interviewer to the next, they learn from comments made, both overt and subtle, the kinds of reactions and responses the interviewers are looking for. They learn which values are prized in the company, what will be expected of them on the job, and which answers result in positive responses from the interviewers.

After having made several home office visits, most students become adept at interviews. Unless company interviewers make frequent use of the self-appraisal techniques, they will be "snowed" by the extraordinary appropriateness of the candidate's responses.

A second change, and one that somewhat offsets the advantage of increasing sophistication, is fatigue. As the day proceeds, students are likely to lose some of their bounce and enthusiasm. Students often report that after four or five interviews, each covering about the same ground, they get bored with the process. Near the end of the day, the student is more interested in getting it over with than in exploring employment opportunities. Thus, the candidate appears to have less interest in the job or the company. This may be especially true of the

Figure 11. Dilutions of evaluations as a function of the beauty parade.

Candidate	Interviewers' Reactions						Group Consensus
	1	2	3	4	5	6	
A	No	Yes	No	Yes	No	No	No
B	Yes	Yes	Yes	Yes	Yes	Yes	Yes

most qualified candidate, who may already have obtained two or three job offers from competitors. The candidate's physical appearance also becomes rumpled as the day wears on.

A third problem is that the attitudes and opinions of the poorer interviewers dilute the judgments of those who are more skillful. Let's look at a typical situation.

Candidate A is bright, aggressive, hard-driving, but frank and outspoken. The applicant has a good record of accomplishment but was once involved in a scrape with the dean's office.

Let us use the hypothetical situation summarized in Figure 11. Assume that six persons are to interview Candidate A. Assume further that Interviewers number 2 and number 4 are astute in evaluating others.

Interviewer 1, a relatively unskillful assessor of others, decides to turn down the candidate. This interviewer sees the candidate as something of a rabble-rouser whose outspokenness is going to rub too many people the wrong way. The interviewer thinks that the candidate will not be able to get the kind of cooperation from others that the job demands. Interviewers 3, 5, and 6 evaluate the candidate in much the same way. Interviewer 2 observes the same flaws in the candidate's behavior as do Interviewers 1, 3, 5, and 6, but also recognizes that the candidate is a highly competent individual whose strengths more than offset the shortcomings. Interviewer 2 votes to hire. Interviewer 4, who is also perceptive, evaluates the candidate in much the same way as Interviewer 2. Now all opinions are combined. In some companies, interviewers write their assessment and submit it to the personnel department; in others, the interviewers meet to arrive at some consensus. Regardless of the method, Candidate A is not likely to be given an offer.

Now let us look at Candidate B. This person is reasonably intelligent, communicates well, seems pleasant, and has a good record (no scrapes with the dean's office). Candidate B did not appear opinionated or outspoken in the interview. Interviewer 1 evaluates the candidate as good; no problems were observed, so the vote is yes. The remaining interviewers also see the candidate as satisfactory. No one sees any significant flaws in this applicant's background; so Candidate B is given an offer.

Candidate B certainly should be extended an offer. The applicant is good but not outstanding. However, Candidate A may well have been the superior candidate. Because the applicant is a strong individual who is more self-confident, aggressive, and forceful, his shortcomings are evident, even to the poor assessor. Self-assured applicants will openly tell you some of their shortcomings because they feel no need to hide them; they are confident of their abilities.

Frequently, inexperienced interviewers become unduly upset by shortcomings, particularly if they identify them early in the interview. They find it difficult to focus on the candidate's strengths and to determine how these assets might more than offset the shortcomings.

Another problem of the beauty parade is that too often it alienates applicants rather than helps them to develop positive attitudes toward the company. A day-long series of interviews, whether designed to assess or sell, probably does not represent the most effective use of time.

The Twosome Approach

One way to cope with problems of the beauty parade is to reduce the number of interviews to which the applicant is exposed. This can be accomplished by use of group interviewers, that is, having more than one person simultaneously interview the candidate. In working with a wide range of clients, I have experimented with combinations of two-on-one, three-on-one, and four-on-one. While I am not yet convinced that three-on-one and four-on-one cannot be made to work effectively, efforts thus far have not proved successful. Good results, however, have been obtained with the two-on-one method. The results are not only good; they are significantly superior to the predictive accuracy obtained by the traditional one-on-one method of interviewing.

A demonstration of the effectiveness of the twosome approach grew out of the chemical company research project mentioned previously. Two interviewing teams evaluated the staff of a newly acquired subsidiary. Team A was trained in use of the Evaluation Model and employed the twosome method to evaluate twenty-five of the fifty-four candidates interviewed. Team B members interviewed singly, using whatever method seemed most satisfactory to each interviewer.

To arrive at their evaluations, Team A members combined the respective ratings of each pair to form a composite evaluation. Team B members, on the other hand, combined the individual judgments to form their composite assessment.

Top management of the acquired company was asked to rate its executives in rank order in terms of their qualifications for their current management assignments. Data about salary progression were also obtained.

The team evaluations were then correlated with top management's evaluations. The results in Figure 12 show clearly that there is a statistically significant difference between levels of correlations obtained by Team A raters, who used the twosome approach, and those scored by Team B raters, who used individual interviews.

A possible explanation of the superior assessment performance of Team A could be that the team was composed of individuals more talented at evaluating others than was true of Team B. To check this hypothesis, the same teams evaluated an additional forty individuals in the acquired company. This time, the persons to be evaluated were at lower levels in the company. On this round of assessments, the two teams reversed

Figure 12. Comparison of twosome and single methods of
interviewing, with Team A using twosome
method.

Interview Method	Team	Correlations with Performance Ratings	
Twosome	A	Managerial Rating	.52
		Salary Progress	.39
Single	B	Managerial Rating	.26
		Salary Progress	.18

procedures, Team B using the pair method and Team A, the
individual method. As shown in Figure 13, the team using the
twosome approach was better able to predict job success than
the team using the individual method.

Making the Twosome Approach Work

When the idea is proposed that two persons simultaneously interview one candidate, the usual reaction from most
executives is that such an approach would be too threatening,
that the applicant would feel "under the gun" and become un-
easy or defensive. This is not the case, however, if the interview
is properly structured. The factor that creates tension in multiple interviews is the problem the interviewee has in relating to
two or more people simultaneously. This problem can be
avoided by structuring the interview so that only one interviewer of the pair is interviewing at any given time. This does
not mean a back-and-forth questioning, with each interviewer
alternately addressing the applicant. Instead, one of the partners (after both participate in the social amenities) starts off the
interview process by covering all the areas in the interview plan.
This is accomplished by using the Evaluation Model (Chapter
13), without interruption by the other member of the interviewing team.

It is helpful if the two interviewers sit at some distance
from each other so that the candidate does not have to try to

Figure 13. Comparison of twosome and single methods of interviewing, with Team B using twosome method.

Interview Method	Team	Correlations with Performance Ratings	
Twosome	B	Managerial Rating	.46
		Salary Progress	.32
Single	A	Managerial Rating	.24
		Salary Progress	.23

maintain eye contact with both. It should be made clear that the applicant should focus on only one of the interviewers.

When the first interviewer has completed all steps in the interview plan, the interview is turned over to the partner. This individual does not follow an interview plan but, instead, inquires about specific technical skills and factual information, or clarifies points brought up earlier. The partner in the second part of the twosome approach may also reexplore some areas already discussed. However, this is not recommended unless it is essential to obtain additional information in the area in question. The portion of time used by the second interviewer is usually from ten to fifteen minutes; the first interviewer spends approximately forty-five minutes. Thus, most two-on-one interviews require approximately an hour to complete.

For the twosome approach to be effective, it must be made clear to the applicant how the interview will be conducted. Unless the interviewers' procedures are discussed, it will seem peculiar that only one person is talking; the candidate may feel sorry for the partner who seems left out and try to involve him in the discussion. It is important, therefore, to explain the interview structure, at the outset and to provide some rationale for the format. The following statement works well:

> In order to cut down on the number of different interviews you'll have to go through today, we would like to interview you together. But, since it might be difficult to talk with two

of us at the same time, suppose I begin, and when I'm finished, Jim will take over. How would that be?

Most applicants will feel no more ill at ease than in the one-
on-one interview. Many indicate that they find it comfortable
and stimulating. This was substantiated in the study described
earlier. As the reader may recall, forty candidates were interviewed by two teams of interviewers. One team used the twosome approach, and the other, the one-on-one interview. When
the candidates completed an interview, they were asked to indicate the degree of discomfort experienced in each interview
by rating the tension felt on a scale of one to nine. The average
degree of tension reported by those interviewed by the one-at-
a-time method was 4.2, and by those exposed to the twosome
approach, 4.8. These differences are not statistically significant.
       Companies that use the dual-interviewer system are able to
reduce by almost half the amount of time they spend in interviews. If the candidate is visiting the plant or home office for a
day, this allows ample time for other activities that might successfully interest the candidate in the company.
       It is interesting to note, too, that almost every client who
has experimented with the two-on-one interviews has remained
with the procedure. The twosome approach has produced
more accurate predictions.

Advantages of the Twosome Approach

One way in which the twosome approach helps increase
accuracy in hiring decisions is that two persons witness the same
event simultaneously. These concurrent observations, when
merged, produce a significantly more accurate prediction than
do two independent observations combined.
       What one interviewer misses, the other observes. Also, in
the discussion and preparation of the balance sheet at the termination of the interview, there is opportunity to share perceptions and to more properly determine the appropriate weight
or emphasis to be placed on the identified characteristics of the
candidate. For example, one interviewer may have confirmed
the hypothesis formulated in his notes that the candidate is

wishy-washy and fails to take firm positions. The second interviewer, however, may remind the first of an instance during the interview when the applicant strongly defended a particular point. Thus, together they may agree to assign less weight to this factor than one of them previously thought appropriate.

The twosome approach also permits one interviewer to study the applicant while the other is busy conducting the interview. Thus, the silent interviewer has the opportunity to make many observations that may escape his partner. When it is the observer's turn to take over the interview, that person can follow up on hunches and unresolved questions that the other interviewer may have forgotten or for some reason decided not to pursue.

Another advantage of the twosome approach is that it allows interviewers of diverse skills and backgrounds to combine observations and judgments. A practical combination, for instance, is an interviewer who is particularly effective at evaluating intellect, motivation, and personality teamed with a technological expert who can evaluate the candidate's knowledge and experience. In this combination, the personnel specialist usually interviews first, using the Evaluation Model, and the technological expert follows, asking specific technical questions.

Some companies have found the twosome approach helpful when several persons want to make judgments about the applicant but time does not permit individual interviews. While an applicant is interviewed in the standard two-on-one format, others, seated in the background, can observe and make notes on the basis of the interview being conducted in front of them. If the group is not too large (that is, not more than six or seven), a conference discussion can follow the interview, with a balance sheet developed from the consensus of the entire group.

Use of Interview Rating Forms

It is important not to complicate the recruiting process by requiring interviewers to complete complex evaluation sheets or forms. On the other hand, there obviously is a need for the interviewers to record their impressions at the conclusion of each interview. Such records are also essential if the organization is interested in evaluating the effectiveness of its recruiting effort. Thus, some evaluation format is necessary. Unfortunately, in an effort to develop easy-to-complete evaluation forms, most organizations lean heavily on the checklist approach, at least for a portion of the form. An example of this type is shown in Figure 14.

Parts of this form clearly are helpful and deserve the space allotted to them. For instance, the section labeled "Interviewer's Recommendations" is efficient and helpful. On the other hand, serious objection must be made to the use of a checklist in which the interviewer is asked to give an evaluation of the candidate's initiative, maturity, and other qualities.

Problems With Checklists

There are a number of problems with checklists that make them inappropriate for use as interview evaluation forms. There is the assumption that the factors listed account for success at work. Of course, there can be no argument that these skills or qualities are desirable. The question is, are they valid predictors of success? In two studies that I conducted, ratings made on client evaluation forms from campus interviews were correlated with ratings of subsequent job performance on the basis of the same characteristics. There was almost no significant correlation between the traits checked on the form (factors similar to those shown in Figure 15) and ratings on these same qualities made after a year's observation of job performance. The only factor for which there was a slightly significant, positive relationship was appearance.

The evaluation of specific personality qualities or traits contributes little to accurate prediction of job success. There may be other, far more significant factors that explain the individual's ability to perform successfully in a given job. For instance, a candidate may not show much evidence of initiative but is successful at work because of a conscientious, persistent

Figure 14. Example of a trait checklist interview form (not recommended).

Interview Evaluation	Instructions—Complete this form for each applicant interviewed whether or not you are recommending them. Attach this form to the front of other material pertaining to the applicant (i.e., application, résumé, etc.). Return all campus interview information to College Relations.

Last Name	First Name	Address

College	Degree	Date of Degree	Grade Point Average

		Poor	Average	Excellent
Appearance	(Neatness, personal habits, manners)	Poor		Excellent
Communication	(Verbal, expression, organization)	Poor		Superior
Maturity	(Aspirations)	Immature		Very Mature
Initiative	(Self-reliant, industrious, motivated)	Lazy		Vigorous
Leadership	(Participation in activities, offices held)	Inactive		Very Active
Technical	(Comprehensive, theory)	Poor		Excellent
Overall Evaluation	(Consider all of above factors)	Poor		Superior

Comment on Evaluation (include Honorary Societies)

Interviewer's Recommendations

☐ Reject

Invite For:

☐ Engineering Program
☐ Manufacturing Program
☐ Graduate Study Program
☐ Research Training Program

☐ Computer Sales and Systems Program
☐ Financial Management Career Program
☐ Manufacturing Information Systems Career Program
☐ Operations Research Career Program
☐ Materials Management Development Program

☐ Marketing Program
☐ Personnel Management Development Program
☐ Direct Hire Referral
☐ Other (Specify)

Specific Vocational Interests Expressed by Applicant	Applicable Work or Military Experience

Locations to Which Applicant Should Be Referred	Application
	☐ Attached ☐ Send To ☐ Not
	☐ Given to Applicant Applicant Required
	Recruiter's Name (Please Print) Facility Ext Date

approach that enables that person to accomplish more than many of his peers.

Because a candidate displays a certain positive characteristic is no guarantee that it will prove good or desirable in practice; that will depend on other elements in the individual's makeup. One may find that an applicant takes initiative, but if he is also highly egotistical, the initiatives will be self-serving and possibly even detrimental to the company.

Another problem with using rating scales on interview evaluation forms is the implication that all the factors checked were observed equally well. For example, the interviewer's rating on "appearance" obviously results from a more complete observation than the rating on "maturity," which may be based on a fleeting and superficial "gut reaction." Yet the credence given to each scale is almost equal.

The presence of several factors on the rating form implies that the interviewer should be making observations on each of them, and that it is realistic to do so. Consequently, ratings are frequently checked off so that the form will look "properly" completed. If for some reason the interviewer did not learn anything about a particular characteristic, he will usually make a rating on a "best guess" basis, if only to avoid being judged a poor assessor.

A more meaningful format for recording information from a campus interview is shown in Figure 15. Notice here how the interviewer is asked to comment only on realistically observable issues. And, because the spaces are completely open, only actually observed behavior is apt to be recorded. The ideal form might simply provide a large open space for comments and reactions.

The Sell Portion of the Student's Visit

Use of the twosome approach can substantially reduce the time spent in evaluation interviewing. This time can be put to good use in selling the student.

An effective approach to selling students is to provide an opportunity for them to develop an identity with the company. One way to accomplish this is to allow the student to participate

Figure 15. Example of a semistructed campus interview form.

INITIAL INTERVIEW REPORT		RECRUITING YEAR 19 19		Interview Date
Name of Candidate		Home Address and Phone No.		
Campus Address and Phone No.				
School		Degree/Major		Graduation Date
Candidate's Geographic Preference or Limitations				
ASSESSMENT OF INDIVIDUAL QUALIFICATIONS (NOTES AND COMMENTS ABOUT OBSERVATIONS)				
Accomplishments and Work Experiences				
Interpersonal Skills				
Intellectual Abilities				
Direction and Interests				
Summary Comments and Reactions				
Overall, I would rate this candidate as				

Below Average   Average to Below Average   Average   Average to Above Average   Above Average

Referral Recommendation: (check one)   [ ] Refer
   [ ] Reject

Interviewer	Title	Unit	Date

in some of the activities and situations he would encounter as an employee. For example, a large oil company uses the morning of the visit for assessment interviews and in the afternoon assigns the student to a young employee recruited a year or two earlier, so that the student can accompany that employee as he performs his afternoon tasks. The student attends meetings, helps write reports, talks with other managers, questions the employee. The student is allowed to spend as little or as much time with the employee as he likes.

The advantages of this work-along-with-me approach are numerous. As the student accompanies the employee on his rounds, he is naturally introduced to other company employees. During the course of the afternoon, the applicant often feels as though he is already on board. Moreover, students often report that the key factor that attracted them to this particular oil company was that they could visualize exactly what they would be doing. The offering letters they received did not represent abstract employment situations but rather called to mind specific people, tasks, and the overall company environment.

The work-along procedure might be difficult or even impossible to implement in certain job situations—for example, when security measures prohibit such tours—but many companies have adopted it to good effect in sales offices, research laboratories, and plant locations.

It is recommended that companies give consideration to ways of selling students other than through a series of interviews. Work-along procedures, tours, discussion meetings with last year's graduates, and a give-and-take conversation with the company president have all proved effective in recruiting. It is usually expensive to bring in students for these visits, and if the candidate is evaluated as good, at least as much care should be given to the sell portion of the day as is given to the assessment.

Summary

The manager who is hiring college seniors may engage in two types of interviews—one on the college campus and the other at the home office. The model for conducting a campus interview takes into account that the campus interview is fundamentally a selling interview with limited assessment goals. The interviewer establishes rapport simply by being natural and structures the roles in the interview by telling the candidate that there will be time to ask questions later. The manager begins the assessment section with make-or-break questions, learning immediately if the student possesses the fundamental requirements for being hired, such as willingness to travel. If the candidate is not disqualified, the interviewer continues the assessment with self-appraisal questions designed to allow time to record observations and formulate hypotheses about the behavior and qualifications of the candidate. In the selling section of the interview, one approach that helps the campus interviewer relate remarks about the company to the interests of the student is to ask what the student is seeking. In closing the interview, the manager should tell the student what the next step in the employment procedure will be.

The purpose of the home office interview is to make a hire/not-hire decision about the candidate and to sell him on the desirability of accepting an offer with the company. An approach that allows for sales time and yet permits accurate hire/not-hire decisions is the use of dual interviewers. Companies using the twosome approach reduce by half the amount of time spent in interviews, and the candidate has time to participate in such selling activities as accompanying a young employee on his rounds in the afternoon.

Chapter 6

The Screening Interview

There are few things more annoying to an employment interviewer than to spend nearly an hour with a job candidate only to discover, near the end of the interview, that a disqualifying fact could easily have been determined at the beginning. Basically, screening interviews help minimize such problems; screening interviews are time savers. They are designed, as the name implies, to screen out those who are clearly unqualified so that those who pass the screen can then be more thoroughly investigated.

Screening interviews are usually brief, taking no more than fifteen minutes; some can be accomplished in less than two minutes. The amount of time spent depends upon the complexity of the job. In screening candidates for a data processing job, for example, only one question may be necessary: "How much experience have you had in programming FORTRAN?" If the applicant's answer reveals insufficient experience, the screening process can end right then and there.

Screening interviews are most helpful when:

1. *There are numerous candidates for a particular job.* When processing many competing applicants, it is almost mandatory to develop a "screen" in order to weed out those who are unlikely to succeed in the job. This happens most frequently when staffing up for nonexempt positions, but can also occur with professional or managerial assignments.

2. *There are one or more critical job requirements which, if not possessed by the applicant, will result in inability to perform the job.* Typically, these requirements are specific know-how or essential

work experience, which can be easily defined or readily determined. "Must know how to read blueprints and extend to quantities" is an example of a clear-cut, essential job requirement.

3. *The candidate is being hired primarily for technological expertise.* If, for instance, a company is looking for high-tech software engineers with experience in rocket propulsion, it often makes sense to have a technological expert screen the candidates before more extensive interviewing is initiated.

Developing a Screening Interview

Screening interviews can be conducted face-to-face or over the telephone; the techniques and questions are essentially the same. The key to successful screening is preparation.

Nature of the Screening Questions

In preparing for a screening interview, it is important to keep in mind that its use is justified because it is cost-effective: it saves time and money. This means that you will have to fight any tendency to add unessential questions to your screening interview.

The most effective questions for a screening interview are those to which only one answer is satisfactory. The questions then become a series of "barriers," the next one being asked only if the applicant satisfactorily answers, or "passes," the previous one.

Screening questions are derived from an analysis of whatever skills, experiences, preferences, or behaviors are *essential* for success on the job. If behavioral specifications (see Chapter 15) have been developed for the job in question, then the source for the screening questions is already available. An item can be considered essential if you can clearly say no to this question: "If the candidate did *not* have this particular experience or capability, could he successfully perform the job?" If your response to that question is at all equivocal, then that particular requirement should not be the basis for a question during the screening interview—because it would not in fact screen out a candidate.

Sources of Screening Questions

The location of a job, its salary level, the work conditions characterizing it, and the knowledge and experience demanded by it are the usual sources of screening questions. A candidate's negative response on any of these factors could immediately disqualify him. For instance, applicants generally have quite decided ideas about where they are willing or not willing to work. Thus the interviewer should mention the location of the job at the outset.

INTERVIEWER: This job is located in New York City. Does that pose any problems for you?
APPLICANT: You mean the job is not in Honolulu?

Or

INTERVIEWER: Are there any areas of the country to which you would not be willing to relocate?
APPLICANT: Well, New York would be my least favorite place, and my wife and kids would hate it.

Obviously this candidate has stumbled at the first hurdle, and can be promptly eliminated.

The salary a job commands is not an equally clear-cut item because candidate and company alike are sometimes willing to compromise on this point. It is nevertheless a leading indicator if the salary level mentioned by the candidate is way out of the ball park. Let's say the company has in mind a yearly salary of $38,000 for the position in question.

INTERVIEWER: Would you mind telling me your minimum salary requirements?
APPLICANT: $50,000. I couldn't make do with less.

Or,

INTERVIEWER: Would you mind telling me what you are currently earning?
APPLICANT: Thirty-six five. And one of the main reasons I'm considering changing jobs is to substantially increase my earnings—and to better my position.

In the first instance, the candidate has clearly disqualified himself. But in the second, the interviewer may well decide to continue talking to find out what aspect of the job is really most important to the job seeker.

Unusual or very demanding work conditions are generally useful screening items. If the job requires substantial travel, extensive overtime, or frequent relocation, or if it involves an unusual physical environment (such as one of excessive heat or cold, or one in which there are risks of radiation), these should be mentioned in the expectation that they will quickly screen out a number of candidates. For instance, the interviewer might say:

INTERVIEWER: This job involves a significant amount of overtime each week. Would that be a problem for you?

Or,

INTERVIEWER: How do you feel about living in a place where the average temperature in winter is 15° below zero?

Or,

INTERVIEWER: If the job involved traveling, how much would you consider excessive?

As mentioned in Chapter 3, interviewers should be especially careful in phrasing their questions to women applicants so as to avoid implying any prejudgment about the woman's capacity or willingness to meet the requirements. Children should not be dragged into these questions. Men are just as likely to screen themselves out in response to the mention of some condition of the job. For instance:

INTERVIEWER: How would you feel about relocating to the Midwest in another two years?

MALE APPLICANT: I've recently found the perfect home—bordering on a golf course and just five minutes from the sound—and it would depress me greatly to leave it.

Where knowledge and experience are concerned, it is sometimes not possible to phrase questions so that only one answer is acceptable—or conclusive for rejecting the candidate. Sometimes it's more a matter of quality than quantity. In these cases, it helps to focus exclusively on *essential*, specific know-how and to develop a series of questions that will elicit data about the extent of the applicant's knowledge or experience. Note, in the following series of questions, how the interviewer qualifies the candidate.

INTERVIEWER: I note from your résumé that you have been selling electronic switches for the past six years. What specific switches have you sold? [*Note, the question is not, "Have you sold XYZ switches?" That would give too much away should the interviewer subsequently have to ask questions about the depth of the applicant's XYZ experience.*]

APPLICANT: I've sold Bellco, Tellco, and XYZ switches. [*Note, if XYZ's are not mentioned, the screening interview can be terminated at this point.*]

INTERVIEWER: Can you put them in order for me? Which ones have you sold the most and least?

APPLICANT: I've sold mostly Tellcos and XYZ's. Not too many of the Bellcos. [*Note, if the applicant placed XYZ's at the bottom of the list, the candidate might be eliminated at this stage.*]

INTERVIEWER: You've certainly had some broad experience. Would you please tell me the approximate dollar worth of sales you've made for each of the three switches?

APPLICANT: Well, of course, it's difficult to do that right off the
top of my head and without going over all my records, but
if a rough estimate is okay, I'd say it went something like
this: I sold more of the XYZ's than the others—this past
year about $450,000 worth. The Tellcos were about
$100,000, and the Bellcos were only about $25,000.

A Model Screening Interview
(For Face-to-Face as Well as Telephone Situations)

Because brevity is one of the principal values of the screening
interview, the opening will usually be short and to the point. It
is not necessary to spend time creating a relaxed climate provided the normal social amenities are observed.

The beginning stage of the interview typically consists of
three relatively easy parts: (1) an introduction, in which you
introduce yourself and your organization (if on the telephone);
(2) an explanation of why the interview is taking place—for
example, "We have received a large number of applications
and, at this point, from your background it looks as though you
could qualify. However, I would like to review just a few points
to be sure we have a good match"—and (3) an explanation of
how the interview will proceed. It is quite important that the
applicant develop the expectation of a short interview. Otherwise, should the interviewer end it after just a few questions, it
would be awkward to terminate and might leave a negative impression of the company. Often, the interviewer has only to say:
"This interview will be quite brief, so I won't be taking much of
your time."

The Questioning

Because most interviews will include several cut-off "gates,"
the series of questions must be developed in advance. Ordinarily, it is best if the questions are arranged in descending order
of importance—the most critical items first, the least essential

last. In this way, the interview can be terminated at any point an applicant "fails" a gate. It is easier to end the interview quickly (when an applicant doesn't meet an essential qualification) if the first questions are the most categorical. These are items from which the *applicant* can immediately determine, without much comment on the part of the interviewer, that there is no match.

A second consideration in developing questions is the degree to which the interviewer can be misled if he "telegraphs" the desired answer. Sometimes it's not a problem. For example, the interviewer states: "This job requires driving a company car." He then asks: "Do you have a valid driver's license?" It's no problem because either the candidate has one (and can produce it) or he does not.

For other questions, however, where a qualitative assessment is needed, the questioning must be more circuitous. This usually means starting with a broad question and then following up with questions of a more specific nature. An example of this line of questioning is shown in the following interview dialogue, where it can be supposed that the interviewer is looking for someone to fill the position of human resources director. The need is for an individual with extensive experience in staffing, particularly at the managerial and executive levels.

INTERVIEWER: Good evening. This is Margaret Smith calling from the General Electronics Corporation. May I speak with Mr. James Kirk, please?

APPLICANT: This is he.

INTERVIEWER: Mr. Kirk, we have received your letter and résumé for the Director of Human Resources job we advertised in the Boston papers. At this point, you may qualify, but I need to get a little more information about your background. Do you have a few minutes now?

APPLICANT: Yes, this is fine. Go ahead.

INTERVIEWER: This interview will be quite brief, Mr. Kirk. It's just a preliminary review. First of all, this job is located at our operations in Portland, Maine. Does that pose any problems for you?

APPLICANT: No, none at all. In fact, it sounds great. We have vacationed there several times, and we have often talked about the possibility of moving there one day.

INTERVIEWER: Good. I can appreciate what you're saying; we go there quite often for skiing. The second question I have is about travel. What would you consider an excessive amount? On the average, how many nights a month would be excessive for you?

APPLICANT: Well, first of all, I don't mind travel. In fact, I like getting out of the office and meeting new people. But, I do have a young family, and if it got to be more than ten nights a month, I think that would be a bit too much.

INTERVIEWER: Thank you. I can appreciate how hard it is to be away too much. Let's spend a few minutes now reviewing your work experience. Your résumé indicates that you have a fairly well-rounded background in human resources. You've had experience in recruiting, benefits, compensation, training, and organization development. Would you mind telling me which one of these areas is your greatest strength, the one in which you have the most competence? [*Note that the interviewer does not risk telegraphing the kind of experience being sought. In this way, it is hoped that a more accurate estimate of the candidate's capabilities can be obtained. This approach usually works quite well, provided too much was not given away when the position was advertised.*]

APPLICANT: That's a difficult question for me to answer. As you said, I've had experience in all of those areas and I feel comfortable about my skills. [*Interviewer remains silent, pauses.*] But, if I had to pick one, I'd say it's in the training and development area. As you know, I've spent the last four years developing an extensive in-house training program. It serves all levels of the company, and has been well-received. I know how to determine training needs, I think I'm quite good at designing effective training programs, and I'm pretty good at delivering some courses myself. I'm also quite strong in performance appraisals, having helped design the one we currently have in operation.

INTERVIEWER: I'm sure all those skills will be helpful in the future. It looks as though you've been real busy. Mr. Kirk, how about the other end of that list? Which of those human resource experiences do you believe represents your least strength—maybe the one in which you would like more experience?

APPLICANT: I don't think I'm really weak in any of the areas, but the one in which I've had the least hands-on time is employment. I've done my share of interviewing, but I haven't been directly assigned to our employment section.

INTERVIEWER: Is there any particular achievement you can tell me about in your recruiting or employment activities?

APPLICANT: Let me think. Oh, yes. I was part of a team that staffed-up a new plant we were opening. It was tough because we had to hire a lot of nonexempts who had never had any plant or production experience.

INTERVIEWER: What role did you play in that project?

APPLICANT: I interviewed at the plant site four or five times.

INTERVIEWER: Mr. Kirk, I want to thank you for the time you've spent here with me on the phone. What you have told me is most helpful, and I'm pleased to say that you're still in the running. However, we have had a large number of responses to our advertisement, and I won't be able to get back to you until we've reviewed the other candidates. We will try, however, to get back to you within two weeks and let you know how you stand with us for this position.

Closing the Interview

The interviewer has two basic options for terminating the interview: the "cutoff" and the "soft" closing.

In the *cutoff* method of ending the screening, the interviewer informs the candidate that there is "no fit." It is used when it is clear to both applicant and interviewer that the candidate is not qualified. In these instances, applicants are unlikely to become defensive or antagonistic because they readily recognize the misfit. An obvious example of such a point occurs when asking about job location. Either the location is acceptable or not. Another misfit occurs when the candidate has weak experience in a critical job area. Here is a way the interviewer could have terminated the interview in the example just described:

INTERVIEWER: Mr. Kirk, you have a good human resources background in development and compensation, but for this job we need someone with outstanding strength in employment and staffing. We'd like to keep your résumé on file for future HR openings, but we have stronger candidates for this particular one.

The up side of this kind of closing is that it can be a time saver, enabling you to close out the discussion in its early stages. The downside is that the applicant may put forth an effort to convince you that you have misunderstood what he said or that he is qualified in some ways not yet mentioned. The situation can become awkward. However, sometimes this kind of applicant reaction can be an advantage. As you listen to the applicant's appeal, you may discover that, indeed, there are strengths you failed to recognize earlier in the interview.

In the *soft closing* approach to terminating the interview, the interviewer does not "close out" the candidate. Instead, the interview is billed as a simple "checking-out" procedure that will be conducted with many applicants. It is "soft" in the sense that the applicant is not overtly rejected, even though the interviewer may no longer be interested. This approach was used with Mr. Kirk in the first example of a screening interview close given. Mr. Kirk is allowed to think that he is "still in the running."

The obvious advantage of the soft closing is that it minimizes the likelihood of prolonged or defensive responses by the candidate. It is easier on both the interviewer and the applicant. From the public relations standpoint, it leaves a good taste in the applicant's mouth. In most cases, it is the closing of choice when the candidate is being eliminated for reasons that are not categorical.

The disadvantage is that it might set up false expectations in the mind of the applicant. This is an issue that will have to be settled by the conscience of each interviewer.

If the soft closing is used, it is helpful to end the discussion with some comment about *next steps.* The interviewer should provide information as to how soon and by what means (phone call, letter) the applicant will be notified of the company's decision on his job application.

Summary

The screening interview should be an integral part of processing job applicants. Candidates who pass the screen can then be given the evaluation interview described elsewhere in this book.

Most screening interviews should take no longer than fifteen minutes. Effective screening interviews require careful preparation of the questions to be asked, their purpose being to eliminate at an early stage obvious "misfits." For screening purposes, the best questions are those that help determine if the applicant meets the most essential qualifications for the job. Care must also be taken in selecting the most appropriate method of terminating the interview—the cutoff or soft closing. Each of these two endings is appropriate in different circumstances.

Chapter 7

The Most Frequent Mistakes Made by Employment Interviewers

The problems depicted in this chapter are gleaned from an analysis of more than 200 tape recordings of employment interviews. The interviews were conducted both by managers who had had little interviewing experience and by professional interviewers who had had lots. The interesting finding is that both amateurs and professionals seem to make the same mistakes. If you have done a fair amount of interviewing, you will probably spot your own errors in this list of most frequently observed mistakes:

- Talking too much, not listening enough
- Jumping to conclusions
- "Telegraphing" the desired answer to questions
- Failing to translate data about past behavior into on-the-job performance predictions

Let's examine each of these problems in more detail.

Talking Too Much

By far the most common error encountered in interviewing is the tendency of the interviewer to dominate the conversation.

This occurs for many reasons. Many managers achieve their positions of leadership, in part, because they have good verbal skills. They find little difficulty in expressing themselves and they usually enjoy communicating. Thus, it is more natural for them to verbalize and to dominate the discussion than to be quiet and listen.

A second reason many managers talk too much in interview situations is that they feel more comfortable when they are in command. They wish to avoid the discomfort of silence or the awkwardness of trying to get the candidate to talk about a topic that may put them on unfamiliar ground. Consequently, they discuss subjects about which they are knowledgeable (the company, the industry, or themselves), but tend to avoid the unknown—the applicant sitting across from them.

A third factor that gets in the way of listening is that some output and communication from the interviewer is both expected and desired. After all, it is necessary to ask questions, explain about the job, sell the applicant on the company, and even engage in some relaxing small talk. The problem is one of balance. In a high proportion of interviews, there is far too much telling and not enough listening. There is a need to control the interview and yet not to engage in so much conversation that the interviewer dominates.

Obviously, the interviewer learns little or nothing while talking. It is only creating a climate that encourages the applicant to speak freely that the interviewer can gather information helpful in making an accurate assessment. The interviewer must strive to keep the conversation going with minimal input. The Evaluation Model, which is presented in Chapter 13 is designed to help minimize the problem of talking too much.

Good interviewing is not merely a matter of trading questions for answers. Instead, it requires the skill to create a purposefully directed casual conversation, one that allows the interviewer to guide the discussion from one topic to the next. Thus, the effective interviewer must learn to lead the discussion but not to dominate it. Such a role requires the interviewer to be a good listener, to show genuine interest in the comments of the applicant. Of course, proficiency in listening can serve managers well in a number of other business activities, such as coaching subordinates or influencing customers. It is an art that has broad application, but it is particularly essential for assessing others.

Jumping to Conclusions

When interviewers hear applicants offer information about themselves or when they observe some behavior pattern, there is a tendency to accept the first logical explanation of the fact or behavior that comes to mind rather than to recognize that many alternative conclusions are possible. An interviewer might learn, for example, that an applicant graduated in the upper 10 percent of his class. The interviewer may think, "Here is a really bright individual." Now, it is quite possible that the person is very bright; it is also quite possible that the applicant is a person of only modest intellectual endowment who worked hard for his grades. The high grades may have been achieved as a result of considerable motivation and not as a function of above-average native intelligence. It may also be true that the applicant's uncle is dean of the school. A number of reasons apart from high intellect could account for the good grades.

Facts or data gleaned from an interview often lend themselves to alternative explanations. To be effective in assessing others, the interviewer must avoid making judgments too soon and must learn to evaluate data so as to select the correct interpretation of any piece of information. Chapter 11 will outline a specific procedure, the Hypothesis Method, that will enable interviewers to reduce the tendency to draw incorrect conclusions.

Another common tendency, particularly among inexperienced interviewers, is to allow a relatively minor attribute (positive or negative) to determine a hire/not-hire decision. For example, an interviewer may be unduly influenced by a candidate who graduated with good grades from the same college as the interviewer. This problem is increased if the applicant also participated in many of the same extracurricular activities.

Sometimes candidates are summarily rejected because they have a "weak handshake" or because they "didn't look me squarely in the eyes." Often other strengths and weaknesses that could lead to a different conclusion are not given sufficient weight.

In most organizations it is policy, either explicit or implicit, to seek out only above-average candidates. Translated into operational behavior, this desire to hire "only the best" is often interpreted to mean that the company doesn't hire people with shortcomings, although a minor one here or there may be allowed. This, too, is jumping to conclusions. Each applicant represents a balance of strengths and weaknesses, so interviewers need to guard against being turned off by shortcomings in applicants. A weakness is often the flip side of a strength. For instance, a candidate who is highly creative and innovative may be judged by an interviewer to be too theoretical, too "blue sky." More will be said on this topic in Chapter 10, "Evaluating What You Observe and Hear: A Conceptual View."

Telegraphing the Desired Answer

Managers often ask how they can avoid being fooled by experienced interview-takers. That is not easy because many applicants, particularly M.B.A.'s or college seniors, have had the opportunity to complete a course on how to take interviews; some may even have participated in more interviews, or be even better trained, than the interviewers themselves.

How difficult or easy it is for interviewers to be fooled has to do with the practice of "telegraphing." This is, most interviewers—through their method of questioning—inadvertently suggest to the candidate what answers they would like to hear. In listening to tapes, for example, one frequently hears the question, "Did you take part in any extracurricular activities on campus?" It is obvious to the applicant, of course, that participation in extracurricular activities must be important to the interviewer. The candidate assumes it would be poorly regarded to indicate little or no involvement in such activities. Another example of telegraphing is the question, "Did you assume any leadership roles in your extracurricular activities?" Again, the interviewer fairly begs the applicant to give the appropriate answer. The interviewer thereby makes it easy for applicants to create a desirable impression.

Another procedure that communicates valuable cues to the applicant is to describe, early in the interview, the job requirements. To illustrate this problem, here is an example taken from an actual tape recording.

INTERVIEWER: Now one thing you should know about this job is that it requires a lot of self-starting ability. You are going to be out on your own a great deal and may see your boss only once every two weeks. And, of course, you're going to have to get your hands dirty, move crates and boxes, and there's plenty of paper work too. There are a lot of records you need to keep. I think you should know these things before we get into this any further.

With such a description in hand, the applicant will obviously understand the best way to respond when the interviewer asks questions about self-starting ability, willingness to get hands dirty, or attitude toward report writing. The applicant who really wants the job can easily supply the correct answers. Candidates who know exactly what is expected may even engage in misrepresentation. The problem is that even though an applicant indicates the ability and desire to do the job described, there may be other areas of work for which he is better suited and from which he would derive greater satisfaction, but by inappropriately telegraphing, the interviewer is not likely to learn about these.

Failing to Translate Facts Into On-the-Job Behavior

Of the four most commonly observed mistakes, the most serious and, at the same time, the most difficult to overcome is the failure to evaluate information heard or observed during the interview. The interviewer may spend quite a bit of time with a candidate and yet at the end have little understanding of the applicant's ability to perform the job. The interviewer, of course, has gathered a great many facts; the difficulty is in translating these facts into a meaningful estimate of on-the-job performance.

When the great variety of data available from the typical employment application form is considered, the question must be raised as to whether the interviewer needs still more facts. Although additional information may help round out the applicant's life story, most interviewers, who already have substantial data available from résumés, application blanks, and college transcripts, need to concentrate on trying to understand what these facts mean rather than on gathering additional historical data.

The point can be easily illustrated in the evaluation of recent M.B.A. graduates. Most students who graduate from the better graduate schools of business have good college records, have participated in extracurricular activities, and perhaps have assumed some leadership roles in undergraduate school. Most of the M.B.A.'s interviewed probably will have done quite well academically in both graduate and undergraduate school. They are, for the most part, articulate and ambitious. What distinguishes Candidate A from Candidate B? Surely there must be differences even though a close examination of their histories shows the two candidates to be almost equally acceptable. The differences, in large measure, center not around the facts themselves but around how and why the students achieved their records. For example, how important is it, per se, to know which subjects a candidate liked or disliked, or what grades were obtained in high school?

INTERVIEWER: What subjects did you enjoy most in high school?
APPLICANT: Well, as I think about it, I really did enjoy math and the science courses best.

Gathering a series of facts such as these just for the sake of gathering them usually contributes little to an understanding of the candidate's on-the-job behavior. However, a discussion about why one applicant had an interest in math or science could be helpful in understanding which job activities will prove rewarding.

INTERVIEWER: What would you say there was about the math or science courses that made them appealing to you?

APPLICANT: I think one thing I liked about them was that there was always a right answer. They weren't as ambiguous as the social studies or history courses in which anybody's answer was as good as anyone else's. With math, particularly, there was one correct answer, and when you got it, you knew you were right!

In this example, the applicant may be telling us something about the kind of job environment in which he will function best. The applicant may be communicating an uncomfortable feeling about ambiguity and a need for a job setting in which procedures and responsibilities are structured or well defined. The message may be that the applicant is likely to be uncomfortable, and perhaps ineffective, if a boss were to give an assignment by saying, "OK, it's your baby. Handle it any way you like." Of course, we cannot be sure at this point about our hypothesis. But if this same desire for structure or black and whiteness comes up several times during the interview, we have begun to learn something about how the candidate will behave in an actual job setting.

Let's examine another example, this time focusing on the "how."

INTERVIEWER: In which subjects did you obtain your best grades?

APPLICANT: Oh, I usually got A's in history.

INTERVIEWER: What would you say there is about yourself that might account for those fine grades you received in history?

APPLICANT: Well, I guess I can attribute them to my writing ability. In the history courses we always had a lot of term papers and, you know, those blue-book exams. I suppose that writing those papers and tests just came easily to me.

In this brief dialogue, the interviewer obtains some clues as to what the applicant might be good at on the job. The hypothesis that must be checked out is that the applicant can in fact communicate well in writing.

In essence, the interviewer needs to concentrate on the primary mission—that of trying to predict how the applicant will perform at work. To accomplish this prediction task, the interviewer must find a method of relating data and information from a person's past to the job for which the applicant is being considered. Chapter 11 describes a clearly defined procedure for helping the interviewer to convert information and facts into meaningful behavioral patterns.

Summary

There are four key mistakes that all interviewers make: talking too much, jumping to conclusions, "telegraphing," and failing to convert information obtained into predictions about on-the-job behavior. As specific techniques can be employed to minimize the impact of these problems, interviewers need not be limited by them.

Chapter 8

What to Ask About

One of the most puzzling aspects of interviewing, particularly for those who do not interview frequently, is to know what to talk about. Much energy is expended in attempting to keep one step ahead of the applicant. Some interviewers follow the sequence of items as printed on an application blank; others follow some prepared guide or interview checklist. Regardless of the device used, the result is rarely the smooth-flowing discussion that most interviewers want to achieve.

One problem in deciding what to talk about lies in the almost limitless number of factors that could potentially explain an individual's behavior or job performance. There are so many bits of information that seem tantalizingly interesting. To illustrate this point, forty-three managers were asked to list those factors they thought were important to learn about in order to make accurate assessments of candidates for supervisory positions. They produced this list.

Analytical skills	Stability
Self-confidence	Persistence
Poise	Maturity
Quantitative skills	Ability to organize oneself
Job interests	Technical know-how
Relevant job experiences	Drive
Social perceptiveness	Ambition
Goals and objectives	Cooperativeness
Energy	Educational background
Ability to communicate	

The managers were saying, in effect, that they could predict the candidate's job success if they were able to learn about all these items. However, they also doubted that all these topics could be meaningfully explored during a typical interview. And their doubts were well taken; the subjects are numerous and complex. An interviewer might acquire a certain "feel" for some of the topics and achieve a reasonable understanding of others. But some qualities, such as maturity, often take years to evaluate. To develop a dialogue that would comprehend all of them is not feasible in a typical assessment interview. Such a dialogue would require at least three or four hours. Every interviewer wants to obtain a well-rounded picture of the applicant, but it is seldom practical to question or evaluate the candidate on all these matters.

A second reason for the what-to-talk-about problem stems from the absence of a plan for organizing the sequence in which topics are to be discussed. The mechanics of conducting the interview should be made easy so that energy and attention can be invested in evaluating what is heard.

This chapter provides both a description of the topics the interviewer can explore and a plan for conducting that exploration. It should be emphasized that the interviewer does not initiate the interview with the intention of determining whether or not the applicant possesses a certain set of traits or qualities. Instead, the interviewer uses a broad topic outline that provides a springboard for conversations from which the applicant's particular strengths and limitations can emerge.

Four Basic Factors

In planning an agenda, the interviewer must first be aware of the kinds of information that are essential to have at the conclusion of the interview. A tool that can help determine which data are most critical is the statistical technique of factor analysis. This method condenses a variety of items into relatively discrete and homogeneous units. When human traits and skills are factor analyzed, psychologists are usually able to distill them

Figure 16. Basic factors in each individual's makeup.

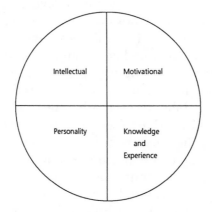

into the following four basic factors that account for success or failure at work:

1. Knowledge/experience
2. Intellectual ability
3. Personality strengths and limitations
4. Motivational characteristics

Supposing that the circle in Figure 16 represents a total person, then it is essential to acquire information about all four factors to obtain a complete picture of the applicant. Should the interviewer fail to obtain at least some data about each of the four factors, his understanding of the applicant will be incomplete and the assessment distorted. At the conclusion of the interview, the interviewer should be able to write a descriptive paragraph about each of the factors that would include something about the candidate's basic aptitudes, thought and problem-solving processes, motivation, relationships to people and temperament, and the relevance of his knowledge and work experience to the job. In a sense, the four factors provide a gauge by which the interviewer can measure his success in developing a comprehensive analysis of the candidate. It is not to be inferred, however, that each of the factors has equal weight or importance for every job. Obviously, the weighting will vary from position to position, but in no case can any one of the factors be dismissed as unimportant. For a research position, for instance, the intelligence and knowledge-experience factors may carry the heaviest weight. However, neither motivation nor personality factors can be ignored. If the research scientist lacks the ability to persuade others of the merits of his ideas or speculations, that researcher may receive little or no budget to accomplish his work. Similarly, motivation and personality factors may command more weight in the selection of successful salespersons, but the intellectual and knowledge-experience factors must also be evaluated.

Later in this chapter, techniques are described that will help ensure that the interviewer obtains information about each factor. The interviewer will be shown, through a discussion of the candidate's life history, how to accumulate information about each of the four factors. First, however, let's try to gain an understanding of the composition of the four factors.

Knowledge and Experience Factor

The fourth fundamental factor, that of knowledge and experience, requires little explanation. Basically, to form a rounded picture of an individual, the interviewer must obtain data about the relevancy of a person's educational background and previous work experience. Is the applicant's training and job experience appropriate for the task at hand? In what ways will the applicant's knowledge help or hinder performance? Most managers typically overestimate the specific skills required for any given task and underestimate the ability of individuals to learn what is needed to perform a new task. The interviewer must be satisfied as to how capable the person is of learning the skills needed for the job in question.

For some jobs, especially those involving technology, it is obvious that the depth and extent of the applicant's capabilities must be carefully explored. Even in these cases, however, if the interviewers are experienced in the particular field, it is usually not difficult to develop a line of questioning that will reveal strengths and weaknesses in knowledge. The depth of know-how can often be revealed by asking the candidate to discuss how and why key projects were completed in past assignments. It is frequently helpful to ask applicants to explain their perceptions of the current state of the art in their respective field.

In attempting to evaluate a candidate's technical competence, some interviewers like to use short verbal tests. They pose a hypothetical problem situation and then ask the applicants what solutions they favor.

There is nothing wrong with the use of such tests, so long as the conclusions drawn from them are not based on whether or not the correct answer is given. The probability of a one- or two-item test being able to accurately predict success is extremely low. Predictive reliability is largely dependent on the number of test items. If the interviewer asked thirty or forty "how-would-you-solve" questions, for example, much more confidence could be placed on the meaning of the applicant's responses than if only one or two such problems were presented.

On the other hand, it is valid and appropriate for the interviewer to ask how the applicant would solve a specific technical problem if the interviewer uses the test question as a basis for observing how the candidate handles himself, what methods he uses, and the sophistication of knowledge displayed instead of as a basis for determining whether or not the answer is correct. In other words, if the test question is used not as a pass–fail sort of quiz but rather as a means of observing the application of knowledge, then its use can be helpful.

Intellectual Factor

In order to understand a candidate's intellectual capabilities, it is necessary to examine intelligence from two different points of view. On the one hand, there is intellectual capacity, the innate ability to solve problems. All people are born with basic capacities that define the limits within which they can function. On the other hand, there is the question of application and effectiveness, that is, how well the individual applies and uses his intellectual capacity.

There are many individuals who possess considerable capacity but who do not apply it well. For example, a person may have good basic intellectual capacity and hence the potential for arriving at good solutions to complex problems, but, because of an impulsive or action-oriented nature, may reason too quickly and superficially. This person has good capacity, but does not apply it effectively.

Another example is the person who has excellent basic intelligence but does not conceptualize well. Such a person focuses on detail and can rarely see the forest for the trees.

A third example of good capacity but poor application is the person who has fine solutions to problems and no lack of creative ideas but does not express them. Most executives know of individuals who leave a problem-solving meeting without having expressed themselves but who, on the way back to their offices, verbalize a solution that would have been ideal. These persons are often afraid of being wrong or of being cricitized: they have good ideas, but they tend to keep them to themselves.

Unfortunately, there is no good way of obtaining an accurate reading of a candidate's intellectual capacity during an interview. The best capacity estimates are made on the basis of certain intelligence tests, tests that do not depend upon the test taker's knowledge and for which scores are not substantially affected by either reading ability or time pressures. These tests have no time limits and provide a measure of the ability to solve increasingly complex problems.* For example, the test items may be like the ones following in which the subject is asked to complete several series by adding the next number or letter:

(a) 2   4   6   8   10   ?
(b) a   b   x   c   d   x   e   f   x   ?
(c) 3   7   23   95   ?
(d) a   c   c   b   e   a   ?

*An example of such an instrument is the *Analytical Judgment Test,* published by Psychological Publications Company, Box 1516, Kennebunkport, Maine 04046.

Because the test items are graded in difficulty, that is, each one slightly more difficult than the preceding one, each applicant eventually reaches items for which he cannot conceptualize correct solutions despite having all the time that is desired. There is no way, however, that similar estimates can be made on the basis of interviewing.

When an estimate of the applicant's intellectual capacity is deemed necessary (and it should be of great concern if the potential for advancement is a consideration in the hire/not-hire decision), then capacity must be measured by tests or inferred from past school or work achievements. Reasonably accurate inferences about capacity can often be made if the applicant has an extensive work history. In such cases, the interviewer can obtain some estimate of capacity by evaluating the complexity of the tasks the applicant has successfully handled. Similarly, when inferring capacity from schoolwork, one can reasonably assume that adequate capacity exists if the applicant received upper-third grades from one of the better colleges or universities. One investigation into innate ability conducted by research psychologists found that the basic capacity of seventy-six top executives for several *Fortune 500* companies was ten percentile points above average when compared with scores on the same test of a cross section of recent college graduates. Of course, these top executives are very superior in capacity when compared with a general cross section of male adults. In any event, in order to get to the top in large U.S. corporations, executives usually need above-average, but not extremely high, capacities when compared with college graduates.

Apparently, an executive's ability to advance, given the capacity level defined here, depends on qualities other than sheer brainpower. If the applicant is an excellent student at one of the better colleges, his intellectual capacity is likely to be sufficient for potential growth into most key positions, all other factors being satisfactory. The question that must be answered is: How effectively can the candidate use this capacity?

A second element of the intellectual factor (basic capacity and its use being the first) is the applicant's preferred manner of processing his thoughts. Most people have a favorite way of thinking. Some like to think in an orderly, deductive manner; others intuitively link one thought with the next; still others like to think quickly, off the top of their heads.

The manner in which a person thinks has much to do with job success. If, for example, Bob, a logical, deductive thinker who likes to study problems thoroughly before acting, is thrust into a fast-paced, action-oriented work environment, he is going to experience much frustration. He will want to opt out of that situation. When evaluating candidates, it is important to compare how the applicant functions intellectually with the nature of the intellectual processing needed for job success.

Personality Factor

The personality factor refers to three different but highly interrelated elements: psychological adjustment, interpersonal relationships, and temperament. To obtain data for these elements, the focus should be on acquiring information about two basic abilities: the applicant's skill in interpersonal relationships and in coping with work demands.

Adjustment   This element has to do with the applicant's general state of mental health. Obviously, if the interviewer is not trained in psychology or psychiatry, the accurate diagnosis of a mental or emotional condition is unrealistic. However, the interviewer can and should be alert to the presence of self-defeating behavior patterns. A blatant example would be an applicant who shows evidence of being a problem drinker. More subtle self-defeating adjustment patterns might be seen in the applicant who is so forceful and aggressive that others avoid contact with that individual. Or, a candidate may have learned to adjust to stresses in the environment by retreating from or avoiding problems and difficulties rather than by confronting them.

Destructive or self-defeating psychological adjustments are not encountered in a large proportion of applicants. Where the evidence indicates a consistent patterns of problem behavior, the impact of such behavior should be judged in relationship to all the other strengths and limitations of the applicant.

Interpersonal Relationships Information about interpersonal relationships is obtained from two sources: observed behavior during the interview, that is, how the applicant interacts with the interviewer, and evidence of how the candidate has interacted with others in the past.

Let's look first at the input from the applicant's ongoing behavior vis-à-vis the interviewer during the interview. Here is a source of information that can be obtained in no other way—how the applicant relates to you as a person, that is, the chemistry that exists between the two of you. This information is critical if the applicant is going to work directly for you. Thus, as interviewers conduct the session, they should note their feelings about the candidate as well as the applicant's apparent reactions to the interview discussion. Is the applicant shy? Confident? Aggressive? Withdrawn? Forceful? Persuasive? Bitter? Arrogant? Open? Outgoing? Passive? Dependent?

What is the person like? If the interview is conducted properly, the interviewer should have ample opportunity to begin developing a picture of how this person typically behaves when he is attempting to create a positive impression and of how comfortable and compatible the applicant might be to work with on the job.

Many books about interviewing point out that interviewers need to guard against judgments that are distorted by bias. Such caution is well taken. But, at the same time, there is no magic switch that the interviewer can turn on that will automatically ensure objectivity. Biases are always with us. One effective way to cope with prejudice is to recognize its presence and to try to understand how it affects the employment decision.

Once in a while, an interviewer may see a candidate about whom he has vague, but negative, feelings. The interviewer, if pressed to explain why he does not like the candidate, would probably find it difficult to give a logical explanation. The interviewer is often inclined to attribute negative impressions to some bias or prejudice. They do this because there is a psychological need to provide a reason for their feelings; if none is apparent, they make one up. The interviewer who encounters an applicant he does not like but who cannot explain these vague I-can't-put-my-finger-on-it feelings should not dismiss them. Many subtle and nonverbal clues are transmitted in face-to-face encounters. If the candidate creates a negative impression upon the interviewer, something is definitely causing it.

Usually, the negative feelings of the interviewer result from the applicant's attitude. The applicant may have been too aggressive, snobbish, pushy, or arrogant. It may be that the applicant talked down to the interviewer. It is not so much what the applicant said but more how he said it, and the subtlety of this is not easy to detect.

Let me cite an extreme example of what can happen when interviewers do not act on their feelings about an applicant. A large machine-tool company had hired a plant manager and now the president and his two vice-presidents were lamenting that they had to fire him after only one week of employment. During the discussion, one of the vice-presidents said, "You know, when I was interviewing that man, I had a funny feeling about him. I couldn't put my finger on it, but something just didn't seem right." The other vice-president made a similar comment. The president, too, said, "You know, I had the same kind of feeling." They had just learned that the man they had hired had not graduated from the college he had indicated and that he had falsified much of his employment record. In the interviews, he was polished and articulate. And he knew the industry sufficiently well to make a favorable impression on the president, two vice-presidents, and the company's personnel director. It was only through a somewhat delayed routine credit check that the discrepancies were uncovered.

Here was a case in which three individuals all had the vague feeling that something was wrong but dismissed it. It is important that the interviewer consider how the candidate impresses him as a person and try to understand how and why this impression is occurring.

Understanding an applicant's interpersonal skills involves

learning how the candidate has interacted with others and handled various confrontations. Information can be acquired by reviewing the candidate's life history. Throughout the interview, the interviewer should obtain a description of how each personal interaction was handled. For instance, if a woman applicant indicates that she earned all her spending money at college by selling subscriptions to *Time* on campus, the interviewer might ask, "What would you say you did, in talking with the students, that led to your success in selling the magazine?" Or the interviewer might pose this question: "Suppose you ran into a student who was particularly negative to your sales presentation and really gave you a hard time. How did you usually manage a situation like that?"

Here's one more example.

INTERVIEWER: You mentioned that you left your last job because of limited opportunity for advancement. I was wondering, did you talk with your boss about possibilities for growth in the firm?

APPLICANT: Oh, yes, several times.

INTERVIEWER: Well, when you went to discuss promotion possibilities with your boss, tell me what you said and how you approached it.

Each time the applicant mentions an interaction with others, it is important to try to get a description of the behavior pattern followed. This information, when added to the observations of the applicant's behavior made during the interview, should enable the interviewer to confirm certain hypotheses about interpersonal relationships and to write a meaningful paragraph or two about how the candidate relates to others in a wide range of situations.

Temperament The third element that helps to explain the personality factor is the individual's approach to work situations, namely, the applicant's temperament. Is the applicant compulsive? Rigid? Energetic or lethargic? Cautious? Sensitive? Impulsive? In other words, how does the candidate behave?

Here again, the interviewer should not look for certain traits or characteristics but rather should let them emerge from observed behavior and from hypotheses developed in the course of self-appraisal questions about the applicant's life history. Subsequent chapters describe the exact procedures for doing this.

Motivational Factor

The motivational factor can be evaluated by learning what a person likes to do or finds satisfaction in doing. Some writers refer to motivation as the "will do" factor, while intelligence, knowledge, and personality represent the "can do" factors. In learning about a candidate's motivation, it is helpful to explore three basic areas: the applicant's interests, aspirations, and energy level.

Interests   The easiest way to learn about an individual's motivation is to inquire about likes and dislikes. Each time interviewees tell you they have done something, you can easily inquire what was liked or disliked about that activity. However, when inquiring about interests, it is not enough to ask only about reactions. It is usually necessary to take a "second cut" at the question; that is, the interviewer must follow up the first question with a second inquiry into the reason for the applicant's preference. The point in asking about the "why" of an interest can be illustrated by examining the following interview segment.

INTERVIEWER: Which of those three summer jobs would you say you enjoyed the most?
APPLICANT: The drafting job.

At this point, what has the interviewer really learned? Merely knowing that the applicant enjoyed the drafting work reveals almost nothing about the applicant's motivational pattern. It is almost always essential, therefore, to follow up the fact-seeking question with a second, motivation-seeking question.

INTERVIEWER: What was it about the drafting job that made it appealing to you?

APPLICANT: I think what I liked about that job is that they left me pretty much on my own and weren't always looking over my shoulder. I had my drawings to do, but as long as I got them done on schedule, how and when I did them was left up to me.

From the applicant's explanation, we see immediately that it wasn't so much the nature of the work that he enjoyed but rather the freedom to work on his own. In the example cited, the follow-up question helped the interviewer avoid a mistaken interpretation that might have been inferred from the first response, namely, that the drafting work itself was the main source of satisfaction.

It should also be recognized that the interviewer is not likely to learn whether a candidate likes a given job by asking directly how the candidate feels about doing that kind of work. For example, it would be inappropriate to ask. "Now that you have had a chance to learn something about the work here, do you think you would enjoy being a technical service representative with us?"*

The question virtually invites the applicant to deceive the interviewer. If the candidate really wants the job, the correct answer is obvious. Of course, there are some applicants who will be frank concerning their feelings about the job in question. However, it is difficult to distinguish between those who indicate they would like the job because it is the right thing to say and those who indicate a positive preference because they truly like the kind of work being offered.

Thus, the prudent strategy is to inquire frequently throughout the interview about the candidate's likes and dislikes in a wide range of activities, many of which may be quite unrelated to the job. In this way, a less distorted picture of the

---

*This kind of question can be used near the end of the interview. At that time, it is appropriate to inquire what there is about the job that might be appealing and not appealing.

applicant's true activity preference is likely to emerge. For instance, suppose the interviewer asked the candidate what he enjoyed least about summer jobs held while attending college. The applicant usually will not relate the question to the job to be filled and, consequently, will speak quite honestly. It is in this manner, by asking many "like" and "dislike" questions, that the interviewer learns about the applicant's true feelings and acquires an accurate picture of the candidate's motivational pattern.

Aspirations Discussion of the applicant's objectives or goals is another way of obtaining information about an individual's motivation. In particular, it can provide clues as to the candidate's value system and perception of the world and as to the rewards expected from an expenditure of labor. However, these are matters about which the applicant can easily deceive the interviewer. Deception is particularly likely when interviewing college seniors or M.B.A.'s. Almost all have been counseled by placement directors as to the importance of having meaningful goals and objectives. Even the untrained have the sophistication to know that it is not desirable to tell a potential employer that they have no particular targets or goals. Most applicants will be able to delineate in rather careful detail their goals and objectives. However, the mere fact that they describe them in a way that suggests they have a clear career path in mind is no guarantee that they are actually committed to such objectives. How interviewers can manage the discussion of goals and objectives is taken up later in this chapter.

The interviewer can test the validity of a polished answer by asking the candidate why he has picked a particular career path or why his particular goals seem most ideal. The individual who has thought through the process and has valid reasons for selecting certain goals usually can handle this question quite effectively; those who are simply attempting to impress the interviewer usually find it difficult to express sound reasons for their decisions, and their thinking will appear shallow and superficial. Again, the motivational input interviewers are seeking comes not so much from the specific goals or objectives mentioned but from the reasons the applicant cites for selecting the goals.

Energy Level While analysis of an individual's interests and goals provides some understanding of the kinds of activities that will motivate the candidate, there is also a second question to be asked, namely: How far down the road will this motivation take the applicant? In other words, direction is one thing, but strength and force in that direction is another. The amount of energy an individual can apply to work activities is a significant variable in job success. Thus, energy level is an important component of the motivational factor.

Energy refers to the physical and biological potential that an individual possesses. A high energy level implies the ability to work long hours without tiring and the ability to get by with relatively little sleep and yet show considerable zest and vitality. This physical energy potential is usually ascertained by inquiring about the current activity level of candidates. A person with a high energy level seems to keep going effectively for long hours in fairly demanding activities. One way to obtain a rough assessment of a person's energy level is to ask the candidate to describe a typical Tuesday. An executive with a high energy level might respond as follows:

APPLICANT: Well, I'm usually up pretty early. I like to get into the office before the staff and get most of the paper work out of the way, so I'm up at 6 A.M. and usually on the 7:30 train. And I'm at the office usually till about 5:30 or 6 P.M. I get home around 7 o'clock and then have dinner. Let's see now, Tuesday is Board of Education night. I'm on the board and usually get out to the meeting at 8 and try to get home by 11 or so. Most nights I try to catch the 11 o'clock news. By then, the house has quieted down and I find it's a good time to go over papers I've brought from the office. I usually try to get to bed around 12:15 or so.

Persons with high energy typically show a fair amount of zest and vitality in the employment interview. It should be recognized, of course, that energy, as with most human traits, distributes itself on a normal curve. To be an acceptable candidate, not everyone need be a bundle of energy. It is important, however, that the interviewer be alert to individuals who appear to have relatively low energy levels, particularly if growth potential is of importance or if the job involves extraordinary physical demands, such as extensive travel and/or long work hours.

Obtaining Data on the Four Factors

As was stated earlier, in order to do a competent and thorough assessment of any job candidate, it is necessary to obtain some information on each of the four factors described here. Obviously, it is impossible to know everything about a candidate's knowledge and experience, intellectual makeup, personality, and motivation, but if data relating to any one of these factors are omitted from the assessment, a large portion of what figures in job success will not be accounted for, and the predictions of the interviewer will be seriously handicapped.

Interview Plans

Chapter 13 will provide a model or procedure for conducting the interview that will help ensure that all four factors are explored. At this point, it may be helpful for the interviewer to institute an interview plan. This means that the interviewer sets up a series of significant topics to be discussed in the interview, and then proceeds in every interview to follow the same organizational format and topic sequence. There are a limited number of topics that can be legitimately covered in an interview. Here are the major life areas that the interviewer is likely to touch on:

1. High school
2. College and/or specialized training
3. Military experience

4. Work experience—full-time
5. Work experience—summer and part-time
6. Attitude toward job, company, or industry
7. Career goals and/or ambitions
8. Candidate's own assessment of strengths and limitations
9. Present activities and interests

Obviously, if the candidate did not attend college or did not serve in the military, these areas would be omitted from the interview plan. The plan should not necessarily follow the order enumerated here. In evolving your interview plan, it is probably best to start off with topic areas that are relatively easy for the applicant to talk about. For example, if most of the candidates to be interviewed are young college graduates, you might start off talking about education and their college experiences. On the other hand, if the interviewer typically interviews mature senior executives, the best plan might be to begin by asking applicants to review their work experience.

The interviewer may also want to include, early in the interview plan but not necessarily as the first topic, parts of the person's life that are especially critical. For example, with a candidate who defies categorization, it may be better to begin the interview with recent accomplishments rather than with high school or full-time work experience. Also, it is helpful to put the more threatening areas such as self-assessment of strengths and limitations near the end of the interview. Other than that, there is no magic to the sequence followed. The main point is to establish a plan and to follow that plan in every interview in which it is applicable. Figure 17 shows examples of two different interview plans that have proved effective.

There are two main reasons why the interview plan is a good idea. First, it simplifies the mechanics of conducting an interview. It removes from the interviewer's mind the problem of what to ask next. With the plan, the interviewer always knows what will come next and, as a consequence, will have a comfortable feeling of being in control. The interviewer will always know when he is half way or a third of the way through the interview. So, a topic sequence plan makes the conduct of the

Figure 17. Samples of two interview plans.

Relatively inexperienced (College Grads, Middle Managers*)	Experienced Senior Executives

High School
College
Work experience
  summer or part-time
Work experience
  full-time
Goals and ambitions
Reactions to job
Self-assessment
Military experience
Present activities
	Work experience
	  full-time
	College or studies
	Goals and ambitions
	Reactions to job
	Self-assessment
	Military experience
	Present activities
	High school

*For relatively inexperienced high school graduates, the same plan can be followed, omitting the college section.

interview relatively easy. It also makes possible a smooth transition from one area to the next.

A second and perhaps more important reason for having an interview plan is to ensure that the interviewer covers a broad cross section of the applicant's life. As we shall learn when we talk about evaluating data, it is important to develop hypotheses for all four factors. If the interviewer restricts his questions essentially to education or job experience, the profile will emphasize those factors and may not yield enough data about motivation and personality.

Life Areas to Explore

There are nine life areas that can be expected to yield relevant information.

High School

It is important to note that if it has been many years since the candidate attended high school, the interviewer should not be concerned with the details of what the applicant did or did not do there. After all, if the applicant attended high school twenty years earlier, the relevance of specific incidents from that period is open to question. However, even in these cases, the area is worth exploring because it can provide a rich source of data and hypotheses about current behavior. The reason for this is that the applicant is interpreting the past (how and why things were done) not through the eyes and mind of a sixteen-year-old student but through the perceptions of a present-day adult. For example:

INTERVIEWER: You mentioned that you played basketball in high school. Sometimes people learn something from playing team sports; sometimes, of course, we get nothing in particular from them. But, as you think back on that period in your life, is there anything you think you learned from playing on that team?

APPLICANT: Yes, I think I got something from it. I learned that if you want to do something hard enough, you can.

INTERVIEWER: Could you elaborate on that a bit?

APPLICANT: Sure. I wasn't very tall in high school, and when I went out for the team, the coach said that I could try out, but he doubted I'd be big enough to make the team . . . but I'll tell you, I was really determined, and somehow I made it. I was just more scrappy and outran the bigger guys; I was always after the ball. I guess what I am saying is I learned that if I set my mind on doing something, I'm usually able to do it . . . and that's true for me even now.

Topics to Explore

■ *Best subjects, subjects done less well*
  What made them easy? Difficult?

- *Subjects liked the most, subjects liked the least*
  Why was that subject so appealing?
  Not appealing?
- *Extracurricular activities*
  What was learned from them?
- *Early interests and ambitions (even if they now sound silly)*
  What made these appealing?

College and Other Studies

As is true for the high school area, exploration of college experiences provides a good opportunity to learn about intellectual skills and aptitudes, motivational patterns (by asking about likes and dislikes of subjects and school activities), and personality makeup factors such as adaptability, perseverance, and social adeptness.

If the candidate attended several schools, it is a good idea to discuss each school in some depth as a relatively separate issue.

Topics to Explore

- *Same topics as for high school*
- *Reason for selection of major*
- *Reason for selecting school*
- *Reason for changes in curriculum (if any)*
  What were the factors that led to your decision to change?
- *Extent to which education will aid work*
  In what ways do you see your educational background helping you to succeed in this job?

Military Experience

Prolonged or detailed discussion of a candidate's military career is usually not productive for predicting on-the-job behavior. However, from time to time the interviewer may learn about skills acquired, attitudes (particularly toward highly structured environments), and personality characteristics such as adaptability.

Topics to Explore

- *Assignments and duties*
- *Explanation for advancement or lack of it*
- *What was learned from military experiences*
- *What was hoped to be gained (if voluntary)*

Work Experience

It is usually desirable to cover work experiences in chronological order. This procedure enables the interviewer to look for gaps in the employment record and to understand the rationale behind any job changes. A helpful way to start discussion in this area is with a question such as: "Will you tell me about your work experiences, taking them in the order in which they occurred."

If the applicant has a particularly long work history, it is usually easier to split the jobs into time segments. In this way, the interviewer will have better control over the discussion and can focus more time on current work experiences. However, early work experiences can provide meaningful hypotheses about present job behavior, so those portions of the applicant's life history should not be skipped. Here is one way of beginning:

INTERVIEWER: Since you have a long work history, suppose we start off by your telling me about the jobs from college up until the time you joined Allied Corporation (about halfway through the candidate's job history).

As the interviewer explores each job in the applicant's track record, it will be productive to consistently ask about: (1) starting and ending salary; and (2) why the applicant left the job.

When salary information is requested for the first few jobs, applicants thereafter usually pick up on the idea and voluntarily provide their salary levels without the interviewer having to ask for them. Because salary history is relatively easy to confirm, it provides a good means of checking on the credibility of the applicant's statements about job responsibilities.

When inquiring about job changes, a good question to ask is: "What did you see in the new position that made it seem more desirable than your previous one?"

The following outline of a questioning procedure may be particularly helpful for learning *how* the candidate functions at work. The interviewer can start by asking the applicant to describe his job at a particular company and next proceed with such questions as:

1. What was your most significant achievement at the ABC Company?
   a. What is there about you that made it possible?
   b. What was the most difficult aspect of this accomplishment? How did you overcome it?
2. What did you like most about that job? Least? Why were those aspects appealing? Unappealing?
3. If I were to call your boss, what would he say about you and your work?
4. Can you describe for me how you typically manage? Could you give me an example?
5. Do you have any unique technical skills that you acquired on that job? Could you describe them for me?
6. Can you describe how you like to go about solving problems? Can you give me a few examples?

This cycle of questioning, or variations on it, can be repeated for each significant job.

Summer or part-time employment should be considered as a separate area for exploration unless the applicant voluntarily describes such jobs along with the full-time jobs held. The same kinds of topics can be explored for both full-time and part-time work experiences.

Topics to Explore

- *Things done best and least well*
  What skills did you bring to bear that helped you to do well? Is there anything about your personal makeup that might account for your success?
- *Job activities liked best and least*
  What was there about them that was appealing? Unappealing?
- *Major accomplishment on each job*
  How were you able to do it? What did you have going for you that made it possible?
- *Most difficult problems encountered*
  How did you solve them? What made them difficult?
- *How people relationships were handled*
  What did you do to make it work out? If you could do it over, would you handle the relationship differently?
- *Reasons for changing jobs*
  What prompted you to leave the job?

Attitudes Toward Job and Company

In this section of the interview plan, the interviewer solicits the applicant's attitudes and feelings about the company, the job, and the industry for which application is being made.

Topics to Explore

- *Interests in job.*
  What is it about this job that appeals to you? What do you see in this assignment that was not available to you in your previous assignment? What things connected with this job might make it somewhat less than satisfying for you? From what you know at this point, what is the least satisfactory aspect of this job?
- *Reactions to company or organization*
  Is there anything about our organization that might

raise a question in your mind as to how ideal this is for you as a place to work?

■ *Reactions to the industry*
How do you feel about our industry (or line of business)?

■ *Job perceptions*
What do you feel you might have to know more about before you could step in and really do this assignment justice?

Aspirations and Goals

Exploration of the applicant's ambitions is an important part of the interview because it aids in establishing additional data and hypotheses about motivation. It provides the interviewer with information about activities in which the applicant expects to find satisfaction as well as about those that the applicant wants to avoid. It also makes possible further understanding of the applicant's drive and ambitions for the future.

The classic approach to discussing goals is to ask, "Where would you like to be five years from now?" However, anyone who has done a fair amount of interviewing knows that this question, above all others, yields answers that can be quite deceptive; almost all reasonably sophisticated applicants will have a prepared or canned answer. Applicants often respond with a great show of conviction, even though they may be quite uncertain as to their career direction. In effect, they simply give a logical answer in order to appear highly motivated to the interviewer.

Interviewers should be careful not to be unduly impressed by applicants who seem to know where they want to go; likewise, they should not be unfavorably impressed by the applicant who seems somewhat confused as to which vocational or career goals to pursue. Instead, the interviewer should try to understand the underlying reasons for the applicant's choice of goals or lack of decision. In this way, meaningful data can be obtained about the applicant's motivation and interests.

In brief, then, the question about goals and ambitions is

asked not so much for the direct response that is given by the applicant but because the response provides a jumping-off point for the interviewer to further explore how or why the goals were selected. As an example, let's consider a dialogue between an interviewer and an applicant who at the outset seems sure and confident about his goals. As will become apparent, however, the applicant is really uncertain as to his ambitions.

INTERVIEWER: As you look down the road ahead, where would you like to see yourself five years from now?

APPLICANT: Well, I feel fairly confident about what I want to do. I want to move up the sales ladder, and my expectation is that within a year I'll be moving into some first-level supervisory position. Beyond that, it's hard to put an exact timetable on it, but I would think I could be a district sales manager within three to four years. Then, I would hope to move right on up to become a regional manager in maybe five to six years.

INTERVIEWER: Well, that certainly sounds as though you've made up your mind where you want to go and how rapidly you want to move. Tell me, what makes you feel so certain that this is the best career path for you?

APPLICANT: That's a good question. [*Pauses*] As a matter of fact, I have been looking at other opportunities in market research. I think the challenges in the research area could be very appealing. I guess what I'm saying here is that my mind isn't really so closed. I would want to see what market research might have to offer in comparison to the sales jobs.

INTERVIEWER: Well, suppose you tell me a little about what you see market research as offering you that you may not find in sales work?

APPLICANT: That's a real tough one. I guess I'm really going to have to first dig a little deeper into the sales jobs in order to see what there is about them that will be the most satisfying for me. Then perhaps I'll be able to compare better.

People who have thought out their career plans carefully and have a true commitment to them usually have a reasoned approach to stating their goals and objectives and can verbalize these thoughts in a clear, believable way. By contrast, those who define goals according to what they believe is the right thing to say are usually unable to convincingly explain why they made the choices they have indicated. If questioned, some will tell you that they are still uncertain as to what they want to do. In any event, the important point here is that one should not take at face value a person's description of goals and objectives. Instead, inquiries must be made as to how the choice was reached. Hypotheses about the applicant's directional motivation and drive are then formed on the basis of the reasons provided by the applicant.

At times, applicants will seem to be confused about which career paths they wish to follow, but as the interviewer continues probing, the motivational pattern may turn out to be quite straight forward. This is reflected in the following dialogue.

INTERVIEWER: As you look ahead, where do you see yourself going from here?

APPLICANT: Well, I guess I'm still a bit on the fence. I think I want to be in the accounting field, but I don't know whether I really want to go into auditing work with one of the large public accounting firms or take a position in finance, like the one you are offering me here.

INTERVIEWER: I can see that you feel there might be good opportunities in both fields. Tell me a little bit about your thinking on the subject. What is making it difficult for you to decide at this point?

APPLICANT: Well, I certainly want to move ahead in the business world. And it seems to me that the experience and advancement I would get in an operating company like this one are essential ingredients for getting into management. But I keep thinking that maybe the professional training I would get in an accounting firm would provide a stronger base to start out from.

INTERVIEWER: The thing that is really creating a dilemma for you is how much weight to put on the kind of training you'd get in public accounting. You're not in a quandary about what kind of work you would prefer.

APPLICANT: That's right. If I thought I'd get the same kind of training here in a business, then I guess my dilemma would be resolved.

As the example demonstrates, once understanding is reached as to why the individual is confused about career goals, seemingly confused motivation becomes understandable. In fact, the interviewer will often find that no basic goal conflict exists. The interviewer, too, should be aware that many times an applicant cannot decide between career A and career B because the candidate does not have adequate knowledge of what the jobs entail. However, the interviewer should know, by virtue of an extensive review of the applicant's likes and dislikes, what kind of work will be most appealing to the candidate, even if the applicant is uncertain.

Topics to Explore

- *Short-term goals*
- *Long-term career objectives*
    What do you feel you need to do and know before you'll be able to qualify for such a position?
- *Jobs or activities to be avoided in future positions*
    Why?
- *Salary goals or targets*
- *Past experiences that led to present career objectives*
- *Attitudes about travel*
    On the average, how many nights away from home per week would you consider to be excessive?
- *Attitudes about relocating*

Self-Assessment of Candidate's Strengths and Limitations

Because this topic can be a bit threatening, the self-assessment query should not be introduced until near the end of the interview. Basically, the interviewer asks the applicant to provide an estimate of his strengths and limitations. The input from such a question enables the interviewer to develop many new hypotheses about the candidate and, in addition, can help confirm or invalidate those that were developed earlier in the interview.

Usually the self-appraisal question is best managed by discussing it in two parts—one segment devoted to the candidate's strengths and the second to his limitations. An easy way to introduce this topic without labeling it a self-assessment is to make a statement such as, "We've been talking here at some length about the success you've had over the years. What would you say there is about yourself that might account for the fine record you bring to us here today?"

Applicants often have a difficult time verbalizing an answer to this question. They may refer vaguely to their experience of motivation, or they may even become defensive about the question. In either case, some "pump priming" is usually necessary to help the individual get started. For example:

APPLICANT: I just don't know what to say. I guess my success really is based upon the fact that I had good experience in this industry.

INTERVIEWER: Well, sometimes it is difficult to think about ourselves in terms of traits and qualities, but do you remember when we were talking about college and how you were able to go out for sports and still make grades good enough to get on the dean's list? At that time I asked you how you were able to manage it and you said you always had a lot of energy and that you could get along with relatively little sleep—that you were just a very vital person. Well, that might be a good quality or trait that accounted for some of your success over the years. Can you think of any other traits or abilities you have that could explain your success?

If the interviewer receives only one or two statements from the applicant about a trait or ability, he should encourage the candidate to continue. This can be done by asking, "Is there anything else you can think of?" Almost invariably, if applicants are prompted in this way, they will offer additional thoughts. It is quite important, too, to generate a fair number of positive responses about strengths because elaboration of them then makes it easier for the applicant to answer subsequent questions about limitations.

The second part of the self-assessment question centers around shortcomings. Of course, this is a more difficult question for the applicant to respond to, but the extent of the response depends in large measure on how the question is phrased. One approach is to say, "We've been talking here about all the good qualities and abilities you have: now how about the other side of the coin? What would you say there is about yourself that could be improved upon or strengthened?"

The interviewer is likely to receive one of three typical responses to this question. First, the applicant may be open and frank and freely share his shortcomings. The interviewer, in such cases, can explore them in any depth desired so as to understand what the applicant is saying.

A second possible response, however, is less helpful. The applicant may answer the question in terms of areas of knowledge or experience that could be bettered. Although it is helpful to understand that the applicant may feel inadequate as far as some specific knowledge or training is concerned, the stated lack of know-how is seldom a significant issue in the hiring decision. Usually the interviewer has other data about the applicant's training and experience that help determine the extent of the candidate's qualifications for the job. The areas that are most important to explore in the shortcomings section are the applicant's analysis of his traits, personality structure, and temperament. To direct the focus away from education and toward the individual's makeup, the interviewer could ask, "Apart from knowledge—I guess we all could learn more—what would you say there is about yourself that you might wish to improve upon?"

The third typical reaction of applicants is to become defensive and beg off the question. The candidate may say, "I can't think of any serious shortcomings. Anything I've been weak in, I've worked hard to overcome."

In such cases, the interviewer should not be discouraged. It is of primary importance to encourage applicants to analyze themselves critically. In reply, the interviewer might say, "Well, I recognize that there may not be any major shortcomings in your makeup, but what are a few of the small things that could possibly detract from 100 percent performance on your part?"

It is important not to give up too soon. This is one area in which a little pressure is acceptable. After the applicant has voiced one or two shortcomings, the interviewer should prod the individual to continue by asking, "Anything else you can think of?" The reason for continuing in this way is that most sophisticated applicants realize that it is naive to indicate that they have no shortcomings or limitations. Thus they are likely to mention a few "safe" shortcomings. For example, a sophisticated applicant might indicate that she could improve her public speaking ability. Of course, almost everyone could, even the most polished speaker. Or another might say, "I guess I get a little impatient from time to time." Impatience has both good and bad implications: It can account for one's success and self-starting ability, and it can be seen as an undesirable personality quality.

In any event, the strategy to follow when such safe responses are given is to discuss the statements made by the applicant but then to go on to look for more shortcomings. Usually, after the few innocuous shortcomings are mentioned, the interviewer will uncover more significant features of the applicant's behavior or performance.

If all efforts to encourage the applicant fail, one alternative is available. The interviewer can ask, "In what ways would you say you have grown the most over the past two to three years?" Applicants typically respond to this question by talking about a weakness. When the area of improvement is mentioned, the interviewer should draw out the candidate to learn the meaning and significance of the limitation.

Topics to Explore

- *Good qualities as seen by others (boss or teacher)*
- *Natural aptitude or abilities*
    Have you ever noticed any particular skill or ability that came easily to you, almost as a natural talent?

- *Qualities that make applicant a good investment*
- *Areas that need improvement*
    Are there any areas you have been working on recently to help you develop greater job effectiveness?
- *Constructive criticism heard from others*
- *Ways in which applicant might be a risk for employer*
    Are there any things about yourself we haven't talked about that you think would help us to know you better?

Leisure-Time Activities

A review of the activities that candidates enjoy in their off hours often provides helpful input about motivation and skills. However, merely asking what a person likes to do during leisure hours is not sufficient. Usually a second-level question must be asked about the satisfactions the applicant finds in the activities mentioned. It is of little help to know that the applicant enjoys collecting stamps or managing a Little League team or puttering in a garden. The real issue is what it is about this activity that makes the candidate good at it or contributes to his personal satisfaction.

The interviewer should also explore to what extent the applicant actually pursues the leisure-time activities mentioned. Applicants will often reel off a string of hobbies and sports, but, upon closer examination, the interviewer may find that they engage in only one or two of them. The others were of interest earlier in life or represent peripheral interests. It is helpful, therefore, for the interviewer to explore how much time during a given month the applicant actually spends engaging in a particular activity.

Topics to Explore

- *Activities one likes to do in spare time*
    What about _____ do you find appealing?
    What makes you good at _____?
- *How spare-time activities may or may not aid job performance*

Tested Questions

This chapter has suggested a variety of topics that should be discussed to ensure that sufficient data are obtained on each of the four basic factors. Also offered were a number of specific questions that can aid in achieving the same objective. These are known as tested questions: They can be defined as those that the interviewer asks in almost every interview because they have been found to produce meaningful results. If the interviewer is not obtaining adequate data on one of the factors, a definite point can be made to include some tested questions that will in all probability yield data on the factor in question. To assist the interviewer in this regard, Appendix A lists approximately 100 tested questions. They are catalogued by topic area, such as high school, work experience, and leisure time, and also by factor.

This is not to suggest that the interviewer should conduct an entire interview based on a prepared set of questions. However, a sprinkling of these tested questions throughout the interview will help elicit data on all four factors. Most individuals who have done a fair amount of interviewing will already have developed a repertoire of tested questions. Tested questions are asked at specific points during the interview, as will be explained more fully later.

Summary

In order to perform a meaningful assessment of any candidate, it is necessary to obtain data on four fundamental factors—intelligence, motivation, personality, and knowledge/experience. While it is not possible to obtain complete information on all these elements, the absence of data on any one of the factors will be a significant handicap in assessing an applicant's prospects for success at work.

The interviewer should not try to determine each of the four factors in order, but should follow an interview plan that consists of nine major topics to be explored during the interview. The plan helps the interviewer cover these nine topics in the same order in every interview. This procedure will give the interviewer a feeling of control in knowing where he is in the course of the interview and will also ensure wide coverage of the candidate's background. It was also suggested that tested questions be used to ensure input of data on the four factors.

The sequence of topics to be explored in the interview plan depends upon the category of candidates being interviewed. It is recommended that the interviewer develop a plan that is appropriate to the general age and experience level of the individual being interviewed.

Chapter 9

Encouraging Applicant Openness

There are many theories about interviewing. Everyone has heard of the executive who, after a few preliminary remarks, picks a crayon off his desk, thrusts it in the applicant's face, and says, "Go ahead, sell me this crayon. Quick, sell it to me!" Another manager may offer cigarettes in a room in which there are no ashtrays, or three or four executives may simultaneously give an applicant the third degree.

All these techniques fall under the category of stress interviewing. They put applicants under duress to see how well they handle themselves in difficult situations or are able to cope with pressure. The question is whether such techniques really help the executive learn much about the applicant. There is little evidence to suggest that this approach to interviewing is productive. In fact, most studies show, even when one is attempting simply to measure the candidate's skill in coping with stress, that the interview judgment of this ability usually bears little relationship to actual job performance. In other words, the use of situational tests has been singularly unsuccessful in predicting future job behavior. The exception is the use of trial experiences to determine a specific technical skill. For example, actual job conditions can be duplicated by setting up a turret lathe on which the candidate is asked to demonstrate proficiency.

One of the difficulties in using situational interviews is that it is almost impossible to duplicate a truly lifelike situation. For example, if the applicant is a candidate for a sales representative position, the interviewer can never duplicate the same stresses that the salesperson will experience in the field. Such replication is difficult because an individual's reaction to pressure is a function of many different elements—the exact situation, the salesperson's self-confidence level, personality traits, temperament, and skills and abilities. In other words, as the salesperson works on the job, the factors in the equation change. Experience with other buyers, for example, will affect one's confidence level and skill in coping with tough buyers. Thus behavior during such an interview may not give an accurate impression of how the applicant will behave on the job.

Elaborate studies about the effectiveness of situational tests were conducted by the Office of Strategic Services during World War II. The findings indicated that such methods do not lend themselves well to use by amateur assessors. And, even though assessment centers have recently been demonstrated to be reasonably effective in predicting job success, the kind of job simulations to which the candidates are exposed (in-baskets, leaderless group discussions) are far more elaborate than the kind of interview simulations referred to here.

A second reason that situational tests, such as the stress interview, are not recommended is that this interview approach tends to make it more difficult to explore other facets of the candidate's makeup apart from ability to cope with stress or pressure. Indeed, use of such interviews make it difficult to learn even about the positive aspects of the applicant's life history.

The moment pressure is applied, the applicant becomes more guarded and defensive and less open to the interviewer's questions. To make an effective assessment, the interviewer cannot just measure reaction to pressure, or social skills, or whatever. There is a need to look at the person as a totality in order to accurately evaluate future performance. Thus the best approach is one that creates a climate in which the candidate feels comfortable and in which threat is kept to a minimal level.

Lowering the Threat Level

It is quite apparent that getting applicants to talk about themselves during interviews is really not enough. To make an accurate assessment, the interviewer needs to hear about the bad as well as the good. This means that applicants must be encouraged to talk about things they would prefer not to mention. Thus the problem is to create a situation or climate in which applicants will share some of the negative elements in their past.

To obtain a better understanding of the conditions that lend themselves to openness and frankness, think of the kind of climate that would have to exist before you would be willing to reveal things about yourself that would not make you feel defensive. Most likely, words such as "sincere," "confidential," "friendly," "relaxed," and "understanding" will come to mind. When all the conditions evoked by these words are combined, the situation created could be characterized as being relatively free of threat. It is only the fear of embarrassment, of not being thought well of, or of not being highly regarded that keeps one from revealing negatives about oneself.

Of course, no interview can be completely threat-free. The mere fact that the discussion is an employment interview results in a certain amount of threat, even if the interview is only for practice or to visit a particular city on a recruiting trip. The candidate's ego demands that he make a good impression on the interviewer even in such a case.

There are a number of activities in which the interviewer can engage in order to keep the threat level relatively low during the interview. Conceptually speaking, individuals feel less threatened if they are confident of themselves in the interview situation; that is, the extent to which applicants feel they are doing well and making a favorable impression on the interviewer is the extent to which they are likely to be open and willing to share shortcomings with that interviewer. Self-confidence works in much the same way in any situation. The strong, confident individual is normally not afraid to admit to shortcomings to others; by contrast, those who are insecure or uncertain of themselves find it difficult to admit their inadequacies to others and even to themselves. Making it possible for applicants to feel as confident as possible then poses a challenge.

Creating a Living Room Atmosphere

There are simple social actions the interviewer can take to make the interview situation more informal, more comfortable, and more relaxed. These can include speaking to the applicant on a first-name basis, offering him coffee or cigarettes, or even having a less formal seating arrangement, such as side by side rather than the interviewer behind a desk. Generally, gestures that feel comfortable and natural for the interviewer tend to make the climate favorable for interviewing.

Interviewers should be cautioned, however, not to play a role. Many texts on interviewing suggest that the interviewer should adopt the posture of a "nice guy." The theory is that, if applicants think the interviewer is a person who is pleasant and easygoing, they will feel more comfortable and reveal more of themselves. However, the applicant is also judging the interviewer as a potential boss. Playing a role, therefore, presents the danger that the interviewer may not come across as sincere and may even be seen as a bit of a phony. Thus the applicant may decide that the interviewer is not the kind of manager for whom he would like to work.

For this reason, it is better for interviewers to be themselves and to act in a natural, normal manner. Extra attention, however, should be given to the social amenities to make the situation more cordial and relaxed.

Ensuring Privacy

There is no question but that people are more likely to be open if they feel their remarks are not being shared with others and if there is a sense of confidentiality to the discussion. However, privacy is more than four walls and a closed door; it is also related to interruptions. Whenever an interruption occurs during the interview, whether it is a telephone call or a secretary coming into the office, it provides an opportunity for applicants to think over what they have been saying. It is this review of previous stages of the interview that can create problems for the interviewer. If the interviewer is distracted for any extended period of time, the following thoughts may go through an applicant's mind: "I probably shouldn't have said so much about the fact that I was fired from that summer job in the road department. I bet this guy feels that I don't get along too well with others. I had better be sure to make the point that I'm cooperative and that I rarely have problems with people." Or the applicant might think, "This interviewer seemed quite concerned about the extracurricular activities I had in high school. They must be important to him—I'd better get a few more lined up for college because I'm sure he's going to ask about them."

It may be better to interview in a crowded dining room where there are no interruptions than to talk in a private office where frequent interruptions pepper the discussion. If it is impossible to discontinue phone calls, seriously consider interviewing in a waiting room or conference room or over coffee in the cafeteria.

Making Small Talk

Many interviewers think that a good way to put the applicant at ease at the beginning of the interview is to engage in small talk. The idea of getting the applicant to talk early in the interview is an excellent one. Whether or not small talk produces the desired climate depends a great deal on how it is used. Not all small talk reduces tension. For example, suppose your boss calls you into his office and says, "Have a seat. Say, how are the kids?" Does his attempt at small talk put you at ease?

Getting the applicant to talk at the beginning of the interview is desirable for two reasons. First, once the applicant has heard his own voice in an unfamiliar setting, there is an inclination to continue verbalizing and participating in the discussion. Second, talking tends to reduce tension. Verbalizing usually helps people to discharge nervous energy. Thus applicants are inclined to be less keyed up and to talk in a more spontaneous manner.

For small talk to be effective, it should not be perceived as such. For instance, to raise questions about the weather or last week's football game or to engage in other obvious chitchat may actually increase tension. The applicant is waiting until the interviewer says, "Now to start with the interview. . . ."

While there may be some value to observing how skillfully the applicant converses in a casual, small-talk way, the amount of time consumed by this exercise is probably disproportionate to the gain. Subsequent chapters will point out better opportunities for observing the candidate's skill in coping with relatively nonstructured social situations.

The most helpful small talk stems from topics that arise naturally and spontaneously. Small talk that is obviously related to the interview situation is also good. The interviewer might, for example, ask about possible difficulties the applicant encountered in finding a parking space; or if this interview happens to be one of several, inquiry could be made about how the interviews are coming along, or how the applicant feels after completing several of them.

If the interviewer experiences any strain in trying to generate small talk, it is best to avoid it altogether. After polite greetings, there is no reason not to launch right into the interview, starting off with the first area in the interviewer's scheduled interview plan. This topic should be one that is relatively easy for the applicant to talk about. If, for example, the applicant was recruited on campus and has come to the home office for a second interview, the interviewer might start out by asking about the candidate's college career. This topic is easy for the student to discuss, and it places no particular burden on the interviewer.

Explaining the Structure of the Interview

Anything that can be done to reduce the number of unknowns in the interview process will also help reduce the applicant's tension. One of the easiest things to do is to tell the applicant something about yourself. Don't give a long job history, of course, but simply mention your position in the company and briefly describe what you do. This information will help the applicant to know how much technical detail to provide about his background and whether or not technical jargon would be understood.

It is also desirable to explain what will happen during the interview process. You can mention who else the applicant will be talking with, how long the other interviews will take (if others are already scheduled), what will happen about lunch, and when during the interview the applicant will have an opportunity to inquire about the organization. Letting the applicant know that the interview will be a two-way street can be particularly helpful and might be introduced in this way:

INTERVIEWER: Obviously you're here today to learn about job opportunities with us, just as we need to become acquainted with you. So, let's plan on dividing the time up. I'd like to spend the first portion of our time together learning about your background; then we'll turn it around to give you a chance to ask about us.

Playing Down Unfavorable Information

Whenever the applicant says something that is uncomfortable to admit, it is usually that very topic that the interviewer desires to hear more about. However, a direct question concerning the issue is likely to cause the applicant to become guarded and to give an answer that while reasonable, prudent, and logical may not be a true depiction of the actual situation. Most candidates will not speak freely about a negative point if they think that the interviewer regards that point as highly significant. In fact, the more attention the interviewer gives to a negative issue, the more cautious the applicant will be in talking about it. Thus it is usually desirable to play down unfavorable information when it is heard.

The easiest way to play down a statement is to indicate that it is a common experience for others. If, for instance, the applicant says that he was let go from a summer job because of a personality conflict with the boss, the interviewer might encourage a further explanation of that topic by saying, "Well, there is hardly a person working today who hasn't run into a boss like that at some time or other during his business career. What happened in this particular instance?" Or the applicant might indicate that he failed analytical geometry in college. The interviewer could say. "Well, I know that was a dog course when I went to school. What gave you trouble when you were taking it?" In other words, it is important to let applicants know that they can safely talk about shortcomings without the interviewer becoming negatively prejudiced.

The interviewer needs to be aware that in playing down shortcomings, there is a risk of appearing phony. If, for instance, the topic is a serious one and is played down, but then discussed at length, it soon becomes apparent to the applicant that the topic *is* important. Thus, the interviewer needs not to go "overboard" in playing down very important shortcomings. Instead, it is best to try to convey to the applicant that everyone has problems and makes mistakes—that we don't expect perfection in people. This type of downplaying is honest and will ring true.

Another way to make a negative issue less threatening is to ask the candidate a question that does not imply negative judgment but is still related to the issue at hand. For instance, the interviewer could ask, "What, if anything, would you say you learned from that experience?"

It is also helpful to express appreciation for the honesty and frankness the applicant has shown. If the interviewer makes a statement such as, "I really appreciate your frankness in mentioning that point. I'm sure it wasn't easy for you to bring it up," quite often the applicant will pick up the conversation and elaborate further on the matter.

When an effort is made to play down negative input but the applicant remains defensive and reluctant to talk, the subject can be dropped temporarily. It should be brought up later, near the end of the interview. However, it is important to realize that it will be scarcely less threatening to the applicant when it is raised at this later point in the discussion. Threatening material should be discussed, if at all possible, at the time it is first mentioned.

Avoiding Disagreement

Overt disagreement with a candidate's statement signals to the applicant that the "wrong thing" was said. Thus if more information is desired, the interviewer should not express disapproval or disagreement. This does not mean, however, that the interviewer needs to compromise his principles or pretend agreement with points of view contrary to his beliefs. It simply means that it is necessary to avoid disagreeing or showing disapproval. For example, if a college recruit says that "American business today exploits young college graduates and doesn't allow them to use their capabilities," and the interviewer wants to learn the rationale behind the applicant's views, he might respond in a neutral tone, "Well that's an interesting comment, let's talk a little bit about it."

Paying Sincere Compliments

One of the easiest—and yet most neglected—approaches to reducing threat and anxiety is for the interviewer to sincerely praise an applicant's achievements. For example, if an interview reveals that an applicant has earned spending money since the age of ten years, the interviewer might say, "You must be proud of that." Or the interviewer could simply say, "Good," or "That kind of trait should be a great asset at work."

The interviewer of course ought not to flatter or insincerely praise the candidate. Flattery will be perceived as phony and unrealistic. It is a rare candidate, however, who does not have some achievements that are truly praiseworthy and about which positive comments can be made. The commendation should be simple, straightforward, and not flowery.

It is interesting to note the reaction of applicants when they are praised. Beneath the surface, the applicant usually experiences a feeling of greater self-confidence in the interview situation. This increase in confidence can sometimes be observed in external behavior. Most applicants will begin to slouch, ever so slightly, in their chairs once a sincere compliment has been paid them.

The interviewer should create a climate in which the applicant feels he is making a favorable impression. When this occurs, the candidate will be more self-assured, relaxed, and willing to share openly—sometimes even willing to share some shortcoming. This is likely to occur, however, only when the interviewer provides positive feedback that the candidate's accomplishments are well regarded. In contrast, the applicant who feels he is not making a favorable impression or who is uncertain about the impact being made is likely to become tense and more cautious about what is said, making it all the more difficult to elicit sensitive information.

Use of Threatening Questions

While the primary theme of this chapter is the need to keep a low-threat climate throughout the interview, it should be recognized that there are times when threat cannot be avoided. The interviewer should not leave questions unresolved if an answer can be determined by more thorough exploration or more probing questions.

In such instances, the applicant will be put on the spot and the threat level significantly increased.

Suppose, for example, the applicant has a record of frequent job changes. Over the past six years, he has changed jobs three times—almost once every two years. The applicant in every other respect seems to be an ideal choice for the job, but the question that keeps going through the interviewer's mind is whether the applicant will leave this company after two years. If no clear-cut answer to that concern is gleaned during the course of the interview, then the interviewer should focus his attention directly on it.

INTERVIEWER: Mr. Jones, after reviewing your background, I feel you might be a very fine candidate for the opening we have. However, the one thought that keeps going through my mind is that you left your last three companies after only a two-year stay. Since we're going to invest so much time and expense in training you, I'm concerned about the possibility that you might leave us after a short period of time. Can you give me any reasons why I should believe that you will not leave us, as you did your other companies?

Another example of a situation in which pressure might be applied is when the interviewer gets the feeling that the applicant is a person who is fundamentally rather hostile, one who would react inappropriately when frustrated. Suppose the interviewer had tried all sorts of indirect ways to obtain an understanding of how the candidate deals with frustrations but was unsuccessful. In such a case, the interviewer should not hesitate to put the applicant in a threatening position.

INTERVIEWER: We've been talking here now for almost thirty minutes and I can't help but get the feeling, as we discuss matters, that you might be the kind of person who walks around with a chip on his shoulder. How do you evaluate yourself on this score?

When there are some concerns or unresolved doubts, the interviewer should put them directly to the applicant and make the applicant prove to the interviewer's satisfaction whether the concerns are groundless or in fact quite proper.

The Place for Threat

When threat is purposely introduced in the interview, there is a definite time and place for it. That time is at about the three-quarter mark. Up to the last fourth of the interview, an effort should be made to play down unfavorable information and to keep threat relatively low. But at that time, the threatening issue should be woven into an exploration area that is somewhat related to it; that is, instead of dealing with this negative point in an isolated fashion, it is better to integrate it into the segment of the interview that is going on at the three-quarter mark.

After the threatening topic has been covered, the interviewer should attempt to reduce defensiveness by introducing a number of questions or topics that are relatively easy for the applicant to discuss. Questions that elicit positive answers are helpful here. For example, the interviewer could ask questions about how the applicant went about achieving some big promotion or raise.

Summary

It is recommended that the interviewer avoid trial behavior situations or stress interviews and instead seek open, frank, and revealing responses by creating a climate that is relatively non-threatening.

An environment that is relatively low in threat is achieved by showing a sincere interest in the applicant, by playing down unfavorable information, by avoiding disagreement with or disapproval of the applicant's statements, and by giving recognition to the candidate's accomplishments. Open and free-flowing discussions are most likely to occur when the applicant feels he is making a favorable impression on the interviewer. Under these conditions, the applicant may be more willing to discuss whatever is unfavorable in his personality or background. When threatening topics must be discussed, they should be raised at the three-quarter mark in the interview, not at the beginning or end.

Chapter 10

Evaluating What You Observe and Hear: A Conceptual View

For almost every interviewer, the most frustrating and difficult aspect of interviewing is evaluating data—attaching meaning to what is seen and heard. Part of the interviewer's difficulty stems from focusing on obtaining more information instead of on the meaning of the data already at hand. Another evaluation problem stems from the lack of an effective system by which to correctly interpret the facts already gathered. Let's examine each of these problems in a little more depth.

Importance of Focus and System

Most interviewers finish the interview with a substantial amount of data. But even though they have a plethora of facts, they rarely have a good understanding of just how the applicant will perform on the job. Yet, isn't that the primary purpose of the interviewer, to use past and present behavior as a basis for predicting future performance? The gathering of ever greater quantities of facts is usually not what is required to make this prediction; rather it is the translation of the facts acquired into a meaningful picture of job behavior.

168

Shifting the Focus From Facts to Causes

When managers are given a one-page résumé containing the usual background data on an individual and are then asked if they would make a hire/not-hire decision on the basis of that résumé, the usual answer is no. If asked why not, they respond with such statements as "I don't know what his personality is like. Is he shy? Confident? Aggressive? Or what?" "I don't know how he would interact with me. Will I be able to get along well with him?" "He indicates he changed from a major in accounting to one in engineering. I wonder if he really knows what he wants to do?" "I wonder why he didn't take a summer job during his junior year?"

Give the same group another résumé, but this time include more facts about the individual's work experience, education, and the like, and ask the same question. As before, the managers will give a "no" response. And the reasons will be the same: Basically they want to know more about what lies behind the facts. Why did the person do certain things? What was the motivation involved? What is he like from the personality standpoint? What kind of physical impression does he make? What accounted for his success or failure in various situations?

In most interview situations, the interviewer does not need more historical facts than the application blank provides. What the interviewer needs is to interpret the facts already available.

Need for an Interpretative System

A second factor that makes interpretation of data so difficult is that most interviewers have not developed a system for evaluating the information they obtain. To be effective, such a system must be able to solve or minimize three significant problems that affect objective evaluation of candidates. These problems are (1) overcontrolling or overstructuring the interview, thus narrowing the range of observations and data obtained; (2) jumping to erroneous conclusions about the meaning of the data, and (3) failing to convert the facts of the applicant's background into meaningful behavioral terms. Instead, the interviewer will often interpret each individual fact as being essentially favorable or unfavorable. In this way, the applicant with the most favorables and fewest unfavorables will get the nod, even though the interviewer still cannot describe how that candidate will perform on the job.

There are two procedures that will help interviewers to avoid these pitfalls. The first procedure has to do with conducting the interview in such a way that the data sources are now narrow or circumscribed. This conceptual approach to the interview will be referred to as the *Emergence Approach*. The second is a specific technique to prevent jumping to conclusions and to provide an accurate interpretation of what is seen and heard during the interview. This technique is called the *Hypothesis Method* and will be discussed in Chapter 11.

The Emergence Approach

The Emergence Approach can be described as a philosophical attitude toward the gathering of data. It concerns how the interviewer perceives his role—a role in which the interviewer, rather than directly seeking out behavior patterns, helps applicants to reveal themselves.

The Emergence Approach is based on the premise that if you give people enough latitude to talk about themselves, to just be themselves, then sooner or later their personality, motivation, and thinking patterns will rise to the surface.

It doesn't matter all that much exactly what is covered in an interview. If the applicant talks freely for a sufficient length of time, the interviewer will learn a tremendous amount about that person. The Emergence Principle can also be observed in social situations. Suppose, for instance, you go to a party or business meeting at which most of the people are strangers to you. How do you decide whether you would like to be together again with someone you meet? Do you interview them? Of course not—you talk. What do you talk about? Usually nothing in particular, maybe whatever the other person brings up. But as you listen and observe, you hear attitudes conveyed, you get some "feel" for how smart the person is, you see personality traits and behavioral patterns projected, and interests mentioned. You haven't structured a list of topics to discuss or probe, but simply by letting the other person "be" and project himself, you can learn a good deal about him.

Interviewers can readily learn about others through careful observation, because anything people do represents an extension of their basic selves: How they walk, how they talk, how they laugh, how they write their signatures—all reveal something of the inner person. When this principle is applied to the interview situation, it suggests that if we truly want to learn how someone behaves and functions, then we should provide interviewees with a lot of freedom to "be." We should begin the interview with an open mind and not search for anything in particular. Obviously, it is necessary, during an employment interview, to discover whether or not the candidate has the necessary technological skills or experience (knowledge-experience factor) to perform the job in question. Therefore, time must be set aside to explore and probe for specific factual data. However, when the interviewer is attempting to learn about the candidate in the more difficult-to-assess areas (intellect, motivation, and personality), use of the Emergence Principla becomes essential. Thus an important portion of the interview will be devoted to the exploration of specific information, but for the major portion of the interview time, the interviewer should try to determine what the candidate is like rather than seek out specific qualities, traits, or behavior patterns.

Basically, the Emergence Approach suggests that when interviewers conduct an interview, they should search out nothing (except for qualifying the candidate on the basis of the required knowledge and experence), but instead see what emerges. The interviewer should try to understand how the candidate functions; how he solves problems, relates to others, is motivated, and applies aptitudes and skills. Once the interviewer has developed a mental portrait of how the applicant behaves and functions, then, and only then, should the interviewer relate the emerged qualities to the behaviors critical to success on the job.

Problems With Traditional Methods of Interviewing

As knowledgeable interviewers have probably concluded, the Emergence Approach is completely contrary to the classical approach to interviewing. The traditional wisdom in conducting the interview is to identify what is needed for success on the job, and then to determine if the applicant possesses those particular skills, traits, and abilities. An examination of the "let's-see-if-the-candidate-has-what-we-want" approach, however, reveals a number of significant reasons why interviewers should look to alternative methods of conducting the interview, such as the Emergence Approach.

Obvious Intent

The issue of "telegraphing" the right response was discussed in Chapter 7. This problem becomes acute when the interviewer tries to ferret out a specific kind of information about the applicant. In most cases, if the interviewer looks hard enough, the sought-after quality will be found, whether the candidate possesses it or not. Most applicants are sufficiently perceptive to see exactly what is being sought and, if the quality is desirable, they claim to have it.

Limited Validity of Behavioral Traits Approach

As was mentioned earlier, many personnel evaluation procedures concentrate on finding someone who has the specific traits, qualities, or abilities that are needed for success in a given job. On the surface, such an approach seems logical. As we watch successful people perform in different assignments, we do occasionally notice that the more effective ones tend to be decisive, or forceful, or intelligent, or to demonstrate some other strength. We then assume that to identify successful employees for that job we must look for applicants having the very same qualities. Applicants who do not seem to possess these few qualities are thus eliminated from further consideration.

An extension of the traits approach can often be found on interviewer guide sheets. These forms usually list ten or twelve traits upon which the candidate is to be rated. The assumption in using such guide sheets is that these traits account for the success of job incumbents. An example of this type of interview evaluation guide is shown in Figure 18.

However, there is serious doubt that any particular set of traits or qualities is necessary for success in any one job. Rarely does research reveal a clear-cut pattern or profile for successful people in professional or managerial assignments. While it is quite possible, of course, for psychologists to establish patterns for positions with clearly defined responsibilities, such data do not exist in most companies.

It should be recognized that the combinations and permutations of individuals' talents, skills, and abilities are almost limitless. It is the complexity of the human being that continues to make the process of assessment (and management, too) both an art and a challenge. As a result, we can rarely be sure that a particular profile or set of qualities really accounts for success in a given job.

Moreover, even when research "proves" the validity of certain predictors, these validities have a way of changing dramatically over time. What may predict success today may do the opposite tomorrow.

Uniqueness of Individuals

It is a truism that everyone is unique. Yet, despite our awareness of this fact, most approaches to evaluating others run counter to the uniqueness concept. Think of some job in your organization in which several people have the same job title. Assume further that these incumbents are all reasonably successful in performing their work. Are these people all the same? Probably not. In fact, in most cases, they will be quite different in many respects. It's not their sameness that makes

Figure 18. Interviewing rating form focusing on traits (not recommended).

Trait	Not ascertained; Don't know	1	2	3	4	5
Assertiveness	Not ascertained; Don't know	Easily discouraged; passive; tends to react to events; avoids challenging situations		Initiates activities; continues at tasks despite problems and setbacks; confident; seeks new and challenging situations		
Communication skills	Not ascertained; Don't know	Hesitant and uncertain, has difficulty presenting ideas clearly and logically		Poised, confident and convincing; can present complex ideas in a clear and interesting manner		
Decisiveness	Not ascertained; Don't know	Uncertain, ill-at-ease about decisions, frequently changes mind, takes excessive time to make decisions		Confident about decisions; accurately assesses risks and implications; makes decisions within appropriate time frame		
Energy	Not ascertained; Don't know	Rarely works hard; appears to have difficulty maintaining a heavy workload and performing efficiently		Frequently works hard; capable of maintaining a heavy workload while remaining efficient		
Flexibility	Not ascertained; Don't know	Unaware, oblivious of changing situations; has difficulty adapting and changing goals, directions, etc.		Sensitive to changing situations, capable of changing demands, goals, requirements, etc.		
Interpersonal skills	Not ascertained; Don't know	Has difficulty maintaining relationships; insensitive; lacks tact		Capable of working effectively with others; sensitive to the feelings of others; tactful		
Maturity	Not ascertained; Don't know	Responds carelessly and impulsively; avoids assuming responsibility for own actions; panics under pressure		Carefully considers effects of potential actions; willingly accepts responsibility for handling difficult problems; calm under pressure		
Reasoning/Judgment	Not ascertained; Don't know	Doesn't seek enough information; misses essentials of problem; solutions are superficial		Identifies need for and seeks relevant information; solutions have been innovative and effective		

them successful, but the unique blend of qualities and skills they bring to the job.

Compensating Strengths

Even if it were established that a particular ability or quality was important for success in a position, it could well be that that particular trait or quality would not always have to manifest itself for an applicant to be effective on the job. A person could possess different combinations of strengths that would enable him to perform the same task quite effectively.

Suppose, for example that it is agreed that self-starting ability is an important requirement for a particular position in your company. If self-starting initiative is not in evidence, an applicant is likely to be rejected. This focus, however, tends to downplay other desirable factors that may be present. It may be that a candidate with a good record attributes success to conscientiousness, persistence, and a high energy level. Such a candidate could well become an excellent employee because of persistence and energy, even though he prefers having goals set for him. If a superior is willing to set priorities and targets, this applicant could be a highly effective employee—even without self-starting ability.

The Flip Side of Traits

The traits or pattern approach tends to focus on whatever traits are desired for a particular job but usually fails to evaluate their potential for becoming undesirable characteristics. Interviewers who focus on determining whether a given candidate has certain qualities usually fail to consider the complexity of the human being and the interaction of the traits upon one another. For example, suppose that for a particular position it has been found that the best performers are socially aggressive; that is, they are forceful, dynamic individuals, particularly in face-to-face situations. Most interviewers would tend to perceive aggressiveness as desirable when they encounter it in an applicant. However, this very trait of aggressiveness could become a problem if the candidate is also a hostile person. In such a case, the more social aggressiveness displayed by the individual, the more likely his behavior is to create problems, for both the employee and the company. Thus, the traits approach directs attention away from other qualities the individual possesses—many of which could inhibit effective performance.

With the Emergence Approach, it's not that we don't want to know whether the applicant is aggressive or not, but precisely because we do want to learn, as accurately as possible, just how aggressive that individual is that we avoid searching it out and let the Emergence Principle operate.

If the applicant is truly aggressive, and the interviewer follows the procedures described in the Evaluation Model (Chapter 13), then clear-cut evidence of this aggressiveness should emerge from the discussion of the applicant's background. If the candidate is not aggressive, evidence of passive behavior should appear; if the candidate is neither aggressive nor unaggressive but middle-of-the-road on this quality, that also should be evident.

The point here is that no one quality, skill, or trait has much significance in and of itself. Only analysis of the *total person,* showing how and when these qualities are used, can determine anyone's effectiveness in a given job.

The Emergence Approach and Conduct of the Interview

At this point, it may appear that some amorphous, tell-me-about-your-life kind of interview is being advocated. While such an approach could be very effective, time constraints make this type of interview impractical in most instances. Instead, we propose a rather structured format that will permit the interviewer to control the interview but, at the same time, allow applicants sufficient freedom to project and reveal themselves to the interviewer.

It is critically important to understand the difference between going into the interview with an attitude that says, in effect, "I will search out specific qualities that I consider important to success in the job," and going into the interview with an open mind, relying on the Emergence Approach to reveal the nature of the applicant. In the latter case, the interviewer sets himself the goal of trying to determine how the candidate behaves or functions—how the person thinks, solves problems, relates to and deals with people, what turns him on and off, and how relevant his knowledge and experience are to the job in question. Once the interviewer understands and can describe the likely on-the-job behavior of the applicant, then the question can be asked. "Given that the individual functions this way, could this person do the job for which he is being assessed?" At this point, of course, technique ends and judgment begins. Then the interviewer must relate the behavioral patterns that emerged from the interview to the behavioral patterns required for successful performance of the job.

Keeping an Open Mind

Can the interviewer really be open-minded when conducting the interview? The answer to this question is yes, to a large degree. Interviewing is still a subjective process, and thus the application blank or résumé data, the applicant's personal appearance or body language, and the opinions of others can all contaminate the objectivity of an interviewer. So it is not possible to begin the interview with an entirely blank slate. On the other hand, it is quite another thing to purposely seek out (in an evaluation interview, not a screening-out interview) predetermined qualities and attributes. Obviously, when it comes to assessing the applicant's technical ability to do specific tasks, the interviewer must do a certain amount of searching and probing. In effect, the good interview utilizes the Emergence Approach about three-fourths of the time; and allocates another fourth to determining if the applicant has adequate knowledge and experience to do the job.

Preinterview Data

If there is a significant advantage to conducting the interview with an open mind, using the Emergence Approach, then the question must be raised whether the background data provided on application blanks or résumés should be studied prior to the interview. The research on this question is ambiguous. For some interviewers, awareness of preinterview data enhanced their predictive accuracy; for others, it created a strong bias and disrupted their ability to observe accurately.

There is no essential need to have preliminary data in order to conduct a thorough and effective interview. However, if the interviewer feels it is helpful to know beforehand the track record of the applicant, it would be difficult to make a strong case against looking over this information before the interview. The danger is that if such preliminary reading contains negative information (reference comments, test scores), this input could so bias the interviewer throughout the interview as to make objectivity virtually impossible. Not to expose oneself to data about the applicant prior to the interview therefore seems the safest course. Negative information obtained after the interview is completed tends to have a less prejudicial effect.*

Interviewers should definitely not have the application blank or résumé in front of them as they interview a candidate. Such a practice tends to direct attention away from the applicant and toward the paper.

Problems arise when the interviewer refers frequently to a résumé or application blank during the interview. When a large array of information is directly in front of him, attentiveness to the applicant and motivation to listen with care are substantially reduced. It is quite a different matter when the interviewer must draw all the information from the applicant; then nothing can be assumed. Also, interviewers are subtly influenced by data in front of them. There is a tendency to assume that what

---

*See R. E. Carlson. "Effect of Interview Information in Altering Valid Impressions," *Journal of Applied Psychology* 55 (1971): 66–72.

is printed is fact. Interviewers are inclined to forget that many things happen in an applicant's life that never appear on a résumé. As a consequence, interviewers are less likely to ask such questions as, "Well, then what happened?" or, "What happened next?" In essence, the interviewer's chances of uncovering gaps in the candidate's background are sharply reduced.

When, at the outset of an interview, a job candidate stops the discussion to offer me a copy of his résumé, I usually reply, as I place it upside down on the desk, "Thank you very much. I'll study it later, but for now, I'd like to hear the story from you." Such a procedure has helped me do a better job in really getting to know the applicant, and it should work the same way for others too.

Summary

During interviews, emphasis should be placed on understanding the uniqueness of the individual being assessed rather than on evaluating his sameness to others. This concept, called the Emergence Approach, dictates that the interviewer initiate the interview without a preconceived set of sought-after characteristics (with the exception of job knowledge); that is, the interviewer must not begin the interview with the intention of determining if the candidate possesses specific traits, qualities, aptitudes, or abilities. It is assumed that preliminary screening has eliminated those candidates whose educational background and work experience are inappropriate for the job in question. Consequently, the interviewer should try to understand how this person functions—how he solves problems, relates to others, is motivated, and applies aptitudes and skills. When the interviewer has developed a mental portrait of how the applicant behaves and functions, then, and only then, should the interviewer relate the emerging qualities to the requirements of the job.

Interviewers who follow the Emergence Approach will reduce the likelihood of seeing people as stereotypes, a trap into which so many interviewers fall. With the Emergence Approach, each individual is seen as unique—a more realistic viewpoint than classifying individuals after isolating a few behavior patterns. The Emergence Approach should also help the manager to work with the candidate once he is employed because the method yields an understanding of the dynamics of the individual.

Subsequent chapters will describe clear-cut steps as to how the Emergence Approach can be applied to the interview and how interviewing can be more easily accomplished with this method than with traits or pattern methods.

Chapter 11

Evaluating What You Observe and Hear: The Hypothesis Method

Chapter 10 presented the Emergence Concept, an overall way of approaching the interview. Its primary purpose is to minimize the interviewer's preconceived notions and biases about what is important to seek out during the interview and, at the same time, to allow applicants sufficient time and latitude to project their true qualities and behavior patterns. This chapter introduces a technique called the *Hypothesis Method*.

The Hypothesis Method

Basically, the Hypothesis Method is a technique that can be used to assign meaning to the data elicited from applicants or observed during the interview. In effect, the method requires the interviewer to make a hypothesis, a guess if you will, as to what each input from the applicant will mean on the job. During the course of the interview, the interviewer will formulate many of these hypotheses, perhaps thirty or forty. At the end of the interview, those hypotheses that repeat themselves will be accepted as true and meaningful behavioral characteristics of the individual being interviewed. By "repeat" is meant that the same hypothesis emerges two, three, or four times during the course of the interview. Those hypotheses that are not confirmed are rejected. Out of the thirty or forty initial hypotheses developed, perhaps six, seven, or eight will remain as confirmed hypotheses. These will then be organized, at the end of the interview, into a balance sheet of the candidate's principal strengths and weaknesses.

Briefly then, a large number of hypotheses are gathered. Those that are supported are taken to be true behavioral qualities of the applicant; those that are not supported are rejected.

Sources of Hypotheses

There are two basic sources from which hypotheses are obtained: (1) the behavior observed (what you see in front of you); and (2) historical information from the applicant's past.

As will become clear from a study of the Evaluation Model described in Chapter 13, ample opportunity can be created during the interview process to watch the applicant. The applicant can be observed as friendly, aggressive, nit-picking, conceptual, analytical, shy, hostile, confident, spontaneous, cool, distant, superficial, good at self-expression, and so on down the line of dozens of qualities. Each time the interviewer observes a particular characteristic in the applicant, he can form a hypothesis that that same characteristic or mode of behavior will manifest itself on the job. The observed behavior must be considered as hypothetical because the interview presents only a sample of behavior. For example, just because an applicant is friendly during the interview, there is no guarantee that the same person will be friendly at work. However, the interviewer can hypothesize that he will be so. Similarly, if someone is cautious and analytical during the interview, it is legitimate to hypothesize that he will be cautious and analytical on the job.

Whatever is observed, whatever impressions the interviewer is receiving, should be recorded as hypotheses (more about writing up the hypotheses will be provided later). Note, too, that even fleeting hunches about the applicant should be recorded as hypotheses. Something that appears to be trivial or perhaps even irrelevant can have significance when additional, related hypotheses are gathered from subsequent portions of the interview. Remember, at this stage of the evaluation process, when hypotheses are simply being assembled, they are regarded only as hypothetical and not as true behavioral characteristics of the applicant.

The second source of hypotheses, the historical data and factual information that are obtained as the interviewer explores an applicant's history, include educational background, work experience, and leisure-time activities. Each time a fact is heard, the interviewer should make a hypothesis as to what that fact will mean on the job. For instance, suppose a woman applicant indicates that she graduated from college in the upper 10 percent of her class. Let us assume further that she attended a relatively good school and that her class standing was verified. The Hypothesis Method suggests that the interviewer should now make a hypothesis as to what this particular historical fact will mean in terms of job behavior.

Most people, upon first learning of the need to conjure up a hypothesis each time they hear a fact, express a couple of concerns. The first has to do with the obvious difficulty of trying to formulate hypotheses in the midst of all else that is going on during the interview. What the interviewer is expected to do—control the interview, ask questions, listen, and also develop meaningful hypotheses—is difficult even for the professional interviewer. The executive with limited training in the behavioral sciences faces even greater difficulties.

A second concern is whether one has the right hypothesis; that is, is the interviewer any further ahead than before formulating the hypothesis? This difficulty can be readily illustrated using the example of the applicant who said, "I graduated in the upper 10 percent of my class." During a recent presentation, I asked members of the audience what hypotheses they could think of that might explain this woman's good academic performance. Some of the hypotheses mentioned that the woman:

Was bright, intelligent
Was competitive
Had a strong need to achieve

Was conscientious, hard-working
Had learned how to be a student
Had cheated
"Apple-polished" her teachers
Had good study habits
Was self-disciplined, well-prepared
Was a bookworm, didn't do anything else but study

I then turned to the group and asked, "Which one of these is correct?" Obviously, no one knew. All could have been correct, some could have been correct, or none could be right. And so, use of the Hypothesis Method immediately introduces two problems in its application: the difficulty of formulating hypotheses under pressure of the face-to-face interview, and the difficulty selecting the most correct of the many hypotheses that might occur to the interviewer.

Developing the Best Hypotheses

Fortunately, there is a tool at our disposal that simultaneously solves both these problems. This tool is the *self-appraisal* question. Basically, the self-appraisal question asks the individual to explain in his own words the *how* or *why* of a piece of information. For example, suppose a male candidate indicates that he has been successful in selling *Time* magazine subscriptions while at college. A good self-appraisal question might be, "What did you do as a salesman that accounted for your fine sales record?" Or an applicant might indicate that he was the rush chairman for his fraternity. The interviewer then might ask, "What do you suppose your fraternity brothers saw in you that led them to pick you for rush chairman rather than some other member?"

For the woman who graduated in the upper 10 percent of her class, a self-appraisal question that could be asked might go like this:

INTERVIEWER: What is there about yourself that might account for the fine grades you obtained at the university?

APPLICANT: Well, I'm the kind of a person who likes to do things right. Do you know what I mean? When I decided to go to college, I planned on doing the best I could. I'll have to admit, I had to work hard for my grades—there were many weekends I stayed at school preparing for exams or writing term papers, but that's how I am. I guess I'm just conscientious.

Now, looking back at the list of hypotheses compiled by members of the audience, it is clear that the probably correct one is "conscientious, hard-working." Of course, the woman's response might simply represent something she made up because she thought it would sound good. Remember, however, that the applicant's response to the self-appraisal question is recorded only as a hypothesis. It is not accepted as being true until that same "conscientiousness" emerges from discussions about other segments of the applicant's life. If it recurs three or four times, it is reasonable to accept it as a genuine characteristic of the individual; if it does not appear again in any significant way, the hypothesis will not appear on the list of confirmed hypotheses. After all, if an individual is truly hard-working and conscientious, that fact will not manifest itself merely for a moment and then disappear into the void. If the behavior is at all meaningful in the individual's makeup, it should reappear in other aspects of that person's life, provided, of course, that the interviewer allows the person to reveal such qualities in discussions about other life experiences.

Advantages of the Self-Appraisal Question

Without doubt, one of the primary advantages of the self-appraisal question is that it removes from the interviewer the tremendous burden of trying to interpret the meaning of the interviewee's comments. It really is not necessary to be a trained psychologist to understand how others behave. Interviewers who try to analyze the meaning of data during the interview are often misled by their own hunches and limited understanding of the complex person in front of them. Let's look at it this way. Why settle for a second-order inference (your guess about what something means) when you have readily available a first-order inference (the applicant's analysis of what something means)? Strangely enough, given the right climate, most individuals have an excellent ability to explain their behavior, even though they might not have been aware of this ability before the interview. In a sense, the interview can be a great opportunity for insights, both for the interviewer and the applicant as well.

Avoiding Premature Conclusions

Once the interviewer places the burden of interpretation on the applicant, the temptation to assign meaning to data is sharply reduced, and the interviewer's mind is open to explanations other than those he has thought about. No longer is the interviewer likely to conclude automatically that because someone graduated in the upper 10 percent of her class she must be highly intelligent. Even more important, the self-appraisal question helps the interviewer to avoid jumping to gross, major conclusions because of a certain set or combination of facts. For example, suppose the interviewer is evaluating a candidate who is currently employed by a respected competitor. Assume further that during the interview it is learned that the applicant is in a key management position, earning an excellent salary, especially for someone of his young age and limited work experience. In this case, it might easily be concluded that the candidate must be a good manager to have advanced that far so quickly. And, of course, such a scenario is a logical probability. Notice what happens, however, when the self-appraisal question is introduced.

INTERVIEWER: Considering your few years with the company, you have really made excellent progress. Tell me [*self-appraisal question*], what would you say there is about you that accounts for your rapid progress at XYZ Company, and what, if anything, is holding you back from going even further?

APPLICANT: Well, I'm not really sure exactly what it might be, but I think I'm a fairly bright person. I pick things up rather quickly, and I know when I was moved into several new departments, I was able to catch on very rapidly to what they were doing, so I got a lot of responsibility early on. And, I'll be quite frank with you, part of my progress was probably the result of my drive and ambition. I often talked with my supervisors about my progress and advancement, so maybe it was a little bit of my own push that helped. As far as what could have held me back, I can't think of anything serious. The only thing I can recall is that in my last performance review, my boss suggested that there were times when I was a little too easygoing with my subordinates . . . but I don't think that was a critical thing.

At this point, it might be helpful to clarify the difference between the Hypothesis Method and the usual approach to evaluating data. In Figure 19, the *A* approach represents the typical reaction to a strongly positive bit of information; in short, the interviewer jumps to a conclusion (in this case, that the applicant must be a good manager to have advanced so rapidly). And, of course, this conclusion could be true or not true.

Now, look at the *B* approach. Here the Hypothesis Method develops three hypotheses, making it difficult to jump to a totally erroneous conclusion about the applicant's strength as a manager. And, remember, the example cited here represents the hypotheses generated by only one self-appraisal question. Imagine how difficult it will be to prematurely conclude anything if, during the interview, many self-appraisal questions are asked so that forty to fifty hypotheses are generated.

Converting to Predictable Job Behavior

A third, and perhaps the most meaningful, advantage in using the self-appraisal question is its help to the interviewer in

Figure 19. Role of self-appraisal question in helping develop hypotheses.

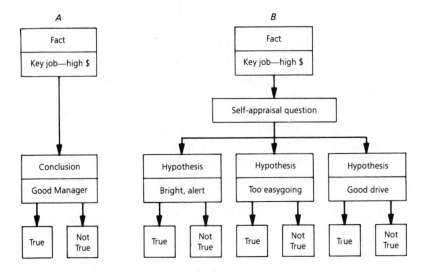

converting the candidate's life history into predictable job behavior. This conversion can be seen in Figure 19. It can be readily observed here how the fact of the applicant's key job and high pay is translated into three significant hypotheses as to how that individual might typically function. This is much more meaningful input for the interviewer to have on hand than the premature (and probably unwarranted) conclusion that the candidate is a good manager.

Even if the interviewer were correct in concluding that the applicant was a good manager, it would not necessarily mean that this particular candidate was right for the interviewer's company. Perhaps the job for which he is being considered will require cleaning out a lot of deadwood. That he might have been too easygoing with subordinates in his former job could be a significant handicap in the new position. Or perhaps the opening for the candidate offers limited opportunity for advancement. Thus, while the applicant's ambition may have been helpful to him at XYZ Company, the same drive might soon result in dissatisfaction on the new assignment. The point is that it is essential to learn what lies behind the success the applicant had at XYZ Company and not to be content merely with the information that he advanced rapidly.

The achievements or historical data listed on an applicant's résumé are in essence his "admission card" to the interview. If the facts are not good, it's not likely that the interviewer would be seeing the candidate in the first place. Once the applicant's background is found to be reasonably acceptable, what is needed is not more facts or achievements, but rather information as to how or why the applicant accomplished them. Only after the interviewer gains an understanding of how the individual behaves and functions is there a sound basis for determining if the applicant can succeed in the job in question. It is the ease with which the self-appraisal helps convert historical data into on-the-job behavior that makes the Hypothesis Method so valuable for the interviewer.

Avoiding Being Fooled

A fourth advantage of the self-appraisal question is that it minimizes the likelihood of being fooled by articulate individuals or those experienced in interview-taking. Most applicants will not previously have been exposed to self-appraisal questions, which require candidates to think on their feet. Here is an example:

APPLICANT: [*Mentions his family*] Bill, my oldest brother, is an engineer, and Charles, my youngest brother, teaches phys ed in a local high school.

INTERVIEWER: [*Asks the self-appraisal question*] You and your brothers certainly took different career paths—you in sales, one brother in engineering, and the other in teaching. What differences do you suppose there are between your brothers and yourself that led them to go their ways and led you toward a completely different path?

In this case, the applicant now has to think out loud in order to answer. And as he responds, he begins revealing things about himself.

APPLICANT: I never really thought about it before, but Bill was always a much more studious person that I was. He had a real flair for math, and I guess I just enjoyed socializing more. I can remember him having a chemistry set and he loved to work down in the basement, while I would much rather be out with the fellows in the street playing ball or something . . . so I guess he went the science route. Now my brother Charlie, he's a little more like me. We both liked dramatics and, in fact, we were even in a few school plays together. I think he went into teaching because it gave him a chance to do a lot of different things. . . . At least, I think that's why he did it. As for me, when I got to college and took a look at the various subjects, I knew that marketing and sales would be right for me; I just like working with people.

As can be seen, self-appraisal questions make it difficult for the candidate to "snow" the interviewer. In order to do so, the applicant would first have to think of an answer to the question, decide that the answer would not be appropriate or not sound good, make up a new story, and tell it—doing almost all these things simultaneously. And, even if the applicant were able to dream up a more favorable explanation than the truth, it is worth remembering that the explanation he gives here is recorded only as a hypothesis. For that hypothesis to become a confirmed hypothesis, the candidate would have to find occasion to lie or stretch the truth two or three more times during the interview, something that is extremely difficult to do.

To carry this thought further, it is important to realize that even though the applicant might lie consistently, other safeguards are available to the interviewer. As will be seen in Chapter 12, in the discussion on recording data, as the confirmed hypotheses are studied, an incorrect one will become evident to the interviewer because, given all the other data available, it will not make sense. The inaccurate "confirmed" hypothesis that occasionally gets through will probably not be given much weight or credence in the final hiring decision.

Self-appraisal questions are the interviewer's best defense

against the polished and experienced interview-taker. Most applicants will not have thought through answers to the self-appraisal questions nor will they be able to gloss over falsehoods or inadequacies.

Self-appraisal questions are also helpful as good stimulators of conversation. Most people like to talk about themselves, and these questions definitely demonstrate the interviewer's interest in the candidate as a person.

Should self-appraisal questions be positive or negative in form? Interviewers rarely hear adverse information from a candidate when they ask direct questions. For example, the interviewer is at a distinct disadvantage when asking a question such as, "How did you get along with your last boss?"

Applicants realize that the answer will be carefully considered, so they strive to give a response that makes them look reasonably prudent and that puts them in as positive a light as possible. Experience has shown, too, that negative characteristics are more likely to be mentioned during discussions in which applicants feel confident than during those in which they feel threatened.

Interview confidence can be engendered by encouraging applicants to talk positively about themselves. The more statements applicants make about the good things they have done and the good traits or characteristics they display, the more likely they will be to venture further and, perhaps even to their own surprise, reveal shortcomings about themselves.

It is recommended, therefore, that a majority of the self-appraisal questions—at the beginning portion of the interview, at least—be of the positive variety. Here are some typical examples of positive self-appraisal questions:

"What good traits or qualities did you display that might account for your being elected president of your class?"

"Are there any particular aptitudes you have that may account for your fine grades in the engineering curriculum?"

"If I were to ask your high school coach what kind of a teammate you were, what do you suppose he would say?"

After the interviewer has asked three or four such positive self-appraisal questions, most candidates will find it embarrassing to go on praising themselves. Secure in the favorable impression they have created, they will then offer clues and direct statements about their shortcomings. For example:

INTERVIEWER: What would you say it was about your personality that might account for your being able to gain the cooperation of the older persons that you supervised?

APPLICANT: I guess I can explain that best by the fact that I'm a kind of even-tempered person. I didn't get upset very easily, and I didn't try to convey the idea I knew all the answers. Of course, I don't mean to convey the impression I never lost my temper or never sounded off. I guess we all do that a little bit, but most of the time I think I'm a pretty patient kind of guy.

INTERVIEWER: Well, we all get impatient with people from time to time. What kind of person or situation is likely to make you sound off?

Briefly then, it's probably better to keep the majority of questions on the positive side, although there is certainly no reason against occasionally asking negative self-appraisal questions, particularly if the applicant has already mentioned a problem or difficulty. In these cases, the interviewer might say: "What is there about you that may have made that part of the job difficult for you?" Or, alternatively, "In what ways would you need to grow stronger in order to be more effective at that?"

Summary

The Hypothesis Method is a technique for assigning meaning to both observed behavior and historical data in the applicant's background. It is designed around the premise that the applicant's interpretation of the data is more likely to be correct than that of the interviewer. Use of the method requires that the interviewer ask self-appraisal questions and then accept as hypothetically true whatever the applicant says in response to the self-appraisal question. If the same hypothesis emerges several times during the interview (thus confirming it), the hypothesis is accepted as being a true behavioral characteristic of the applicant. Of thirty to forty hypotheses generated during the interview, six to eight will usually be confirmed at the conclusion of the interview. For effective use of the Hypothesis Method, it is necessary to adopt an interview approach consonant with the Emergence Approach and the Evaluation Model (actual interview process) described in Chapter 13.

Chapter 12

Taking Interview Notes

How do interviewers remember all that they hear and learn? Must they have prodigious memories? Certainly it would be difficult, if not impossible, to remember some thirty to forty hypotheses that may be generated during an interview. For this reason, the use of the Hypothesis Method requires jotting down the hypotheses as they occur. To many managers taking notes during an interview seems wrong, particularly in view of the need to keep anxiety and threat levels low. The negative implications of note-taking, however, are not as serious as they may seem. In fact, the reverse is usually true. Effective and efficient data gathering for employment interviewing invariably leads to note-taking.

The Pros and Cons of Note-Taking

Those who believe that interviewers shouldn't take notes usually give one or two reasons for their position. They will say that note-taking is threatening and therefore reduces the quality and/or quantity of data obtained. Or they will claim that note-taking is just too difficult for the average interviewer to manage during the interview. They point out that there are too many other things going on simultaneously—asking questions, evaluating information, and observing behavior—and that note-taking becomes too much of a distraction. Let's examine both these objections.

In my view, whether or not note-taking in an interview is threatening or anxiety-creating is a matter of how one takes notes. If the interviewer takes notes by using writing paper on top of the desk that the applicant can peek over and decipher, this may prove distracting and possibly threatening. Or if the interviewer does not take notes consistently but writes only when the applicant says something negative, such action is likely to raise considerable anxiety or even alarm. But if neither of these procedures is followed, note-taking usually does not become a threat.

An effective way to take notes is for the interviewer to keep the notepad on his lap rather than on the desk. In this way, the interviewer can sit back in a chair and relax. If the interviewer's legs are crossed, usually the angle of the page is such that the applicant cannot see what is being written on the pad. The interviewer should make no attempt to hide the fact that notes are being taken but should angle the paper so that the applicant will not be distracted by seeing the writing on the page.

Another helpful note-taking procedure is to take notes fairly constantly during the course of the interview. When done steadily, the note-taking becomes almost a routine part of the scene. Because of its ongoing nature, the candidate may often become oblivious that notes are being taken. This is particularly true if the applicant is busy doing most of the talking. An analogy can be drawn between interviewing and role playing with a videotape recorder. When the participants first begin the role play and face the camera, they are usually tense and uptight; as the role play proceeds, however, they become so involved in the task that they forget about the camera and lose their anxiety. The same is true for note-taking; as long as notes are taken steadily throughout the interview, the applicant's anxiety, if it exists at all, soon vanishes.

By contrast, the likelihood of an applicant being threatened or distracted by note-taking is clearly aggravated by the typical question-and-answer method of interviewing in which the applicant is not required to assume responsibility for carrying a significant portion of the interview. For example:

INTERVIEWER: Why did you decide to leave your last job?
APPLICANT: I didn't think the company gave me a chance to use most of my abilities.

INTERVIEWER: [*Pauses to make notes about answer*] I see, you
    wanted more challenge and couldn't get it there?
APPLICANT: Well, it wasn't so much that, but. . . .
INTERVIEWER: [*Pauses to make notes about answer.* . . .]

Obviously, this kind of note-taking calls direct attention to
the act of note-taking and is disruptive of a conversational style
of interview.

If note-taking is at all threatening, the attendant anxiety
can be significantly reduced by proper positioning of the notepad as well as by making the note-taking a consistent, ongoing
process.

At this point, there may be some concern in the reader's
mind about the ability to take notes on an ongoing basis. While
this is an understandable concern, there is a solution. The solution rests, in part, with the interview procedures described in
"A Step-by-Step Process for Conducuting the Evaluation Interview" (Chapter 13), and in the fact that the interviewer will not
need to write down many words at one time. Usually, the notes
will not consist of sentences or paragraphs but only one- or two-
word descriptive phrases that emanate from the hypothesis
method. The notes might read, for instance: "friendly," "self-
confident about abilities," "highly aggressive," "organizes
thoughts well," "tends to get lost in details."

Before going further, the reader should be aware of recent
research data about the impact of note-taking on the amount
and depth of interview data obtained. In controlled situations
in which persons were interviewed both with and without note-
taking, no decrease in either the quality or quantity of data was
found when notes were used. The results showed that those
interviewers taking notes recalled (really had available) significantly more data than those who did not take notes. These findings were also corroborated by my own research. However, in
one of these investigations, a high proportion of the population
interviewed were from Western Europe—France, Germany,
Belgium, and Holland. There was a slight, but not statistically
significant, decrease in data elicited by interviewers who took
notes. It may be that note-taking could cause similar problems
with people of other cultures. In such cases, the interviewer

must make a decision. Is the potential gain from note-taking worth the potential risk of less meaningful data being obtained? It is my practice to take notes regardless of the cultural background of the candidate. I believe the gain far outweighs the potential loss.

Some interviewers object that it is too difficult to concentrate on asking questions, listening, guiding the interview, and taking notes at the same time. These simultaneous tasks will present a problem if the interviewer burdens himself with the mechanics of conducting the interview. Many interviewers, for example, are more caught up in what they are going to say next than in analyzing what is being said or in recording hypotheses. Fortunately there is a solution to this problem. It rests in conducting the interview in such a way that the burden of responsibility falls on the applicant, so that conducting the interview requires little effort or attention. The model for conducting the evaluation interview, described in Chapter 13, provides just such an interview structure. If the interviewer follows the procedures of the model, there should be ample time to observe and study the applicant as well as to develop and record hypotheses.

Taking Notes After the Interview

Many interviewers, realizing the importance of remembering details, attempt to jot down their recollections after the applicant has left. This procedure has three distinct disadvantages. First, it increases the time that the interviewer spends in the assessment task, because it will take another ten or fifteen minutes to sum up the interview comments on paper, time that might better have been spent in interviewing the candidate.

Second, pressures of the day common to most businesses often make it impossible to write summary notes after completion of the interview: Phones ring, secretaries come in with important questions, and meetings must be attended. These and other commitments frequently impinge on the interviewer, and the intent to do after-interview summarizing frequently goes unfulfilled.

Finally, there is the problem of differential recall. It is a well-documented psychological phenomenon that our mental set has much to do with what we recall. Suppose, for example, the interviewer ends the interview with a generally favorable opinion of the applicant. Then in recalling the findings of the interview, the interviewer will remember more positive than negative factors about the candidate, even though the negative elements were observed. And if the impressions were not positive, the interviewer will differentially forget some of the positive aspects observed and remember more of the negative ones. This phenomenon is often called the "halo-horns" effect. It obviously reduces the validity of prediction of job success.

Basically, there are few, if any, good reasons not to take notes; the alternatives are entirely unsatisfactory. Few professionals do not take notes when interviewing.

Note-Taking Techniques

There is no one best way to record notes. However, the approach used here, which I have developed, has been found highly satisfactory. A few ground rules will clarify the process.

It is not a good idea to use a printed or prepared form. Printed forms incorporating interview categories tend to focus the interviewer's attention on the printed items and questions rather than on the flow of conversation. If the interviewer feels the need for some format as a guide, broad categories such as "Education" and "Work Experience," with ample blank space beneath each heading, are the best approach.

An effective method is to use a blank sheet of lined paper (8½ × 11), and to draw a vertical line down the center of the page. This permits the recording of historical information about the applicant's background on one side of the paper and the interviewer's hypotheses on the other side.

Relatively little should be written on the fact side of the paper since most of this kind of information is already recorded elsewhere: on application forms, résumés, and college transcripts. However, there will be times when the interviewer solicits data that are not found elsewhere and that are impor-

Figure 20. Example of interviewer's notes using Drake's method of note-taking.

Facts	Hypotheses
coll – why leave jr. yr? father ill – needed $ help support fam not enjoy science courses left XYZ Company ? wanted mgt work – recruited by agency	relaxed – seems self – confi- dent communicates well impatient bright and articulate wants quick results for efforts verbally skillful not good at math drives self hard intolerant if not get own way can be "pushy" likes much variety and change in job enjoys people contact

tant to remember. For example, as is shown in Figure 20, the interviewer may have asked why the applicant left college after his junior year; or, in another instance, what prompted the candidate to leave the XYZ Company.

The bulk of the writing, however, should fall on the hypotheses side of the page. Here, as the reader may recall, the interviewer should record hypotheses from two basic sources. The first source is the observations the interviewer makes about the applicant's interview behavior, hypotheses such as "friendly," "confident," "detail-oriented," "conceptualizes well," "expresses thoughts clearly," "appears disorganized," "shows limited energy and drive," or "personable."

The second source of input for the hypotheses side of the

page is the applicant's life history. These hypotheses are obtained by asking the applicant to self-appraise the hows and whys of the facts presented.

During a typical assessment interview of an hour's duration, the interviewer is likely to accumulate three to four pages of notes, most of them containing one- or two-word hypotheses. When a hypothesis recurs, the interviewer can make a check mark next to the already written hypothesis.

The interviewer may also wish to make more detailed comments about some of the hypotheses. For example, the interviewer might ask the applicant why he was successful as a salesman, to which the applicant might respond, "Well, I rarely take no for an answer. I push hard and I'm quite aggressive in trying to close. I don't give up easily." Because the interviewer noted during the interview that the applicant was particularly forceful and quite aggressive in expressing his point of view, the interviewer might write next to his hypothesis, "rarely takes no—pushes hard" and the comment, "can see this." This represents another way of confirming or rejecting hypotheses.

Collating Hypotheses

Some professional interviewers in reviewing their lists of hypotheses are able to see a pattern developing or to gain an overall impression of the balance of strengths and limitations. However, most interviewers cannot do this effectively without in some way organizing their thoughts. Perhaps the simplest way for the interviewer to organize the list of hypotheses is to quickly examine it and eliminate those for which there has been no additional support. It is difficult to pinpoint what represents adequate support in order to accept a hypothesis as being a true trait or characteristic. It is quite possible, for example, that one hypothesis will appear only twice during the interview, yet be evident in such an obvious fashion, or with such strength, that it must be accepted as a true behavior characteristic. Other hypotheses may lack substance and definitiveness. The interviewer might like to see the trait, skill, or ability appear three or more times in the life history or in overt interview behavior

Figure 21. Balance sheet showing confirmed hypotheses.

Strengths	Limitations
Quick thinker—bright and alert Energetic Likes contact with others and to be on the go Good drive—a self-starter Warm and personable Good insights about others Appropriate sales management experience	Impulsive—tends to act before thinking Basically soft—inclined to be too easygoing with others Seeks much credit and recognition for his efforts—likes to be in limelight

before accepting it as true. This is a judgment that the interviewer must make.

The Balance Sheet

The end product of the evaluation process is a balance sheet of principal strengths and weaknesses. It is comprised of a listing of all the confirmed hypotheses. The interviewer must decide for each hypothesis whether it should be considered a strength or a limitation. Obviously, assigning it correctly depends upon a knowledge of the job. What is a strength for one job could easily be a limitation for another. As we shall see, however, this is not a problem for the interviewer to fret about. Regardless of the column in which the hypothesis is entered, it is the interaction of the strengths and weaknesses that is important, not so much how accurately they are placed. A typical balance sheet is shown in Figure 21.

Developing the balance sheet should not require much of the interviewer's time. It can usually be completed in less than five minutes at the conclusion of the interview.

Once the balance sheet is drawn, technique and methodology end; now the interviewer's judgment must prevail. When
analyzing the balance between strengths and limitations, the interviewer's knowledge of the job requirements and understanding of the elements of human personality and behavior are the
ingredients that will help make a sound hire/not-hire decision.
In essence, the interviewer's task is to weigh the strengths
against the limitations and to decide whether the resulting behavior pattern of this unique mixture of traits and abilities will
enable the applicant to perform effectively on the job in question. As we shall see later, the balance sheet is the tool used to
begin the decision-making process. It will be compared against
the job demands as described in the *behavioral specifications*
(Chapter 15).

Interviewers following the Hypothesis Method will probably uncover more shortcomings than would have been revealed by any other method. This makes it hard to see
applicants as simply "good" or "not acceptable." Instead, the
interviewer will list a large number of positive and negative
characteristics. And, of course, this is realistic; each of us represents a constellation of strengths and limitations for any given
job. Unfortunately, in many organizations, the objective of hiring "above-average candidates" is taken to mean that the best
applicant will have few, if any, identified weaknesses. The tendency to overreact to weaknesses is almost universal. This is
unfortunate because often the strongest candidate will manifest
the most obvious shortcomings. For a fuller discussion of this
point, see Chapter 15, "Matching the Candidate to the Job."

Evaluating Weaknesses

No one should be unduly prejudiced against a candidate
simply because a significant number of shortcomings are confirmed and appear on the balance sheet. It is the specific mix
of strengths and limitations that is important, not the fact that
shortcomings exist.

A case in point appears on the balance sheet shown in Figure 21. Would the reader hire an individual with those qualities

for an assignment, let us say, as regional sales manager? In this position the incumbent will be supervising other supervisors. When this question is asked in a classroom of business executives, the answer given is almost invariably no. The executives quite logically point out that such an individual might be too easygoing with subordinates; that customers might "get away with things" they shouldn't; that the manager might make false starts because of impulsiveness; and that he might not have a highly motivated work force because of taking too much of the credit for his subordinates' accomplishments.

All these conclusions seem reasonable. Yet this profile, somewhat simplified, was found to be characteristic of the most successful regional managers of a major food manufacturing company. In other words, the best regional managers in this particular company tend to have these qualities. Because the shortcomings are quite undesirable, how could these managers successfully direct large regions and still have such a configuration of strengths and limitations?

The experienced interviewer knows that the answer lies in the extent to which the strengths offset the limitations. For instance, consider the shortcoming "Impulsive—tends to act before thinking." The regional manager may indeed be an action-oriented, decisive person who finds it difficult to sit down and plan for extended periods of time. But one of the positive characteristics possessed by this manager is that he is bright and alert. So, even though people may be action-oriented, it should not be assumed that their solutions to problems will necessarily be out in "left field." They are intelligent enough to develop reasonably satisfactory answers most of the time. They may not select the best possible answer, but they pick an acceptable answer. If they make a mistake, they may be quick and bright enough to notice the error before it goes too far. Moreover because they have "good insights about others," it is not likely that they will make many serious mistakes in managing subordinates or customers. Imagine, on the other hand, if brightness and insight were absent. There are few executives more dangerous than those who are both impulsive and stupid.

Another consideration when weighing the balance of

strengths and limitations is the extent to which the shortcomings lend themselves to change or development. While some shortcomings may be serious, many can be ameliorated by coaching, experience, and maturity. We know, for example, that impulsiveness tends to lessen with age. We know, too, that even though a person may be basically soft underneath, he can learn to take a tough posture when it is necessary. It may be more difficult psychologically for such a regional manager to make unpleasant personnel decisions, but he still makes them.

A third factor to be considered when evaluating shortcomings is the extent to which a shortcoming can be compensated for by the nature of the organization, that is, the degree to which company supervision, controls, policies, or organizational structure may reduce or eliminate the negative aspects of a shortcoming. For example, in the case of the regional manager described by the balance sheet, the company coped with his shortcomings by organizing the sales function so that each regional manager was teamed up with an analytical, finance-oriented partner. Together, the two of them ran the region. Thus the company did not sacrifice the drive, enthusiasm, and marketing capabilities of the sales executive by insisting on a more analytical or cautious candidate. Instead, the company reduced the risk of his weaknesses. In other cases, it might be recognized that the characteristics of the candidate's future supervisor will offset the shortcoming. For example, if one of the applicant's confirmed weaknesses is limited self-starting ability, such a shortcoming might not be serious if the applicant's strengths are good and if his boss is a hard-driving individual who will provide plenty of stimulation. Or the work environment may be so highly motivating and contain so many built-in pressures that self-starting ability is not required for successful performance.

It is important, then, not to overreact to shortcomings as such. Factors that are limitations for many jobs in a company may be assets in other jobs, depending on the exact situation. In trying to determine the negative impact of any confirmed hypothesis appearing on the balance sheet, three analyses must be made: (1) the extent to which strengths offset or minimize each of the limitations; (2) the extent to which the shortcomings lend themselves to change or development; and (3) the extent to which organizational structure, supervisory personnel, or controls will compensate or offset the weakness.

Numerical Evaluation

It is strongly recommended that interviewers as they finish the evaluation of strengths and limitations, assign a numerical rating to the candidate. Such a procedure takes less than a minute of the interviewer's time but yields some valuable assistance.

It helps to facilitate communication between several interviewers who see the same candidate. It also helps at a later date in distinguishing among candidates, readily permitting the interviewer to place applicants in some sort of rank order.

Let's examine the numerical rating idea in more detail. The range of numbers assigned to the system seems to be of little significance, but the factors that are to be rated are important. A five-point rating scale is as follows:

1. Above average
2. Average to above average
3. Average
4. Average to below average
5. Below average

It is possible, of course, to establish a nine-point or a seven-point scale, but in practice the shorter scales appear to be quite sufficient.

A helpful way to use ratings is to base them on two factors: qualifications for the position in question, and potential for growth beyond this assignment.

Thus, at the end of the interview, the interviewer may simply jot at the end of his page "Q-2, P-4." Such a notation indicates that this candidate is somewhat above average in terms of qualifications for the assignment in question but has limited potential to go beyond that point. On the other hand, a candidate might have a Q-4, P-2 rating. That person is not particularly well qualified for the job but has sufficient underlying strengths that the interviewer believes the candidate can over a period of time develop a good potential to move further.

If several interviewers were asked to list only a candidate's strengths and limitations, they might easily reach complete agreement on these factors yet at the same time arrive at quite different conclusions. Some assessors will focus on the candidate's long-range potential with the company, whereas others will center their evaluation on the candidate's ability to perform the job in question. Rating the candidate separately on each of the two characteristics helps to clarify each assessor's opinion of the applicant.

Assigning numerical values to candidates provides a second advantage in that it permits the interviewer to readily classify applicants at some future time. For example, if one interviews five candidates for a position during a week's time, it may become difficult to decide at the end of the week which candidate was best unless numerical values have been designated. When numbers are assigned to candidates, it is easy to arrange them in rank order of preference.

Summary

To make effective use of the Hypothesis Method, note-taking is required to recollect and to analyze all the hypotheses developed. While it is possible that note-taking during the interview could diminish the quality or quantity of data obtained, the advantages of note-taking, properly done, far outweigh any potential disadvantages. One should take notes consistently during the interview, using a lined pad with two sections, one for factual historical data and the other for the hypotheses. It is also suggested that the interviewer use the Evaluation Model in conducting the interview so as to avoid a question-and-answer approach that calls undue attention to the note-taking.

Once the notes have been gathered and the interview is completed, it is recommended that the confirmed hypotheses be assembled onto a balance sheet of principal strengths and weaknesses. To further clarify the interviewer's assessment, the assignment of a numerical rating, on the basis of qualifications for job and for growth potential, is also suggested.

Chapter 13

A Step-by-Step Process for Conducting the Evaluation Interview

The point has now been reached when all the previously discussed segments of the interview can be integrated. This chapter provides a guide or model that explains exactly how the interviewer can proceed from opening comments to closing remarks.

The interview described here will be referred to as the Evaluation Model. It is designed to provide sufficient information to enable the manager to make an informed, confident, hire/not-hire decision. At the conclusion of the evaluation interview, the interviewer should be able to produce a meaningful description of how the candidate will function on the job. In effect, this interview approach will help answer the question, "Will the applicant fit into our job?" An overview of this process is shown in Figure 22.

It should be understood that the evaluation interview is not a screening interview. Those are usually short interviews designed to weed out the unqualified on the basis of a limited number of essential requirements. The campus recruiting interview is an example of a typical screening interview.

The Evaluation Model described in this chapter allows the interviewer to use the Emergence Approach as well as the talk-generating techniques and Hypothesis Method in one easy-to-conduct procedure.

Figure 22. Model for conducting the evaluation interview.

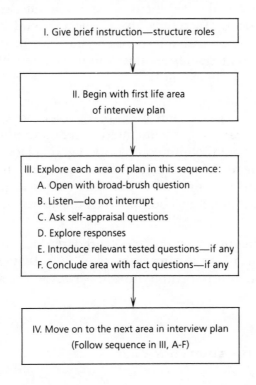

Structuring the Interview

Interviewers should not consciously emphasize small talk when opening the interview. There is little reason to postpone obtaining meaningful input once the social amenities or introductory comments are completed. Instead of starting with obvious small talk about the weather or last week's football game, the interviewer can initiate the discussion with the first topic (life area) in his interview plan. For candidates with long work histories, this might be the life area of work experience; for young first-job hunters, high school is usually the most appropriate place to begin.

It is also helpful at the outset to structure the interview so as to keep interruptions by the applicant to a minimum. Interruptions often cause the interviewer to lose some control of the interview and make it difficult to maintain an easy, conversational discussion. To reduce the applicant's tendency to break into the discussion with questions about the job or the company, a statement that structures how the interview will proceed is helpful. Here is an example:

INTERVIEWER: In the time we have together today, I know that we both want to get acquainted with one another. You want to be certain that our company is a good place for you, and we want to be certain that you're right for us. So let me spend the first portion of our time getting acquainted with you, and then it will be your turn to learn about us.

With this information, the candidate does not feel compelled to interrupt the interviewer; he knows that eventually he will be given an opportunity to ask whatever questions he has on his mind.

Following the Interview Plan

In Chapter 8 the concept of a planned interview was introduced. As the reader will recall, such an interview helps ensure broad coverage of the candidate's life history and thus aids in obtaining information about each of the four fundamental sectors. The planned interview also provides two other advantages. It helps the interviewer maintain control and it also simplifies the mechanics of conducting the interview. When the interviewer follows an outline of the nine major areas of exploration, he no longer has to worry about where he is going next in the interview.

One of the easiest ways to remember an interview plan is to list the preferred sequence of topics on a small card. By keeping the card on the desk the interviewer can refer to it from time to time during the interview. Once three or four interviews have been conducted according to the same plan, the interviewer will no longer need to resort to the list.

The interviewer should consistently follow the plan rather than skip about and should explore each area completely before moving on to the next one. When, for example, work experience is being discussed, that entire segment of the applicant's life should be covered before moving on to some other life area, such as leisure time.

Sometimes, however, the applicant makes only a brief statement about the area being discussed and then jumps to another area of the plan. When this occurs, the interviewer must interrupt the applicant and bring him back to the area under discussion. The following dialogue illustrates one way of coping with this situation.

INTERVIEWER: Suppose you start by telling me a little bit about your high school days.

APPLICANT: Well, there is not too much to say. I went to Hackensack High School in New Jersey and then went on to the University of New Hampshire, where I started my major in economics.

INTERVIEWER: I certainly want to hear about your career at New Hampshire, but before we get into college, let's go back and talk a little bit more about your high school days. What is there of interest that you can tell me about that period in your life?

Exploring Each Area

When the interviewer begins to discuss an area, the conversation is controlled by asking the applicant questions that follow a specific sequence. The questions are arranged in such a way that it is unlikely the applicant will be aware that any particular model is being followed. More important, the sequence of questions lends itself to the development of hypotheses and helps keep the interview on a conversational plane. The pattern to be followed as each life area is explored is outlined in the following sections. This pattern is repeated over and over again as the various areas are discussed with the applicant.

Employing Broad-Brush Questions

The interviewer starts off each area with a broad-brush question, that is, an open-ended question that does not indicate what specific information is sought. One of the best ways to frame a broad-brush question is to begin with the invitation, "Tell me. . . ." A typical broad-brush question is, "Suppose you tell me something about your high school days."

This device is perhaps the single most important technique for effectively conducting a conversational-style interview. Its great advantage is that it places the burden of responsibility for carrying the conversation directly on the applicant. With the "tell me" approach, it becomes quite clear to applicants that they are going to have to talk and to share themselves. Once this burden of responsibility is shifted, the interviewer can almost adopt the role of a third party who is looking in on the discussion. It is this freedom from immediate demand that enables the interviewer to sit back, relax, and take notes —and, of course, to generate hypotheses about observed behavior.

There are a great many different hypotheses that can be formed when the responsibility for determining what to say and how much to say is placed on the applicant. Dozens will come to mind in response to the following considerations.

How well does the applicant communicate? Can the applicant express his thoughts in a clear-cut, intelligible way or does he become tongue-tied? Are the applicant's vocabulary and communication skills adequate to the job in question?

How does the applicant think? Is the candidate able to conceptualize effectively or is his thought superficial and shallow? Does he organize his thoughts in a logical, concise way or does he tend to ramble? Does he look at things from a broad perspective or does he become mired in detail?

The interviewer can also get some feel for the applicant's social perceptivity by asking him to describe his college career, because there is, roughly speaking, a "right amount" of information to give. If the applicant responds by merely saying he "graduated in 1981" and nothing more, he has obviously misjudged what is expected of him in this situation. If, on the other hand, he goes on for half an hour explaining in detail everything that happened to him over a four-year period, this will show an equal lack of judgment. The applicant who has any social perceptivity will judge fairly accurately how much should be said. The uncertain applicant may have sufficient social savoir faire to ask how much detail is required. As experienced interviewers know, some applicants simply go on and on. The interviewer should let such applicants ramble at length for some time in order to estimate just how poorly they judge (or misjudge) what is expected.

The broad-brush question also gives the interviewer the opportunity to get some feel for the applicant's ability to handle structure. Many applicants, upon hearing a broad-brush question, are likely to ask, "What do you want to know?" The interviewer should be prepared for such queries and be ready with a response such as, "I had nothing particular in mind; anything you'd like to share with me would be fine." Observing the applicant's struggle to handle the ambiguity of the broad-brush question provides valuable data that will help the interviewer make hypotheses about the candidate's need for structure.

Another benefit of the broad-brush question is that it does not telegraph to the applicant what information is important to the interviewer. It makes it difficult for the applicant to pick and choose the "right" things to say. The candidate, in a sense, is given a blank slate on which to project whatever he feels will most impress the interviewer. As a result, the interviewer will often learn of topics or situations he never thought about exploring.

An important advantage of the broad-brush question is that it provides the subject matter for the next step, the self-appraisal question. The response to the broad-brush questions is likely to be a paragraph or two about the candidate's achievements, the things that he believes will make a good impression on the interviewer. This is exactly what is desired. Discussion of the applicant's accomplishments keeps the interview atmosphere positive and nonthreatening. The applicant freely reveals information about himself, thereby setting the stage for the how and why questions—the self-appraisal questions—that in turn help the interviewer to develop additional hypotheses.

Listening Without Interruption

Once the broad-brush question is asked, it is essential that the interviewer not interrupt the applicant's response. If the candidate's spontaneous response to the question is interrupted, it hinders evaluation of the candidate's ability to organize his thoughts, to communicate effectively, and to be socially perceptive. In other words, the value of the broad-brush question is ruined when the interviewer interrupts the applicant's thought flow. This is particularly true if the interviewer interrupts with a question. At that moment, the responsibilty of the interview will almost immediately shift back to the interviewer and then the interviewer will be forced to ask another question. Thus, the applicant is now in the role of passive responder and the interviewer becomes the worker.

The no-interruption rule is difficult for most interviewers to adhere to when they are first trying to learn the broad-brush questioning procedure. With so much data flowing from the applicant, there is an almost overwhelming temptation to interrupt with questions intended to clarify or to seek out further information. If the interviewer feels compelled to say something, the listening can be done by using such acceptance phrases as "uh huh," "I see," "I understand," or even an occasional restatement—but no questions should be indulged.

The only exception to this rule against interrupting is when the applicant directs the conversation away from the particular area that is being explored. Then it is necessary to intervene to get the applicant back on the track. The way that the interviewer controls the interview is to keep the applicant locked into the specific area being explored. Only when the questioning sequence (broad-brush, self-appraisal, tested questions, fact questions) for one area is completed does the interviewer move on to the next.

Asking Self-Appraisal Questions

Once the candidate has responded to the broad-brush question, the interviewer must begin developing hypotheses about the information imparted. The manner in which the self-appraisal questions can be used to develop hypotheses is illustrated by the following dialogue.

INTERVIEWER: [*Asking broad-brush question*] Suppose you tell me a little about your career in high school.
APPLICANT: Do you want me to talk about my grades or what?
INTERVIEWER: Oh, I had nothing particular in mind. Just tell me anything you think might be helpful for me to know.
APPLICANT: Well, let's see, I did fairly well in high school, as far as grades are concerned. I remember that I was on the honor roll four out of the eight terms. And I was pretty active in school. I played sports and had a varsity letter in soccer and track. I also had the lead in our senior play. I don't know what else to say. I enjoyed myself in high school; I had a lot of friends and took part in most of the social activities.

Once the applicant has concluded the response to the broad-brush question, the interviewer can begin asking self-appraisal questions about the achievements mentioned by the applicant. In this particular case, the accomplishments mentioned are as follows:

Good grades—honor roll
Athletic achievement—team sports
Extracurricular activities—lead in senior play
Personality development—socially active

The specific accomplishments the interviewer chooses to inquire about depend on which of the applicant's comments are judged to be most productive for the development of hypotheses. Sometimes, only one of several statements will be queried;

in other instances, almost everything the candidate reveals could be profitably explored. Here is how all four of the applicant's statements might be examined with self-appraisal questions, beginning with grades.

INTERVIEWER: [*Self-appraisal question*] You have indicated that you were on the honor roll four out of eight terms. That's quite an accomplishment. What kinds of skills or abilities would you say you have that might account for those fine grades?

APPLICANT: I don't know really, but it seems that whenever I do anything, I like to do it right. I've always been that way; I guess that I was just very conscientious about grades. I've worked hard to get good grades—I guess you could say that I applied myself well.

Possible hypotheses that could be written down on the basis of these statements include "conscientious," "sets high standards for self," "accepts responsibility," and "is hard working."

INTERVIEWER: [*Self-appraisal question*] You also indicated that you obtained varsity letters both in track and soccer. As you think back on it, is there anything you learned from your sports activities that might help you in adult life today?

APPLICANT: Well, yes, as a matter of fact, I did learn something from sports. I guess it was mostly from soccer. I never was a particularly good player, but I really liked the game and for the first two years I sat on the bench most of the time. It was pretty discouraging but I stuck with it and then in my senior year I made the first team and got my letter. I guess there were lots of times I thought about giving it up, but I stuck with it. I think what I learned from that experience is that if you really want to do anything, just persist and you can accomplish it.

The possible hypotheses from this area are "persistent," "hard-driving," and "tends to complete things he starts."

INTERVIEWER: [*Self-appraisal question*] I notice you also mention that you had the male lead in your senior play. That's quite an honor. Tell me, what would you say your dramatic teacher saw in you that led him to pick you for the lead rather than someone else?

APPLICANT: Oh, I don't know. I was lucky I guess.

INTERVIEWER: [*Restatement*] It was only a matter of good luck?

APPLICANT: Well, no, I guess it wasn't only good luck. Like I said before, when I do something, I like to do it right. The night before rehearsal, I read over a section of the script and really practiced it. So when it came time for the tryouts, I went over pretty well. Most of the other fellows more or less read off the top of their heads, and I guess they didn't sound as good.

Possible hypotheses that could be formulated from this are "conscientious" and "needs to feel sure of self in new situations."

INTERVIEWER: You also mentioned that you were socially active in high school, had a lot of friends, enjoyed the dances, and so on. I assume you're telling me here that you got along well with most of the students.

APPLICANT: That's right. I had a lot of friends.

INTERVIEWER: [*Self-appraisal question*] Well, what would you say there is about yourself, say your personality, that might make it possible for you to get along so well with others?

APPLICANT: I don't know. I guess maybe it's my temperament. I don't think I get upset very easily, so a lot of people tend to confide in me. Maybe that's why people get along with me—I don't argue a lot with them.

Here, the possible hypotheses are "even-tempered" and "tends to avoid conflict."

Each of the examples should assist the reader in understanding exactly how the self-appraisal question helps translate the applicant's facts into behavior terms. The only difficult part of this process is the development of a wide variety of self-appraisal questions, so that the interviewer's actions do not become too obvious or repetitious. To help the interviewer build a good repertoire of such questions, some prototypes are listed.

Prototypes for Self-Appraisal Questions

1. What skills do you have that might account for your success in _(school subject, school office)_?
2. What was there about this particular _(job, course)_ that made it a bit difficult for you?
3. What was there about this _(class, job, hobby)_ that appealed to you? Why do you suppose you liked it? (This same question can be asked to elicit negative feelings by substituting "was unappealing" and "disliked.")
4. How would you evaluate yourself as a _(manager, fraternity president, salesperson)_? Good? Fair? Poor? What traits or skills do you have that might account for your success?
5. If I were to call up your _(boss, teacher, coach)_ and ask him what kind of _(salesman, student, team player)_ you are, what do you suppose he would say?
6. You said that you were _(captain, president, chairperson)_. What do you suppose it was that your _(classmates, teammates)_ saw in you that led them to pick you rather than someone else?
7. You indicated that you were _(an only child, camp counselor, very poor)_. What impact would you say that experience has had upon your development as an adult?
8. You mentioned that you _(played team sports, were a "hot-line" counselor)_. What, if anything, would you say that you learned from that experience? What do you see carrying over to your adult life today?
9. You said that you have ambitions to become a _(district manager, nurse, company president)_. What is there about yourself that makes you think you would be a good _(district manager, nurse, company president)_?

What area do you feel you might still need to develop before you could perform at a high level in that position?

The interviewer must make meaning out of the applicant's comments by asking the self-appraisal questions immediately after hearing the responses to the broad-brush questions. It is important not to have other questions intervene between the conclusion of the response to the broad-brush question and the beginning of the self-appraisal questions. If other questions are broached before the self-appraisal questions begin, the interviewer will find it awkward to refer back later to those original points and difficult to make the interview flow smoothly.

When trying to develop hypotheses about the facts or accomplishments presented in response to the broad-brush question, the interviewer should take each accomplishment one at a time. In making the bridge back to the original achievement or accomplishment, it is helpful to start the self-appraisal question with the words, "You mentioned that. . . ." This bridging phrase helps the applicant focus on the topic under question and also give the interviewer some time to formulate the wording of the self-appraisal question. The questioning sequence is shown in Figure 23.

The interviewer should be aware that it is sometimes necessary to use additional questions as well as restatements and acceptances to draw out the applicant's response to the self-appraisal question. When applicants do not answer the self-appraisal question in a way that describes themselves, it becomes necessary to follow up the first answer with additional probing and questioning. For example:

INTERVIEWER: [*Self-appraisal question*] You mentioned that you were a reporter on the school newspaper. Suppose I were to call up the editor of the newspaper and ask what kind of reporter John Jones was. What do you suppose the editor would say?

APPLICANT: I don't know what he would say.

Figure 23. Questioning sequence using self-appraisal
technique.

Interviewer's Activity	Interview Dialogue
Open area with broad-brush question	INTERVIEWER: Tell me about...
Observe response and write down hypothesis about observed behavior	APPLICANT: [*Describes accomplishments*] I did quite well at... ...in my position at ABC. ...in my position at DEF.
When applicant completes response to broad-brush, ask self-appraisal questions	INTERVIEWER: You mentioned that at ABC... You also indicated that at DEF...
Record hypotheses as applicant describes how or why of each accomplishment	

INTERVIEWER:　Well, I realize you don't actually know what he
would say, but you could probably speculate on what he
might say. What would you guess he would say?

APPLICANT:　Well, he would probably say that I always got my
story. [*Notice in this example that the answer does not tell us anything directly about the applicant. The fact that he "always got his
story" really doesn't say anything about how the person functions
or behaves. Thus, some additional probing is necessary.*]

INTERVIEWER:　Can you elaborate on that a bit? What does that
really mean?

APPLICANT:　Well, it was often necessary to interview someone
to get the story, and some of these people were difficult to
reach, like the mayor of the town or the president of the
university.

INTERVIEWER:　Well, how did you go about doing that? What
did you do that made it possible? [*Notice, again, the self-
appraisal to learn how or why he accomplished this.*]

APPLICANT: Well, you see, I wouldn't give up on them. I'd try to reach them at the office; if they wouldn't talk with me on the phone, I would wait outside their office until they came out after work and try to catch them then. If they would not talk to me then, I would wait until that night and call them up at home. If that didn't work, I'd try to catch them as they came out of the house in the morning and went to their car in the driveway. I would just wear them down and sooner or later they'd say, "Okay, I'll give you the story." I guess they used to give me the story just to get me off their backs.

As the reader can see, it took a number of questions before it was possible to extract behavioral meaning from the applicant's work as a school reporter. In this case, some interviewers would have written a hypothesis such as "persistent." Others may have interpreted it as "pain in the neck." In any case, the hypothesis finally arrived at is far more helpful than the fact that the person "always got his story." The critical point to remember is that the most productive information about job behavior comes from *constantly seeking the "how" and "why" of any past accomplishment.*

Introducing Relevant Tested Questions

When all the self-appraisal questions for the respective area have been asked, the interviewer can introduce the tested questions that are appropriate to the area being discussed. Each interviewer should have, at the tip of his tongue, a few questions to weave into the interview plan. For example, when talking about college, the interviewer can always ask the applicant why he selected the college he attended and why he chose a particular major subject. As the applicant responds to these questions, the interviewer, of course, is able to develop and record additional hypotheses.

Readers who have done a substantial amount of interviewing will probably already have developed their own repertoire of tested questions. But for relatively inexperienced interviewers, it is worthwhile learning one or two tested questions for each of the interview areas.

Appendix A lists approximately 100 tested questions that could be added to the interviewer's repertoire. These tested questions are listed by life area and also indicate the likely hypothesis that each question will yield. This list can be especially helpful if the interviewer is experiencing some difficulty in obtaining sufficient data about one of the four basic factors (knowledge/experience, intellectual, personality, motivational). The tested questions to select are those that will produce more hypotheses in the area in which additional information is needed.

Concluding With Fact Questions

Fact questions are inquiries about events in the applicant's life history. For example, the candidate's application blank may indicate that he received a scholarship to college. The interviewer may want to know the basis on which that scholarship was awarded—whether it was for scholastic achievement, athletics, financial need, or some other reason.

Fact questions are most likely to concern work experience. Specific questions about how things were done on the job, what was done, the approaches taken, and the specific skills learned or needed are quite appropriate. Educational background is another area about which many fact questions will probably be asked.

In other life areas, however, fact questions are often not required. For instance, in discussing a candidate's leisure-time activities or goals and ambitions, few fact questions are necessary. The emphasis in these areas should be on questions that emanate from the applicant's response to the opening broadbrush question.

Moving on to the Next Area in the Interview Plan

When the interviewer has completed the exploration of an area, he is ready to move on to the next area in the plan. Because he knows exactly what that topic will be, the transition from one area to the next is made smoothly as part of the on-going conversation. When the interviewer enters the next area, he once again begins with the broad-brush opening question and repeats the step-by-step procedures described in the Evaluation Model.

While the model may appear somewhat mechanistic and structured, the applicant will rarely be aware that any plan is being followed. Moreover, the interviewer is in complete control throughout the process, knows where he is at each point in time, and has a firm hand on the pace and course of the interview. For the applicant, the interview will appear as a generally pleasant conversation with a gentle sense of direction.

Most candidates will like this approach to interviewing because it is so applicant-centered. Many will indicate, "This is the first time I have really been interviewed." What they are saying is that this is the first time anybody tried to understand who they were—as a person rather than as a technician, engineer, supervisor, or student. Interviewers are concerned whether the applicant has the necessary background qualifications to perform effectively, but what makes this type of interview so different is that there is considerable focus on how the person behaves on the job and the reasons behind that behavior. Most candidates find it enjoyable to talk about themselves once they understand that the interviewer is eager to hear details about their lives. Even the shyest applicant will often open up freely when the interviewer seems interested in him as a person.

Many companies indicate that this approach is one of their best recruiting devices because it so distinguishes their interviews from those of other organizations.

Concluding the Interview

Most interviewers who follow the model described in this chapter will require forty-five minutes to an hour to complete the interview. At times, especially when there is extensive work history to explore, the interview can take even longer. Unless the candidate is obviously unqualified, the interview should not be terminated in less than twenty minutes, even if the applicant seems weak. Often, strengths that do not appear at the outset manifest themselves later in the interview as the candidate relaxes and communicates more freely.

Terminating the Discussion

A good strategy for concluding the interview is to let the applicant close it. This can be accomplished in two ways. The interviewer can nonverbally signal that the interview is over by placing his notepad and pencil down on the desk. Or the interviewer can say, "I think we've discussed all that we need to cover for now. Is there anything else that you would like to add?"

The applicant will usually respond in either of two ways to the statement. He may say, "No, I can't think of anything else," in which case the interview is over. Or the candidate may say, "You never asked me about the summer jobs I had. In two of them I had some very good experience in cost estimating, so perhaps I should tell you about some of the projects I was involved in."

In the second instance, the interviewer should encourage the applicant to say what he wants about the summer work and then ask, "Is there anything else you can think of?" At this point, the applicant is likely to say no, and the interview can be terminated.

This strategy is also quite effective when the interviewer desires to terminate the interview before it seems appropriate to the applicant.

In most instances, no additional techniques are needed to conclude the interview. What makes the method described so satisfactory is that the applicant is given the chance to say whatever is on his mind. In effect, the applicant is permitted to end the interview whenever he decides nothing further can be added. It is also helpful if the interviewer strives to select, for the last topic in the interview plan, a subject that is relatively easy to talk about. One life area that is quite appropriate for closing is leisure-time activities.

When an offer of employment is not going to be extended, it is usually best to indicate to the applicant that several other candidates must be considered before a final decision is made and that he will be notified just as soon as that decision is reached. Except in the obvious situation in which the candidate is fully aware that he is not suited to the job, the interviewer should not tell the candidate on the spot that he is unacceptable. If the interviewer follows such a procedure, it could open the door to endless haggling. It is also possible, once the other candidates have been interviewed, that the interviewer might want to reopen the discussion with a questionable candidate. Telling the candidate that he will be contacted soon is usually a gentler way of letting a person down and also a more efficient way of handling the end of the discussion.

Selling the Company and the Job

The selling of the applicant on the job or the company really begins at the outset of the interview—not explicitly, of course, but implicitly by the manner in which the interviewer conducts the discussion. Candidates are often positively influenced by the degree of sincere interest the interviewer shows in them. The formal sell should be initiated only after the interviewer has decided that the candidate is acceptable. There is little value either in trying to evaluate and sell simultaneously or in first selling and then assessing. If the applicant is unacceptable, both these approaches waste time. Of course, a certain amount of selling is good public relations, regardless of how the interviewer feels about the applicant.

The sales portion of the interview can be divided into two distinct phases: the applicant's questions, and input from the interviewer about the job and company.

Applicant's questions. An excellent way to begin influencing the desired applicant toward accepting a company offer is to solicit questions from him. These questions usually reveal the applicant's areas of concern or interest and should receive considerable attention from the interviewer. Each question provides a platform from which the interviewer can relate how the company can meet the candidate's needs and interests. The most effective type of interviewer question is an open-ended one such as, "What is there that you would like to know about us?" or, "Are there any problems or concerns you have, at this point, about the company, the people, or the job?"

Interviewer's input. Once the applicant's questions have been answered, the interviewer can provide additional information to help the candidate make a decision about the company. The most helpful comments are usually those that review job responsibilities, growth opportunities, and company style, philosophy, or policy.

Detailed information and suggestions for selling an organization to the job candidate are outlined in Chapter 16, "Selling the Candidate."

Additional Points about Conduct of the Model

To make effective use of the Hypothesis Method, it is necessary that the interviewer explore a wide range of topics about the applicant's background. The depth to which each area is probed, however, will vary according to the interviewer's judgment about two factors—the number of hypotheses that can be generated from discussion of the area, and the relevance of the area to job success.

Depth of Exploration

It is recommended that every area of the interview plan be explored. This procedure is often called "dipping in." It is important to follow such a process because failure to do so may result in significant information being missed. Even for such seemingly irrelevant areas as early family life, the interviewer has no way of knowing what fruitful hypotheses might develop from a discussion of it unless he inquires about the topic.

When the response to the opening broad-brush question seems to reveal little data upon which hypotheses can be built, the interviewer can simply go on to the next area. It is important, however, to develop as many hypotheses as possible per minute of time. A good rule of thumb for the interviewer is to ask at least one self-appraised question in each area.

The second factor that determines the extent to which a

given area will be explored is the relevance of the area, that is, the area's proximity in time to the job in question. Most of the interviewer's time—65 percent or so—should be devoted to discussion of relatively current life history, such as recent work experience and education, leaving 35 percent of the time for discussion of more remote areas, such as early childhood or high school.

Use of Résumé or Application Blank

It is not recommended that résumés or application blanks be used by the interviewer during the interview. These props make it difficult to keep the interview conversational and often lead the interviewer astray. If the interviewer follows the content of a résumé or application blank, there is a strong tendency to focus on what is recorded there and to assume that that is the whole story. Obviously, many things happen in people's lives that never appear on an application form. What is written there is only what the applicant wants you to see.

There is also a tendency, while following a résumé or application blank, to assign a certain motivational logic to the candidate's activities. The reason for this is that most application blanks are arranged in a logical, sequential fashion. Thus, in reviewing the application blank, it might appear that an activity at one stage of the person's life led to a subsequent one. However, life rarely goes along in such a logical, organized manner. There are zigs and zags and often unexplained and unmentioned time gaps. Thus, the interview tends to gloss over segments of the applicant's life that would have been pursued in greater depth if the interviewer had not been using the application blank as a springboard for the interview discussion.

Following a printed page also makes understanding the applicant more difficult. The interviewer should always try to understand the reasons for the sequence of events and changes in the applicant's life. To accomplish this, it is often helpful for the interviewer to ask, "And then what happened?" If the résumé is directly in front of the interviewer, it is rather awkward to raise such questions.

Candidates will often offer the interviewer a résumé or

completed application form at the outset of the interview. At such times it is best to look at the historical background briefly, noting any red flags or possible trouble spots. Then the interviewer can gracefully put it aside by saying, "Thank you very much. I'll look it over carefully later, but now I would like to hear the story from you."

One great value of the planned interview, with its prescribed areas to explore, is that it makes the conduct of the interview relatively easy for the interviewer. Little energy should be expended in coping with the mechanics of the interview; instead, effort should be directed toward developing the self-appraisal questions and recording the hypotheses.

Summary

The model for the evaluation interview provides a guide for conducting a hire/not-hire interview, from the introductory remarks to the terminating comments. Small talk is not recommended as a way of beginning the interview, but the interviewer should structure the roles in the interview by advising that the applicant will have an opportunity to ask questions later. The interviewer should consistently follow the plan and explore each area completely before moving on to the next one. He should start the discussion of each area with a broad-brush question and listen without interruption to the applicant's response. Once the candidate has replied, the interviewer asks self-appraisal questions and then any tested questions that are appropriate to the area being discussed. He then concludes with fact questions if any are necessary and moves on to the next area in the plan. To terminate the discussion, the interviewer signals the interview is over by a nonverbal sign such as placing his notepad on the desk or by asking if the applicant has anything to add. The sales portion of the interview logically follows the assessment of the candidate.

Chapter 14

The Reference Check Interview

Once the interviewer has completed the interview process with the job applicant, reference checking is usually the next step. It provides an additional opportunity for confirming (or rejecting) hypotheses generated during the evaluation interview. Because of time and economic constraints, almost all these interviews will be conducted by telephone.

Picking the Right Sources and Strategy

Unfortunately, in this age of litigation, the amount of useful information that past employers are willing to provide has decreased significantly. Many organizations have adopted the policy of confirming dates of employment and job title only. Personal references, by contrast, typically provide more information. However, the value of information from such sources is questionable because most job applicants suggest only the names of personal references who can be counted on to make highly positive comments about them. It is easy to draw inaccurate conclusions from such references. Of course, negative comments from these same individuals are significant, but even here the data must be carefully weighed against the interview findings and information from other references.

This chapter describes an approach to the reference check interview that is designed to circumvent some of these problems and to provide meaningful information to help confirm or reject interview hypotheses.

It has been my experience that the most productive reference sources are persons who have worked closely with the applicant. This means the candidate's former peers, supervisors, and subordinates. The key word in the last sentence is "former." It is important *never* to contact individuals in the organization where the applicant is currently employed without that person's explicit permission. When trying to contact former associates of the candidate, it is best to bypass human resources personnel; they will attempt to thwart further inquiries being made of their line managers.

The names of the first-contact references are usually found on the application blank or asked for during the interview. When these individuals are called, they, in turn, are asked to name others in the organization with whom the candidate has worked. Armed with these potential reference sources, the interviewer is now in a position to learn more about the applicant than was revealed in the personal interview.

The basic strategy in conducting the reference check interview is to create a climate of trust—one in which the reference is willing to share his opinions relatively freely. This is accomplished by creating a "we're all together in this" bond, by sharing with the reference some quasi-confidential information about the interviewer's organization, the job in question, and the interviewer's own reactions to the employment interview with the candidate. This strategy works because in essence *it asks the reference to react to already observed characteristics or deficits* rather than to volunteer information in response to traditional questions such as, "How would you describe Richard's job performance?"

A Step-by-Step Approach

The six steps in an effective reference check interview can be outlined as follows.

1. *Introduce yourself*

Mention your name, job title, and the name of your company, and then launch into the purpose of your call. For example:

> "I'm calling because we are considering hiring Carol Smithson and she gave us your name as a reference. We understand that you have worked with Carol."

2. *Openly share what you know about the job situation*

Tell the respondent what the candidate will be expected to do on the job. For example:

> "We are considering Carol for a position as district sales manager for our western region. In this, she will directly supervise eight to ten salespersons and will need to work independently a major portion of the time. This is a new territory for us and. . . ."

3. *Quickly involve the interviewee*

Get down to the nitty-gritty of your concerns. For instance:

> "On the basis of our interview with Carol, a few questions have arisen. If you have a few minutes now, I'd be interested in your reactions."

Do not say "Will you answer some questions?" Asking for reactions is much more open-ended and less threatening than asking for specific answers.

4. *State your observations*

Be diplomatic in your observations by first stating positive things about the candidate. For example:

> "When we interviewed Carol, we felt that she was someone with a high energy level, that travel probably wouldn't wear her down. Does that match your observation of her?"

After listening to the response, continue by saying:

> "We also thought that our customers would like her. All of our staff who met her had very positive 'vibes.' Is she like that most of the time, or was that just her interview behavior?"

At this point, you are ready to move on to some negative observations. For instance:

> "During the interview, several of us had the impression that while Carol was good at selling, she might not be effective at training and developing her sales staff. Do you have any reactions to our observations?"

Another example of a negative hypothesis would be:

> "We also got the impression that Carol might pay too little attention to administrative detail, such as getting weekly sales reports in on time. Are our hunches in the right direction here?"

After sharing a negative observation, it is not prudent to say to your reference, "Is that right?" When this is done, it requires the interviewee to make a categorical response; it puts the reference on the spot. When you say something less definitive, such as "Did you ever observe anything like that?" it becomes easier for the interviewee to continue elaborating on the issue at hand.

To wrap up the "strengths and weaknesses" portion of the reference check interview, a very important question should be asked. It is asked whenever the reference is a former employer. The question is:

> "Considering everything, would you be willing to rehire Carol?"

After asking the question, the interviewer should remain silent and listen carefully. Sometimes more is learned by listening to *how* the question is answered than by the answer itself. If the applicant was a satisfactory employee, most managers, upon hearing the question, would respond without hesitation, with a "yes." If, however, significant problems existed during the applicant's employment, the employer will almost always hesitate and perhaps fumble for the right words. The words spoken may indicate "yes," but it is often easy to detect that the employer's heart is not in it.

If hesitation occurs, the interviewer can always explore for more by making a simple statement: "I know you said yes, but I sensed that you also had some concerns as well."

5. *Begin the close*

In moving toward the close, be sure to leave the door open for any additional comments the interviewee might have. For example:

> "Well, I think that covers what we were interested in discussing. Is there anything else you could share with us that might help us to understand Carol better?"

It is to be noted that this last question should not be phrased as follows: "Is there anything you could share with us that will help us *make a decision?*" The interviewee will probably not want to take responsibility for such a crucial decision, especially if that decision is likely to be a negative one.

6. *Close*

A diplomatic close could yield something positive for the future. For example:

> "Thank you very much for your time and help. We really appreciate your input. If, later on, you happen to have some other thoughts about Carol, my telephone number is _____. If I can be of any help to you, won't you please give me a call? Oh, incidentally, can you give me the name of someone else in the company who has worked with Carol?"

If a reference gives information that runs counter to the interviewer's observations or is inconsistent with that given by other references, it is worth remembering that such puzzling input is just a sample of one. There is no way of knowing what biases or prejudices that reference may harbor. One negative reference should not tip the scales, but rather should stimulate further investigation of the troubling data. In the final analysis, most of the weight should be placed on the interviewer's own assessment.

Summary

Obtaining meaningful data about an applicant, via reference checking, is difficult. Most employers are unwilling, in this age of litigation, to provide much more information about a former employee than title of job held and dates of employment. However, by calling references provided by the applicant, it is often possible to obtain significant information.

This chapter describes a procedure for conducting a reference check interview that gets beyond pat comments. The procedure involves six basic steps:

1. Introduce yourself.
2. Share openly about the nature of the job for which the candidate is being considered.
3. Quickly involve the interviewee by indicating that you would like some reactions to your observations about the candidate.
4. Share with interviewee both positive and negative interview impressions. Start with positive items.
5. Begin the close by asking an open-ended question such as: "Is there anything else that you could share with us that may help us understand <u>(name of candidate)</u>?
6. Close by asking for other possible references and by offering to help the interviewee in the future.

There are two key factors in successful reference checking. First, gain the confidence of the interviewee. After this is accomplished, keep from putting him on the defensive.

Chapter 15

Matching the Candidate to the Job

Once the interview is complete and references have been checked, the time has come to compare the candidate's qualifications with the demands of the job. The information from the interview should be organized into a balance sheet of major strengths and limitations on the basis of hypotheses confirmed. In addition, it is recommended that a paragraph or two be written about the applicant's standing with respect to each of the four basic factors—knowledge/experience, intellectual, personality, and motivational. A format for organizing interview findings is shown in Figure 24.

The data in the summary paragraphs and the balance sheet should describe how the applicant functions, how he thinks, solves problems, relates to others, is motivated, and applies knowledge and experience. This description must be compared with the behaviors required to succeed in the job in question. For example, in fast-paced jobs, a behavioral description about one aspect of the work might read: "Must be able to think quickly on his feet, be decisive, and make good judgments on the spot." In this job, anyone who was evaluated as a "cautious, deductive thinker" might not be successful (depending, of course, on the applicant's other strengths and limitations).

Thus, the entire job can be described in terms of necessary, critical behaviors that account for successful performance. The greater the overlap of the interview findings with the behavioral specifications, the more suitable the candidate is. Ob-

Figure 24. Format for organizing interview findings.

Applicant Assessment	
Name_____EEO Code_____Sex_____	
Position_____Dept._____Job Code_____	
Applicant Source_____Date_____	
Interviewed By_____	
Strengths	Weaknesses

Knowledge and Experience

Intellectual Capacity

Personality

Motivational

Overall Assessment

For Initial Position

Outstanding | Above Average | Average | Below Average

Growth
Potential

Outstanding | Above Average | Average | Below Average

Assessment Summary (a brief, narrative evaluation of candidate)

Recommended Action (if rejection, give reason, be specific)

viously, there will rarely be 100 percent congruence, so good judgment must take over from technique or methodology.

The lack of a carefully delineated description of necessary job behaviors significantly reduces accuracy in predicting job success. No matter how well trained and perceptive the interviewers may be, conflicting opinions and wrong decisions are likely to result if those in a decision-making capacity have differing views as to what is required for successful job performance. For an accurate identification of the candidate most likely to succeed, it is absolutely essential that the job be defined in behavioral terms. These are known as behavioral specifications.

It is important to distinguish between behavioral specifications and other job data that could be used to understand the job (in order to make the candidate-job comparison). Two typical job information sources are job analyses and job descriptions. Both these tools can be helpful in learning about the job, but they rarely provide the information needed to make a good selection decision. These sources do not describe the position in terms of necessary job behaviors. A review of both these sources and their use in the selection process follows.

Job Analysis

In large corporations, personnel experts often perform job analyses in which they describe the essential skills and knowledge required for certain positions. While these analyses can be helpful in screening applicants for tasks that require definite measurable skills, such as stenography or the operation of machinery, their value for analyzing management positions is doubtful. Knowledge and skill represent only a portion of the spectrum that determines effective performance in managerial or professional positions, and it is often difficult to analyze the exact skills and training needed. The talents exhibited by successful managers vary greatly from person to person, and the specific talents required for good management performance are often as much a function of the industry and the nature of the company—its climate and its own growth cycle—as they are indigenous to the job itself. Consider, too, the nature of the manager's position: that is, a manager usually has support staff or subordinates who can compensate for his deficiencies. For example, an executive with a perceived weakness in planning can nevertheless be quite successful when a staff assistant who helps schedule and set priorities offsets this shortcoming. Thus a job analysis of all the skills and knowledge needed for a management or professional position is not likely to prove helpful in matching the candidate to the job.

Job Description

In addition to an analysis of the skills and knowledge required for a certain position, the executive can also obtain a written job description. Such a description defines the tasks that the employee will have to perform. However, as with a job analysis, it does not provide the data needed to make the employment decision. First of all, job descriptions are usually prepared for salary administration purposes; that is, they assist salary administration experts in assigning a grade point value to each particular job so that appropriate salary ranges can be established. These descriptions reflect the tasks that the incumbent must carry out, but they rarely describe in meaningful terms the skills, talents, and aptitudes required. In essence, a job description only outlines the scope and functions of the job and defines the responsibility and authority of the incumbent.

A second reason job descriptions are not particularly useful in matching the applicant and the job is that they are static in nature. They may or may not reflect current conditions.

Finally, job descriptions do not describe the extra-job factors that affect the success of any manager. These include such elements as the personality dynamics of one's supervisor, the company pressures and climate, and the talents and personalities of subordinates.

Despite the limitations of job descriptions, it should not be concluded that a review of a written description is inappropriate. Review of a job description can help the executive recall

all the tasks that must be performed. However, reliance on this tool as the only vehicle for understanding what is required would be inappropriate.

Behavioral Specifications

Behavioral specifications depict the job in terms of how the incumbent must function in order to perform successfully. It is not a question of what duties the individual has to perform, but rather the manner in which they must be carried out. Some behavioral specifications are written in terms of how the incumbent must not function, and others, of course, in terms of the behaviors required. Figure 25 is an example of a list of behavioral specifications drawn up for a district sales manager position.

An examination of the behavioral specifications for the district sales manager will show that the framework for writing the specifications is made up of the four factors that account for job success. In this figure, the required behaviors can readily be compared with the conclusions the interviewer has drawn from the interview, which are in the form of confirmed behavioral hypotheses. Figure 26 shows the sequence of steps to be followed in the selection process.

Before developing the more specific data that go into behavioral specifications, three general principles ought to be considered:

1. *Don't overqualify.* Most managers tend to overestimate what is required to do a given job. Education is a good example. For many managerial jobs, it is categorically stated that the incumbent must be a college graduate. In reality, however, the course materials studied and completed for a college degree may be irrelevant for the successful performance of the managerial tasks. Of course, the attainment of a college degree may indicate something about the applicant's intellectual interests or abilities, but not all the topics covered in a degree program will have much, if any, application in many jobs. The executive should think carefully before deciding how to define the body of knowledge necessary for the job.

Figure 25. Example of behavioral specifications.

JOB TITLE: District Sales Manager
REPORTS TO: Regional Sales Manager

KEY RESPONSIBILITIES
- Directs activities of eight sales supervisors.
- Maintains direct contact and control over six key accounts.
- Develops methods and programs to assist sales supervisors in training sales representatives.
- Recruits and hires sales representatives to adequately staff the district.

Critical Behavioral Specifications

KNOWLEDGE AND EXPERIENCE FACTORS
- Minimum of one-year experience in retail grocery trade.
- Minimum of one-year experience in supervising salesmen—needs good insight and trial-and-error experience in directing others.
- Needs good knowledge of sales techniques and principles.
- Must have valid driver's license.

INTELLECTUAL FACTORS
- Needs to be able to solve problems at college graduate level; most subordinates and buyers will be college graduates.
- Must have good verbal skills; should be able to express self effectively in face-to-face situations.
- Needs to be decisive; must make many quick decisions in field.

PERSONALITY FACTORS
- Needs to be warm, affable, and outgoing; must make good initial impression.
- Must be able to cope with frustration; should be able to roll with punches; will be subject to many frustrating sales situations.

MOTIVATIONAL FACTORS
- Must like extensive people contact in everyday work.
- Must find satisfaction in physical mobility—not a desk job.
- Must have high achievement needs; should show evidence of being a self-starter; will have very limited field supervision.
- Must have good energy level; show evidence of being able to travel and work long hours.
- Should have ambition to advance up sales ladder; must be able to advance at least to regional manager.

Figure 26. Block diagram of selection process.

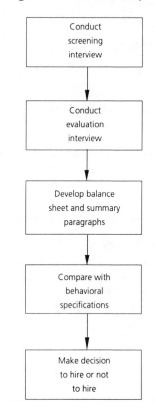

A good way to check whether or not a specification is really essential is to see how individuals currently performing successfully in the job in question actually manifest that particular behavioral specification. Another similar check would be to ask, "How many of our best employees now doing this job would be hired if we used these behavioral specifications as the criterion for the job offer?"

2. *Don't overstress technical qualifications.* The need for specific technical know-how diminishes as a function of the organizational level attained. Moreover, rapidly changing technology results in knowledge quickly becoming obsolete. The applicant either is going to be a technician or a manager;

rarely can one be good at both. If effective management is desired, technology should be of relatively less importance.

3. *Orient behavioral specifications to the present and future.* Felix M. Lopez writes of the changing nature of behavioral specifications:

> They should be oriented, first, to the situation now existing in the company and in the outside managerial market. They should also be oriented toward the future, toward the corporation's long-range goals, toward the likelihood of change in managerial needs and attitudes. By all means, they should ignore the past—and failure to do so is a fault that most companies are addicted to. The fact that the company president was born in a log cabin is no justification for requiring all future presidents to be born in log cabins. We are exaggerating, of course, to emphasize the futility of hiring what has been successful in the past. Data from research should be evaluated only in terms of what they portend for the future.*

Writing Behavioral Specifications

Behavioral specifications, as mentioned earlier, are written for each of the four basic factors that account for success at work. They require the description of the knowledge and methods needed for functioning on the job. Most managers should not find these specifications difficult or time-consuming to write. Many management groups have said to me, "We just can't agree among ourselves about what's really important in this job." These same individuals, however, after a little instruction in writing behavioral specifications, found to their surprise that agreement was not difficult. The secret, if there is one, is to limit the list of specifications to those that are absolutely essential. To keep the list realistic and meaningful, ask, "If the candidate were not able to do this particular thing or did not possess this quality, could he successfully perform in the job?"

*Felix M. Lopez, *The Making of a Manager* (New York: AMA, 1970), p. 169.

If the answer is yes, then that element should not be included in the list of behavioral specifications. Usually no more than fifteen will be listed. All the other qualities or skills that managers might like to list are no doubt good attributes to have, but they are not essential and will only confuse the decision-making process.

It is also helpful to keep in mind that the more specific each specification is, the more helpful it will be. Each should describe a particular form of knowledge or pattern of behavior needed. Specifications should not be simply a list of adjectives. For example, to write "mature" is not adequate. If maturity is an essential specification, then it should describe the behaviors needed such as, "Must come across to others as professional—should not appear kiddish, hucksterlike, or overly aggressive."

What follows are some guidelines on how to write the specifications for each factor area. Also included are a few questions that may help in formulating the critical behaviors and know-how.

Knowledge and Experience Factor

The manager must avoid the temptation to describe knowledge and experience requirements in overly general terms and instead focus on the specific elements that are absolutely necessary. For example, a meaningful behavioral specification for a training director might read, "Must have sufficient knowledge of current training techniques such as sensitivity training and confrontation methods to evaluate cost effectiveness of programs offered by consultants." Two specific questions should be considered in describing knowledge and experience behavioral specifications.

First, "Is there any particular body of knowledge that the incumbent must have in order to carry out the functions of this job?" In answering this question, consideration must be given to whether or not the knowledge can be acquired on the job. The interviewer should also consider whether the know-how can be supplemented by subordinates or others in the company, such as staff experts. Often the potential to learn is more important than what has been learned.

The second question is, "What particular kinds of experience would be necessary for effective performance in the job in question?" For many management assignments, the response has to be previous managerial experience at a specific level. Usually what is needed is the maturity that comes from exposure to problems similar to those that the manager will encounter in the new assignment. Often it is not necessary that applicants have specific experience in the same industry or field of endeavor. There are many instances in which nontechnically trained individuals have successfully managed high-technology operations. In these assignments, many doubted that nonengineers could successfully manage the groups, and yet because of their excellent ability as managers these nonengineers proved highly successful.

Intellectual Factor

How critical are communication skills for success in the job? For most management positions, the specification will probably read, "Must express self well, both in writing and in face-to-face situations." The behavioral specification should note the kind of communication skills that must be demonstrated. In many technological assignments, for example, the ability to communicate in writing is far more critical than the ability to communicate in face-to-face encounters.

How complex is the task to be performed? The requirement for intellectual capacity depends in large measure on the number of variables the individual must consider in decision-making activities. The Peter Principle—that people rise to the level of their incompetence*—has validity for the very reason that many managers get in over their heads because of their inability to cope with the additional variables they encounter in

---

*Laurence J. Peter and Raymond Hill, *The Peter Principle* (New York: William Morrow & Company, 1969).

new assignments. If the job being studied is narrowly circumscribed, a high capacity for dealing with many variables may not be necessary.

Some questions that can be asked to help formulate specifications for the intellectual factor include: Are any specific intellectual aptitudes (for example, mathematical or mechanical) necessary? How should the candidate go about problem solving (impulsively, cautiously, deductively)?

To assist the executive in preparing a list of behavioral specifications, a format is shown in Appendix C.

Personality Factor

Are any particular personality traits essential for success in this assignment? This is often a difficult question to answer. The temptation is to list such obvious qualities as initiative, decisiveness, and self-confidence. Rarely, however, are these specifications meaningful except when these qualities are necessary in the extreme. Whether a trait is helpful or not depends in large measure on the other traits with which it is combined in the individual. Thus it is more helpful to look at specific issues relating to personality strengths and limitations when considering possible specifications.

How much pressure is involved in this job? Does the incumbent need the ability to roll with the punches? In analyzing possible sources of pressure, the interviewer should examine the number and importance of deadlines, the extent to which pressing demands are made on the incumbent by others, and the number and nature of internal conflicts.

Does the person need to be reflective or action-oriented? Is the type of work best managed in a cautious, analytical way, or is it important to get things done immediately? If the former situation prevails, the behavior specifications might indicate that the applicant should manifest a behavior pattern that is characterized by reflectiveness, restraint, and caution. For an action-oriented job, the specification might read, "Incumbent should be highly energetic and be able to make decisions under pressure."

Does the incumbent need to be socially dominant? Will there be many conflicts with others—subordinates, peers, or supervisors? Is a strong dominant personality necessary to minimize the possibility of being buffeted by conflicts and pressures? Here are some additional questions to think about when determining the specifications for the personality factor: Are any essential personality qualities needed for success in this job? How must the incumbent handle stress or pressure? What kind of interpersonal behavior, if any, is required to perform the job? Up the line? Peer level? Down the line? Outside the organization (customers and others)?

Motivational Factor

What will the incumbent be doing most of the time in the job? Planning? Directly supervising others? Solving complex technological problems? Whatever it is, specifications can be drawn indicating the activities the manager should *like to do* in order to be motivated in this assignment; that is, specifications can spell out what the incumbent's interests must be. For example, let's examine a research and development job in which the incumbent spends much time alone monitoring a pilot plant operation. A motivation specification for this kind of job might read, "Life history should show enjoyment in independent or solitary activities." Another specification could be, "Incumbent should have a strong preference for working with concrete, tangible results as opposed to abstractions."

In general, the behavioral specifications should include two or three kinds of activities that a person would probably have to like doing in order to find the work tasks satisfying. Referral to the discussion of interests in Chapter 8 may prove helpful here.

In writing motivational specifications, thought also should be given to the goals and objectives that the applicant ought to have. Many positions tend to be dead ends. Consequently, specifications must indicate the extent to which the applicant can have ambitions for further advancement. A specification for a position in which advancement cannot be rapid might read,

"Applicant needs to be willing to invest at least two years' development time in the Wilmington plant before promotion to the director of manufacturing position."

Some questions to think about when determining the specifications for the motivational factor are: What should the applicant like to do if he is going to enjoy working in this job? Is there anything the applicant definitely should not dislike doing? Are any goals or aspirations essential? Does the job require any unusual energy demands (long hours or constant travel)? How critical is the drive level? Must the incumbent overcome many obstacles?

In Figures 27–33 are more examples of behavioral specifications developed by managers in their respective companies. These lists may suggest how behavioral specifications can be assembled.

An Important Consideration

One reason why little attention has been given to examining what is required by the job is that so many different kinds of individuals can perform a given task—and perform it successfully. The variations with which most professional or managerial tasks can be approached suggest that any definition of what is required to perform a job be undertaken in a cautious and conservative way. To be sure, matching abilities to the job requires some appreciation of what it may take to perform the job successfully. But the danger is great that the interviewer may come to believe that particular skills, traits, or aptitudes are essential, whereas, in reality, varying combinations of attributes will also result in successful job performance.

The interviewer should recognize that the tendency of most evaluators is to hire people who satisfy the overall needs of the company rather than to seek a variety of individuals who in combination might fulfill company needs. For example, if executives were asked to delineate the ideal characteristics for a good manager in their company, they might say:

(text continues on page 258)

Figure 27. Behavioral specifications for a sales trainee.

Knowledge/Experience
- Must rank high (in upper half) in sales knowledge test
- Must have demonstrated success in persuading others

Intellectual
- Must be able to communicate orally and in writing at a level acceptable to customers and company management

- Must be able to approach problem solving in a broad, rather than a detailed, manner

- Must show flexibility in thinking and approaches to problems

Personality
- Must be socially outgoing (as shown in interview and past activity)

- Must have optimistic attitude, at least show no evidence of being easily discouraged

- Must show ability to sustain long-term relationships

- Must demonstrate persistence and perseverance

Motivational
- Must show good internal drive, evidence of at least one self-starting activity

- Must demonstrate high energy level and strong competitive nature

- Must like mobility, have no objections to travel or moving about, or to a nondesk-type job

- Must enjoy people contact

Figure 28. Behavioral specifications for a project manager.

Knowledge/Experience
- Must be apt at scheduling

- Must be apt at estimating

- Must be apt at cost analysis

- Must be apt at "scoping out" jobs

- Must be apt at administrative aspects of projects

Intellectual
- Must have engineering degree or track record demonstrating quantitative aptitude

- Must have ability to make quick decisions, to think "on feet"

- Must have common sense, or the ability to think practically

- Must have the ability to simplify complex situations

Personality
- Must have consistently demonstrated ability to function in an aggressive and "take charge" manner

- Must be a team leader, with ability to work effectively with a wide range or people

- Must show self-confidence and decisiveness even on unfamiliar ground

- Must exhibit a strong sense or urgency (be action-oriented)

- Must possess ability to operate with minimal structure and/or supervision

---

Motivational

- Must derive great satisfaction from tangible, measurable results

- Must like working with people and managing them

- Must thrive on challenges

- Must demonstrate significant self-starting ability

- Must evidence high physical energy, stamina to work long hours

- Must feel strong need to complete projects, to get things done

Figure 29. Behavioral specifications for a construction superintendent.

Knowledge/Experience

- Must know how to read blueprints and extend to quantities

- Must have a working knowledge of geometry and trigonometry

- Must know how to do "near-term" scheduling (can be tested during interview)

- Must have knowledge of construction methods and materials, including building structures, concrete, material handling equipment, and carpentry (formwork)

(continued)

(Figure 29 continued)

Intellectual

- Must be decisive, able to think quickly on feet

- Must have ability to relate many variables to the "big picture"

- Must orient thinking to the future, with capacity to "deal with today's details while planning for tomorrow"

- Must be able to think methodically, logically, and systematically

Personality

- Must demonstrate ability to be firm and decisive with others

- Must exude a positive, "can do" attitude to subordinates

- Must come across as self-confident and self-assured

- Must move quickly in confronting problems and conflicts

- Must be impatient, eager to get things done quickly

- Must have ability to understand and reach to the needs of others

Motivational

- Must thrive on challenge, competition, and the overcoming of obstacles

- Must show evidence of a "mountain climbing" mentality

- Must be able to tolerate pressure, conflict, change, complexity, and ambiguity

- Must possess a high energy level, ability to work long hours

- Must have strong leadership ability (need for control and ability to tell and sell)

- Must like variety and change in the work

- Must prefer concrete, tangible things to theoretical concepts

---

Figure 30. Behavioral specifications for an insurance
company president.

Knowledge/Experience

- Must be financially knowledgeable (with ability to understand balance sheets, PVLs, pro formas) and experienced in working with financial data as part of management responsibility

- Must offer a minimum of five years' insurance company experience

- Must have managed, simultaneously, several different departments at upper levels

Intellectual

- Must have good verbal/writing skills

- Must be quick at thinking on feet

- Must be able to look at problems from a broad perspective

- Must have good integrative skills

Personality

- Must have a high degree of credibility (openness, integrity, knowledgeability)

- Must make a good public appearance

- Must have sufficient strength to make tough decisions

- Must relate well to a wide range of individuals

- Must be teamwork-oriented, with a participative, rather than an authoritative style

- Must have ability to cope with politicians and regulators, and to roll with punches without getting emotionally involved

- Must have a low level of distractability

(continued)

(Figure 30 continued)

Motivational
- Must have a strong inner drive to accomplish and to see results

- Must find satisfaction in representing company in community organizations, delivering speeches, and other public affairs activities

- Must possess a high energy level

Figure 31. Behavioral specifications for a pharmaceuticals field representative.

Knowledge/Experience
- Must have two to four years of field sales experience or its equivalent in knowledge

- Must have experience in closing sales, working a variety of customers, managing self in field, and handling finances

- Must have experience in successfully managing personal finances

- Must have the ability to talk effectively with veterinarians of pharmaceutical products relevant to animal health

- Must have the ability to communicate effectively with college-level personnel (usually shown by a college degree or evidence of equivalent ability)

- Must have a valid driver's license

Intellectual

- Must possess good ability with numbers so as to be able to calculate prices, dosages, and percentages

- Must communicate easily in face-to-face situations without sounding disorganized or at a loss for words

- Must be able to write effective letters to customers

- Must evidence ability to make frequent decisions, to plan, and to exercise good judgment

Personality

- Must be able to handle pressure

- Must come across to others as professional, not as a huckster or as an immature amateur

- Must appear to care about others, show ability to empathize, and convince others of sincerity

- Must project self-confidence in interview

Motivational

- Must like extensive contact with people

- Must enjoy travel or at least not dislike it

- Must like being on own and show some evidence of self-starting ability

- Must preferably enjoy engaging in competitive activities, such as sports or cards

Figure 32. Behavioral specifications for a college recruiting
            coordinator.

Knowledge/Experience
- Must know how to keep on top of many people/papers simultaneously—be able to keep many variables "in the air" at the same time

- Must know how to use a personal computer

Intellectual
- Must be able to make quick decisions, "shift gears" quickly

- Must have good verbal skills and be able to enunciate clearly and concisely

- Must be able to work effectively with and be able to organize details

Personality
- Must be outgoing, personable, and diplomatic

- Must come across in a confident, self-assured way

- Must be able to cope with many pressure deadlines

- Must have demonstrated persuasive skills

Motivational
- Must enjoy and be able to work on the phone

- Must find satisfaction in extensive people contact

- Must be service-oriented and find satisfaction in helping others

- Must be willing to travel extensively

Figure 33. Behavioral specifications for a book
management trainee.

Knowledge/Experience
- Must show knowledge of business practices through actual business experience or through completion of business management courses

Intellectual
- Must demonstrate ability to learn business and technical information at the college-graduate level (usually by completing college degree)

- Must be able to solve problems analytically and in detail

- Must show good insight into the motivation and behavior of others

Personality
- Must demonstrate ability to wear well, to maintain long-term relationships with groups

- Must make a good initial impression on others, come across as poised and mature

- Must be flexible, able to adapt to rapidly changing situations

- Must show enthusiasm

Motivational
- Must show evidence of persistence

- Must feel satisfaction in being helpful to others

- Must desire to advance to management level

- Must possess self-starting ability, so as to be able to assume initiative in branch locations

---

- "We want him to be creative but not too blue-sky."
- "We want him to be practical and down to earth but not just a nuts-and-bolts man."
- "We want him to be a good planner, but he also must be action-oriented."
- "He should be very bright but not so advanced that he cannot communicate and identify with those around him."

And so it goes. It is true that the company could not effectively use only creative thinkers any more than it could be successful if it were composed entirely of action-oriented individuals. A successful company needs both these kinds of people and their skills, but needs them in balanced proportions. As David A. Whitsett, a professor at the University of Northern Iowa, points out, the tendency is to seek the balance in each individual hired. Thus unusually creative persons are passed by because they are not practical enough, or careful, conceptual planners are passed by because they do not get things done fast enough. Much thought should be given to meeting the company's needs through the diversity of its personnel rather than by trying to find this balance in one person. The company that consistently hires individuals with a balanced range of talents, none of which are extraordinarily developed, is likely to end with a static organization. But a company composed of mediocrity will find itself losing out on the innovative thrusts and perceptive changes of direction that usually emanate from the not-too-well-rounded mavericks.

Thus it may not be so important for overall company requirements to be mirrored in each individual job candidate. Job tasks can be shifted, incumbents can team with others to supplement deficiencies or augment strengths, and the interplay among relatively narrow-gauged, highly talented personnel can also produce an effective coordinated whole.

Figure 34. Worksheet for comparing applicants.

Evaluation of Candidates vs. Behavioral Specifications

Job Title_____   Interviewer_____

If candidate meets specs,   Names of Candidates
make a ✓ under name.

BEHAVIORAL SPECIFICATIONS:

Knowledge/Experience
1._____
2._____
3._____
4._____
5._____

Intellectual
1._____
2._____
3._____
4._____
5._____

Personality
1._____
2._____
3._____
4._____
5._____

Motivational
1._____
2._____
3._____
4._____
5._____

Making the Decision

As was mentioned at the outset of this chapter, the hire/not-hire decision is predicated on the extent to which the candidate meets the required behavioral specifications. A convenient way to do this—especially if several applicants are being considered for the same position—is to use the worksheet shown in Figure 34. Since this device gives equal weight to all specifications, the best choice may not simply be the candidate with the most checkmarks (although this often proves to be the case). However, the checkmarks do provide a meaningful springboard for focused discussion about the qualitative merits of each candidate. It is at this point that technique and methodology end, and good judgment must be relied on. In many ways, making the right decision about potential employees is still an art form.

Summary

This chapter introduces a concept for defining jobs—behavioral specifications. These describe the essential knowledge and behavior patterns that must be evident for an incumbent to successfully perform a particular job. They help increase the accuracy of employment decisions because they are the ruler against which the interview findings are compared. Having a consistent frame of reference by which to measure applicants helps ensure more objective decision making.

Behavioral specifications are written on each of the four basic factors that account for job success. Mention was made of the need not to overqualify, not to overstress technical qualifications, and not to focus too much on past success patterns. In developing specifications, consideration must also be given to the future direction of the organization.

Chapter 16

Selling the Candidate

There is nothing more frustrating (and costly) than to go to the trouble of recruiting and evaluating an excellent candidate only to have that applicant turn down the job offer and then to have to start the whole process over again. Effectively marketing the company and the job is as important a part of the selection procedure as recruiting or evaluating. Unfortunately, companies often give scant attention to determining whether the applicants they want also want them. They assume that if the company offers employment, the candidate will readily accept it. A company that seeks the most desirable individuals, those other organizations also want, must remember that the candidate is evaluating the company just as it is evaluating the candidate.

This chapter describes an effective procedure for attracting candidates, particularly to job situations or locations that are not considered highly attractive or desirable. What is considered desirable of course varies from person to person but, typically, remote plant locations, harsh climates, and large cities (even though glamorous to some) are viewed as undesirable, despite good pay and benefits. Sometimes an organization attracts candidates because of its preeminence in the industry or because it is situated in a highly desirable location. Even so, to get the most sought-after candidates, a company must pay attention to the sales aspect of the employment process.

That the selling approach outlined here is successful is shown by the experience of a large chemical organization that was faced with the problem of filling a large number of vacancies in locations that were physically unattractive or remote. Using this approach, the company obtained an extremely high acceptance rate of 80 to 90 percent of the candidates it made offers to. It was pleased to discover, too, that it made very few mistakes in selection. An indirect benefit from this method of selling a candidate is that it can strengthen the esprit de corps in the organization because key people are involved in the hiring and integration of new people.

Some Basic Assumptions

Before depicting the selling approach, let's make some basic assumptions. First, let's assume that the candidate has passed some initial screening or filtering. The candidate may have been recruited by an executive search firm or on campus, interviewed by the personnel department, or sent to headquarters for approval following assessment by a regional office. The assumption is that the company would like to attract this candidate, who seems well suited to the job. The procedure, of course, provides ample opportunity for conducting the evaluation interview, discussed in Chapter 13, so there remains the possibility that the candidate may be eliminated after the sales visit. Let's also assume that the compensation and benefits are competitive, that there is a career path—a place to grow—for new employees, and that the organization is reasonably successful.

In examining this approach for increasing the acceptance rate of the best candidates, it must be recognized that many things besides the job need to be "sold" to the candidate. It is also necessary to sell the company, the location, and, most important, all the personnel the candidate meets. All these factors enter into the candidate's decision whether or not to join an organization, and all should be addressed in any effort to recruit the new employee. The premise on which this procedure is built is that familiarity is the best antidote to resistance to something new or different; that "hands-on" exposure to job, potential co-workers, and community environment are all important in helping the applicant overcome possible objections to accepting the employment offer. Ultimately, the probability of a positive reaction to the offer depends on the candidate's ability to identify with the employment situation, to see himself happily engaged in the life style of that company and the community in which it is located.

Essential Ingredients in Winning Top People

Here are the steps it takes to build up that essential positive reaction:

Involve all key managers. The visit to the location should involve more than the personnel department and the candidate's future boss. All individuals with whom the applicant is likely to interface, once on the job, should be briefed on the candidate's background before the visit takes place. When the applicant is being shown around the facility, the key employees he meets should not be caught unawares. They should know enough about the candidate to provide a warm welcome and to make constructive comments by way of positive support for the recruiting effort. This briefing of key people can be made during a staff meeting when the group is together for other purposes. At that time, the candidate's background should be reviewed and agreement reached on which aspects of the operation are most meaningful and best suited to being highlighted during even casual discussions with the candidate.

Organize a team operation. The on-site visit should be a carefully structured team operation in the sense that many individuals will be involved, including frequently the spouses of some of the executives. Specific assignments should be delegated to various members of the executive group.

Allow adequate time. It is not cost-effective to bring an important candidate for an on-site visit only to whisk him through many interviews, a quick lunch, and then off to the airport. About thirty-six hours will provide the right amount of time from arrival to departure; and twenty-four hours should be considered minimal. Before a candidate can successfully identify with the operation, he must have firsthand exposure to company activities at the site. He needs to see how the company operates and to learn how he would function, fit in, and be accepted. The applicant also needs time to view the nonjob aspects of the position (such as the character of the community and what type of schooling and housing is available) and to digest what was discussed and seen during the first day of his visit. Therefore, a period of time overnight, when the candidate and his spouse can discuss and reflect on these issues and prepare questions for the following day, is vitally important.

Involve the candidate's spouse. In this age of dual careers, emphasis on the quality of life, and concern about family stability, it is inexcusable not to involve the candidate's spouse (if one exists) in the visit. Usually the spouse will be a significant factor in the candidate's acceptance or rejection of the offer and in the longevity of his stay with a company. If upon relocation the spouse finds work opportunities limited, or the children unhappy, or the community lacking in satisfying experiences, the likelihood of the candidate remaining with the organization is, of course, greatly reduced. It makes good sense therefore to win over the candidate's spouse when trying to gain commitment from a top candidate.

Designate a host and hostess. To make sure that the candidate is treated as an honored guest and not simply as a job applicant, an executive and his spouse should be assigned the role of host and hostess for the duration of the visit. The host might be the candidate's future boss or a more senior executive. In any case, the host should not be slotted lower in the organizational hierarchy than the level at which the candidate will be placed. If the key person the company is attempting to sell is slated to come in as the president or top official in the location, it may not be practical for a headquarters couple from outside the location to serve as host and hostess. In this case, the host and hostess should be selected from among those who are actively involved in the community, people who are warm and friendly individuals and also well respected by the organization.

Provide on-the-job contacts. An effort should be made to involve the candidate with people he can identify with, that is, individuals of similar age, job function, and life style. Candidates want to know what people like themselves are doing, how they live, and what they think of the company and community. Making available persons with whom the applicant can relate and talk is analogous to sending a recent graduate from a particular university back to that campus to recruit graduating seniors. The prospective peers of a candidate will often have more success in recruiting him than a senior manager would have.

Involve the prospective boss. If executives in an organization are going to be held accountable for productivity, then they should be directly involved in making the decision as to who will be working for them. For this reason, and because "chemistry" between individuals is an important ingredient in successful work relationships, the prospective boss of the candidate should participate directly in the interview process, the final decision, and the job offer. Often, it is this individual who actually extends the final job offer. However, there is no reason to wait until the first day the candidate reports to work to start building this relationship. It should begin at the time of selling the candidate.

Offer real-life activities. An effective way of selling candidates is to let them get a feel for what it is really like to work in the organization. This sort of knowledge cannot be gained from verbal descriptions of "how we operate here" or from assurances that the company is a "good place to work." It is important for the candidate to experience something more concrete, more tangible. The usefulness of this approach is demonstrated by a study I did for a client organization. For this company, fifty-six college seniors were asked why they had accepted the company's offer of employment. Of that group, thirty-three, or 57 percent, indicated that "a clear image of the job assignment" was their primary reason for accepting the offer. In effect, they were saying that when they got their offering letter they could actually visualize the job they were going into; it was concrete, not some vague abstraction.

In this company's selection process, the evaluation interviews were conducted in the morning. During the afternoon, the candidate was assigned to an individual who was new in a job similar to that the candidate would fill. The candidate was allowed to "tag along" with the employee as he carried out his daily job responsibilities—writing reports, answering the telephone, and attending staff meetings. Thus, by the end of the afternoon, the candidate had a real feel for what the job would entail and for the nature of the work environment, and even a sense of identification with the organization. Many candidates said that during the afternoon they felt as though they were already "on board."

. In essence, it is important to involve the candidate in real-life, day-to-day activities at the location. These could include morning production planning meetings, project review conferences, and the like.

Deal with hidden needs. To be effective in selling key people, it is important to consider their hidden needs as well as those customarily expressed. The expressed needs will be formulated as explicit questions about the challenge of the work, the nature of future opportunities, and the compensation and benefits offered. Obviously, the organization should be prepared to answer these clearly and definitively. But there are also hidden needs that affect the candidate's decision. These needs are sometimes not articulated because the candidate fears that they may be interpreted as signs of insecurity or weakness. Following are a few hidden needs that any effective selling program should consider.

Picture the working atmosphere. The candidate needs a chance to see the whole business picture in order to have a sense of completeness and a clear understanding of what makes this organization tick. At a more subtle level, most candidates are trying to determine for themselves: "Is this a stimulating kind of environment? What are the possibilities for my personal growth and involvement in the organization?" Most candidates want to know, for example, the true extent to which they will participate in goal setting or have autonomy in their jobs. Candidates may fear that they will find the environment stifling or will be narrowly boxed into a small segment of the business. They worry about whether they will be cut off from the mainstream or have much control over their own environment, work flow, or decisions. The degree to which the company can deal with these hidden concerns, which center about the person's ability to be a meaningful part of the organization, will in large measure determine the probability of acceptance of the offer.

Focus on nonjob possibilities. Many organizations focus so entirely on the job and the organization that they fail to address the concerns candidates may have about what it's like to live in a particular area or community. The candidate may not always ask outright, "Is this a place that I want to live and raise my family in?" But obviously that is a question of major importance. Essentially, the candidate's concerns are about opportunities for off-the-job activities, association with people of like interests, the quality of the schools, the opportunity for personal growth, and opportunities for family recreational activities.

The more positive the answers supplied to these questions are, the less concern the job candidate will have. It is not enough merely to link the candidate up with a real estate agent and hope that their trips around town will satisfy his concerns and needs. Perhaps the most critical question of those mentioned is association with people of like interests. The candidate and his family naturally wonder about how they are going to fit into the community in much the same way that a single job applicant wonders about fitting into the organization. It is important, therefore, to show the candidate what the community offers to make life satisfying. This usually requires during the interview a direct question about what is important to the candidate and his family's life style. It might be helpful to ask what the candidate's family enjoys where they currently live, so that information can be gathered on opportunities in the local community that might satisfy these same interests.

Provide a bridge to the new life. This really has to do with such questions as, "What will it be like living here?" and "Will I succeed?" It has much to do with the individuals the candidate and his spouse have met during the visit and the extent to which they see these people as welcoming them into the company and community. It may mean that some of the people doing the interviewing and meeting with the candidate ought to share some of their activities and life style. They should be instructed to be genuine and to reveal some of the negatives as well as the positives of life in the community. Without being obvious about it, those involved in the selling visit should be prepared to provide answers to the questions mentioned in this section.

An Effective Format for Visiting Candidates

This section presents a list of suggested activities for a two-day visit. In this example, let's assume that the candidate is male and that he brings along his wife. If the situation is reversed, or if the candidate's wife is employed, some revisions in the suggested schedule must be made to allow time for the candidate's spouse to explore employment opportunities. In such cases, it would be helpful if the personnel department worked directly with the spouse, describing employment opportunities in the area, salary levels, and major industries. The personnel manager might also be requested to line up interviews with local executive search organizations, employment agencies, and personnel departments. Short of that, supplying brochures from the major employers in the area would be desirable.

The procedure outlined here has been tested and has worked effectively with a large number of candidates but, obviously, represents only one of many ways of making a visit effective. Local situations may require adaptations.

Before the Arrival of the Candidate

Mr. and Mrs. Candidate should be contacted well before their arrival by the assigned host and hostess. They should know where they are going to stay, who will meet their plane, and what they will be doing. They can be informed by letter, but it is often best to combine a written communication with an informal telephone conversation to learn if the candidate has any questions about the visit. There may be, for example, some questions about the climate and the appropriate clothing to pack.

Arrival

If possible, it is desirable to have the candidate and his spouse arrive the evening before the first full day. The host and hostess should meet the plane, conduct the guests to the hotel or motel, and at that time explain the next day's activities. Essentially, it will be a busy day at the plant or office for the candidate, a relaxed day around town or a busy one investigating employment possibilities for the spouse, and dinner with the company host and hostess for both.

It is also helpful to provide the visitors with a packet of information regarding the community and the company. These could be Chamber of Commerce maps, brochures describing local places of interest, company benefit package outlines, annual reports, or company house organs or magazines. The meeting the first evening should not be long. The travelers may be tired, and so, after explaining briefly what will happen the next day and what time they will be picked up, the host and hostess should let the guests retire.

Next Day: Spouse's Program

A designated host or hostess picks up the candidate's spouse at about 9:30 A.M. and spends the morning showing off a few community points of interest, including schools if they are of interest. In cases where the spouse will be job seeking in the new area, meetings can be arranged with local employment agencies, executive search firms, and human resources managers. The host or hostess arranges a lunch with two (or a maximum of three) carefully chosen hosts or hostesses.

The host or hostess offers to turn the visitor over to a local cooperating realtor for a couple of hours during the afternoon.

Arrangements are also made to return the spouse to the hotel at 4:30 to freshen up before a happy hour at 6 P.M., to be followed by dinner.

Next Day: Candidate's Program

The following is a typical first-day schedule for candidates.

8 A.M.—Plant (or location) briefing. This should be kept short, to no more than twenty minutes. For this it is helpful to use an expert who is skillful at presentations, perhaps someone from the training department. The briefing might include slides or a film, or maps and exhibits, to brief the applicant on the nature of the operation, what is done, and how it is accomplished. In effect, this gives the person a good overview of what the place is all about.

8:30 A.M.—Plant or location tour with future associate. In this portion of the day, the applicant is assigned to someone who is in the same type of job he will be filling. The candidate is given the opportunity to follow this employee around as he goes about his morning chores. It would be helpful if they could drop in on morning meetings, such as a project review meeting, a production or maintenance planning meeting, or perhaps the plant manager's staff meeting. These should be ongoing meetings conducted in the usual way, whether or not a candidate is present. If the employees are preparing a report, they might involve the candidate in this process.

11 A.M.—Candidate visits his future department and is introduced to other associates in the operation. A round-table discussion may focus on the objectives of that particular department, the problems it is currently facing, some of the hopes for solving them, and how the members of the department and the potential incumbent might work together. Some description of how the department functions as a team should be included.

12 noon—Informal lunch during which the respective groups discuss goals, their views of the organization, and the business or industry. Again, this is a shop talk kind of meeting where the candidate gets a chance to see who he will be dealing

with, how they view his department, and the way they will probably be working together in the future.

1:30 P.M.—Interview with the manager and future boss. In this time segment, the manager should use the evaluation model discussed in Chapter 13. It should be a serious attempt to make a sound, qualitative assessment of the candidate. After completion of the assessment portion of the interview (completion of the Evaluation Model), the manager will explore the candidate's reactions and perceptions. Open-ended questions should be asked as to what the candidate's reactions are thus far, what he sees as some of the positive aspects of being in the organization, and what concerns he may have. In addition, the manager could invite comments on how the candidate would like to contribute to the organization. This is a good opportunity for the manager to practice listening skills. Finally, the manager might end the meeting with a review of the total picture. Some topics that could be touched upon are:

1. Business strategy of the organization and its competitive position
2. The management style of the organization and how the manager likes to operate
3. Investment planning
4. Objectives for the future

The purpose of this interview is to bring the candidate into the "fold" by really giving him a feel for what the company is about, where it is going, and how it is managed.

3:15 P.M.—Session with personnel manager. Here the candidate is exposed to company policies, benefit plans, and information about where personnel in the organization are living, the location and quality of schools, and other community data. It also provides a time to inquire how the candidate feels about the company and whether he has any unanswered questions about the company or the community.

4 P.M.—Return of guest to motel. The company representatives who have been seeing the candidate during the day can now get together to share their views on the suitability of the

applicant and what the next steps in the selling process should be. Usually this gathering includes the manager, the host, tour guides, and the personnel representative. At this discussion, it would be well to evaluate the candidate by comparing numerical ratings on qualifications, potential, and any other concerns that anyone has. At this time, it can also be decided who will explore any questionable areas and how this information will be fed back to the decision maker (the manager). This new information will ordinarily be gathered that evening or during the following morning.

6 to 6:30 P.M.—Pre-dinner drinks.

6:30 to 8:30 P.M.—Dinner with manager (if seriously interested), spouse, host, and others. A party of six is recommended, but never more than eight. The brief period keeps drinking moderate and ensures an early adjournment. There does not seem to be any advantage to "doing the town" or making this a lavish affair. Dinner in a good but quiet restaurant affording an opportunity to talk in a relaxed manner is probably the best plan.

During dinner, which should be on a pleasant social level, questions from the candidate or his spouse can be answered, but no explicit attempt should be made by company staff to probe or question at this time.

If the organization is still feeling quite good about the candidate, positive comments (though not a job offer) should be made during the dinner simply to show a favorable disposition. It would be well if the candidate and his spouse could retire that evening having positive feelings about the organization and also feeling optimistic about employment possibilities.

Second Morning

The second morning is when efforts are made to "close the deal." And this is when the manager should play the major role. It is helpful if three major points can be made at this time.

We like you. Indicate that all who have met the candidate feel that he would be an excellent member of the team, that he's the kind of person who would fit in well. It could be mentioned further that all foresee a working relationship that would be cooperative and enjoyable.

We need you. Point out that the offering is a critical job that really needs doing, and that the applicant is believed capable of accomplishing it.

You will succeed. Point out, in an optimistic way, that you believe the candidate could make an excellent contribution. Indicate confidence that the candidate will find much satisfaction in completing what needs to be accomplished.

If the terms of the job offer have not been put forth already, this is the appropriate moment to do so. Be sure to allow time in the morning schedule for negotiations, should they become necessary. The following should be done to end the visit.

1. Ask for an early acceptance, giving one week maximum for the candidate's decision. Mention that you will be seeing other candidates but would like to go ahead with this one; emphasize that "we need to know soon."
2. The manager should present his business card and phone number, both at business and home, in the event that the candidate has further questions to ask.
3. Offer the candidate a confirming letter. If possible, have it typed and ready to give to him before he leaves the site.
4. Mention physical examinations if they are required by the company.
5. Have the host and hostess facilitate the candidate's departure, picking spouse up at the hotel, getting to the airport, and waiting until the plane departs.
6. Write a warm follow-up letter. This letter can mention again the main points suggested earlier, that is, that the company likes the candidate, needs the candidate, and believes the candidate will succeed. Mention should also be made of the spouse and that the manager believes the candidate and his family will fit into the community and find it enjoyable.

Summary

This chapter deals with the most important factors to be considered in trying to sell the candidate, particularly when the location of the plant or industry is not particularly attractive or in vogue. It stresses satisfying the hidden needs of candidates, as well as their more explicitly stated needs. It provides a format for a thirty-six hour visit. It is strongly recommended that the candidate's spouse be included in this visit and that the focus be on how the person will fit into the organization and the community. This is accomplished by providing an opportunity for the candidate to have close contact with persons of similar background, age, and life style.

Chapter 17

Job Coaching and Performance Appraisal Interviews*

Of all the methods used to improve job performance, the most widely used is some variation of the "good old-fashioned talk." It can range from a casual chat over lunch to a formal, annual performance appraisal. But whatever the approach, the objective is the same: to help the subordinate grow or commit himself to doing something differently—in short, to improve.

As can be noted from the title of this chapter, I distinguish between job coaching and performance appraisal. Actually, performance appraisal is a form of job coaching. However, for convenience in discussing interview approaches, I will define performance appraisal as a formalized annual review, usually involving a summary of how objectives or performance standards have or have not been achieved. In some organizations, performance appraisal also involves discussion of developmental plans, career planning, and salary/bonus decisions. Job coaching, on the other hand, is defined here as a more informal discussion with the subordinate about job performance.

This chapter discusses the difficulties involved in developing staff and provides four helpful models for talking about a subordinate's behavior or job performance. The model the

---

*Parts of this chapter have been taken from *A CEO's Guide to Interpersonal Relation.* Study #77. The Presidents Association.

manager selects depends on the objective of the interview. But, before describing these models, it will be helpful first to gain an understanding of the problems likely to be encountered when the manager initiates a discussion of the subordinate and/or his job performance.

What Makes Job Coaching and Performance Appraisal So Difficult?

On the surface, it would seem that discussions about a subordinate's job performance should be a relatively simple matter. The boss wants to share an observation about the subordinate's work; he may even have a positive suggestion or two that will enable his subordinate to do the job better or more easily. But as anyone who has attempted this kind of discussion can testify, good intentions rarely lead to a satisfying discussion and even less often do they produce improved performance.

Here are the major reasons why job coaching and performance appraisal discussions are often disappointing:

Coaching is perceived as risky. One difficulty is the awareness that the interview could make things worse. Many managers have lived through the experience of trying to help a subordinate only to find that, as a result of their initiative, the employee became less motivated, more antagonistic to the boss, and perhaps even quit! It is no wonder, then, that managers approach job coaching with some trepidation.

This fear in turn often yields to feelings of resentment or hostility toward the subordinate. At such times, it is easy to think: "Things may not be perfect now, but if I mention this topic, things could get worse." As a result, if the manager proceeds with the interview, he is likely to be defensive and so make the climate tense—all of which reduces the likelihood of success.

There is uncertainty about how to proceed. Many managers put off job coaching or formal appraisals because they just don't know a good way of going about them. They may wonder, for example, how to manage it if the subordinate disagrees or gives them a hard time. Some are perplexed even about how to begin, especially if what has to be communicated is a touchy issue. Others are concerned about how to terminate the interview or how to proceed should the subordinate get upset and become emotional.

Motivation to conduct the interview is low. A third factor that leads to a low success rate in job improvement discussions is the expectation of many managers that not much good will come from the meeting, particularly if it is an annual performance review. Even when the subordinate appears to agree with the manager and says, "I'll work on it," these words are seldom translated into changed behavior. As a result, many managers enter the discussion in a routine way, attempting to get it over with as quickly as possible.

Bosses and subordinates become defensive. Of all the problems mentioned, this one is the most difficult to deal with. Defensive behavior occurs whenever it is stated or implied that something the subordinate is doing is not being viewed favorably. Instead of learning from the criticism, the subordinate typically responds with reasons justifying the actions or behavior the manager wishes to see corrected. While it is normal for people to protect their egos, these defensive reactions naturally hinder objective discussion of the problem.

The problem of defensiveness begins when subordinates, protecting themselves, respond to criticism with normal reactions. An interesting point about defensiveness is that it becomes the reaction of both parties to the discussion. The subordinate becomes defensive in an effort to demonstrate that the improvement suggestion is not valid or necessary; and the boss becomes defensive because the subordinate is rejecting his feedback. *In most interviews concerned with improving job performance, the discussion boils down to a battle between two defensive systems.* It is the dynamics of this interaction that leads to failure in gaining improved performance.

Four Types of Interviews for Improving Performance

Before readers go on to the procedures (models) designed to minimize the problem just cited, it would be helpful if they recognized that job coaching interviews can take either of two paths, depending on the objective of the interview.

One objective can be to provide an opportunity for growth. This can be called *developmental coaching.* This kind of interview is used when the manager has no particular problem to discuss and is not seeking to bring about a specific change. *The technique is employed when the manager wishes to teach the subordinate something that the subordinate wants to learn about.* Alternatively, it can be a discussion in which the boss wants to give the subordinate an opportunity to talk about his work, future, or career path. The distinguishing aspect of developmental coaching is that the subordinate is likely to be receptive to what is said and will not react defensively.

The second type of coaching situation is one in which there is a problem or an implied lack of success that the manager wants the subordinate to overcome or to change in some way. This type of interview can be called *change coaching. The objective of this technique is to correct or change ineffective performance.* It is difficult because here again the subordinate is quite likely to become defensive.

In this chapter, four models will be presented, two for developmental coaching and two for conflict coaching. Each one is designed so as to minimize the interviewing difficulties previously referred to. They are depicted in Figure 35.

The Teaching Model

Although teaching a subordinate may seem a relatively simple thing to do, there are some pedagogical principles that, when employed, help ensure that the training will "take." The Teaching Model incorporates many of these concepts and techniques for helping people learn.

This model is used when two conditions exist: (1) when the

Figure 35. Four types of interviews for improving job
performance.

Developmental Situations	Conflict Situations
1. The Teaching Model To transmit information so that it is likely to be learned	**1. The Change Coaching Model** To get a commitment to changed behavior or performance
2. The Growth Model To create an opportunity to discuss growth, career path, or other concerns	**2. The Performance Appraisal Model** To review the past year's successes and failures and seek improved performance

manager knows more about the subject at hand than the subordinate does; and (2) when the subordinate is desirous of
learning what the manager has to share. If these conditions are
not present, then the manager should use the Conflict Coaching Model, described later in this chapter.

The sequence of steps to be followed for the Teaching
Model are given below.

Step 1: Provide an Overview

In broad terms indicate what you wish to teach or explain
and what can be expected as an end result. For example:

> "Mary, I'd like to talk with you today about how we
> put together our division's annual profit plan. When we
> finish, I hope that you'll be able to develop your depart-
> ment's segment of the plan for the coming year."

Step 2: Outline What You Wish to Convey

It is usually helpful to describe first how your explanation
will unfold so that the subordinate has a sense of what material

will be covered. In this way, as your comments unfold, the sub-categories and details will have more meaning and can be placed in perspective. For example:

> "There are four different parts of the report I would like to explain. . . ."
> "I'd like to start by explaining why the report is prepared as it is and after that I'll get into the mechanics of putting the data together. . . ."
> "This process has six different steps. Let's take them in order, one by one."

Step 3: Provide an Example for Each Major Point

Examples are especially helpful when what is being taught is a concept or an abstraction. Examples help make the vague more concrete. Use of visual aids such as graphs, charts, or physical displays are good ways of doing this.

Step 4: Summarize Whatever You Have Explained or Demonstrated

Clearly, the manager doesn't want to patronize his subordinate by "beating to death" something that is simple or readily understood. But it is usually prudent to summarize the key points, especially when what is being taught is rather lengthy or at all complicated. Starting the summary with words like these is usually appropriate:

> "So as I see it, the key points in putting the profit plan together are. . . ."
> "When I think about all that we've covered in our discussion, the main idea that I hope you're coming away with is. . . ."

Step 5: Ask for Questions or Needed Clarification

While it is generally helpful to encourage questions throughout the interview, it is especially important to ask if there are questions or points needing clarification at the end of the discussion. Most subordinates are reluctant to tell their boss that they don't understand what has just been explained. This is why asking, "Do you understand what I've just told you about?" is hardly ever productive. The boss has to make it easier for the subordinate to admit that what was said was not all that clear. Here are some ways to do this:

> "Mike, of all the things we have just talked about, which things would you say are most clear in your mind, and which ones are you not that sure about?"
> "I've been talking for awhile here, and probably some questions have popped into your head. Are there some that I could answer for you now?"
> "I realize that I've hurried through some of this material. Are there some parts you'd like me to go back over and discuss in a little more detail?"

Step 6: Schedule a Follow-up

Ideally, the follow-up should be scheduled for a time when the subordinate will have begun to implement the suggestions made in the initial interview, but not yet gone so far as to get into much difficulty. Ideas, steps, or changes that appeared easy and quite intelligible to the subordinate during the training often turn out to be more complicated when the attempt is made to implement them. Also, many subordinates hesitate to come back to their boss to admit that "it's not working out." The safest course is for the manager to take the responsibility for checking on progress. Sometimes this is best accomplished through an informal "How's it going?" discussion.

The Growth Model

One of the greatest favors a manager can do for his subordinates, especially if they have underutilized potential, is to invest time in helping them to better capitalize on their abilities. This can be accomplished by creating a climate of trust and understanding in which subordinates can share their thoughts and feelings about such topics as areas for improvement; concerns about present job effectiveness; and their future in the company.

If the subordinate accepts the invitation to talk about any of these issues, the manager has an unusual opportunity for building a more trusting relationship, strengthening two people's ties to the organization, and providing direct suggestions for enhancing job performance. When the potential payoff of such an effort is considered, it is shocking to realize how few managers take advantage of this kind of interview. In fact, discussions of this sort are likely to give a far more significant return on the investment of the manager's time than traditional performance reviews. It is therefore unfortunate that more companies do not train their managers to conduct periodic growth interviews.

The sequence of steps for the Growth Model follows.

Step 1: State the Purpose of the Interview

In any coaching situation, an understanding of what is expected from both parties helps to reduce anxiety and to keep the discussion focused. Here is an example of an opening statement of purpose:

> "Once a year or so, I like to take some time out to sit down with each staff member and talk about how things are going for them. I have no specific issues in mind or problems I want to discuss, but I would like to see if there are any ways in which I can be of help to you, either on your job or in connection with your future in the company."

At this point, the employee will either accept the invitation or decline it (perhaps by reacting in a negative way). The most obvious "acceptance" is when the subordinate embarks on some topic. But a question about the purpose of the interview or whether it is permissible to discuss a particular topic also represents a form of acceptance. Since you should not attempt this kind of interview if certain topics are off limits, you can indicate to your subordinate that you're "open to talk about anything he would like to bring up or ask about." When the employee's questions have been answered, the discussion can then proceed to Step 2.

If the offer of the growth interview is declined, one option is to gracefully terminate the discussion but to leave the door open for future talks:

> "I can understand that there may be nothing on your mind right now. But, at a later time, if you think a discussion of this sort would be helpful, please let me know and we'll get together."

A second option is to take a hard look at why the invitation was declined. To be sure, subordinates with poor verbal skills or self-images or those with limited ambition may find a growth interview with the boss unappealing. More frequently, however, the negative response is a function of the manager's relationship with the subordinate. The subordinate's opting out of an interview of this sort suggests a limited trust in the manager. Very likely, the relationship needs strengthening.

One way to strengthen the relationship is to explore the subordinate's reluctance to engage in the interview. This discussion can be started by describing to the subordinate what seems to be happening. For example, suppose the employee says, "I can't think of anything that I really need help with right now." Some possible responses from the manager could be:

> "You feel that everything is going along about as well as you could hope for."
> "You're finding it a little difficult to talk about anything at this point."
> "You'd really prefer not to discuss anything right now."

Each of these statements allows an opening for the subordinate to mention what is making it difficult to continue the conversation. If this second invitation is not accepted, it is likely that the subordinate is intimidated and fearful of making any comments. At this juncture, it is very important that the manager not succumb to the temptation to give advice or lecture the employee. This action will only confirm the subordinate's suspicion that there really was an underlying motive for embarking on the interview, and that his mistrust of you is justified.

At this point, the recommended approach is simply to state:

> "If there is nothing you wish to discuss now, that's fine. I'll put aside some time later on in the year; maybe at that point you will have some topics you'd like to bring up."

The basic idea of the growth interview is to work with issues that the subordinate is willing to share. Even sensitive or negative topics, when volunteered by the subordinate, can be comfortably discussed because defensiveness levels in these circumstances are likely to be low. As a result, the time can be profitably spent discussing solutions to issues that are of significance to the subordinate—and there may well be a transference from the discussion to job performance. Perhaps most important, this kind of discussion helps establish a communication climate that will lead to greater openness in the future on the part of both parties.

Step 2: Listen Nonjudgmentally

Once your subordinate starts talking, shut up and just listen. For all of us, the temptation to give advice is at times almost overwhelming. This is a time to resist it. It is helpful to recognize that at the outset most subordinates are not going to bring up their most significant concerns. Most employees will first assess your sincerity. They will "test the water" by mentioning something they believe is safe and then observe how you react.

At this point in the interview, the best course of action is to try to maintain an open, nonjudgmental attitude. It will be most helpful if you listen, are supportive, and provide advice only if you are directly asked for it. Remember, it is not necessary for this interview to end up with any specific conclusion or plan of action. As manager, you may never directly observe the internal changes that take place in the subordinate's attitudes, motivation, or commitment to the company. In this kind of interview, the medium often *is* the message.

All this does not mean, however, that the manager must simply play the role of a passive listener. In a typical growth interview, employees will talk about the future or even about current job problems depending on their assessment of the situation. Their diagnosis of the situation or evaluation of their capabilities could be erroneous, however. In these instances, the manager ought to help the subordinate obtain a more accurate picture of the situation before proceeding further.

One of the most effective ways to help the subordinate obtain a more accurate picture of his situation is to encourage self-appraisal. Such action allows the employee to examine the issue nondefensively and often results in changed, more correct perceptions. Here's an example of an effort to encourage self-appraisal:

> "Bill, I understand your desire to move into the regional manager slot, but what do you think you'd need to learn first before you'll be ready to step into such a position?"

Step 3: Decide on a Plan of Action

Even though a plan of action does not necessarily emanate from this interview, in most cases a discussion of growth will lead to planning some course of action. A practical question to ask when discussing courses of action is:

> "What is going to be done differently tomorrow that will make possible the improvement we want?"

Use of this question will help both parties avoid falling into such generalities as, "I'm going to look into that. . . ." Such vague statements are a recipe for ending up with nothing happening.

Sometimes the subordinate wants help, but the manager cannot think of specific ways to be of assistance. At these times, a joint review of a list of developmental activities could be useful. The following two lists have been successfully used by the General Foods Corporation. The first lists activities an individual employee can take to enhance his development:

- Map out a planned program of reading
- Make an inventory of strengths and determine how they could be enhanced
- Ask for a "special" assignment
- Visit other managers and/or facilities
- Join task forces for special projects
- Ask others, especially superiors, for input about areas for development
- Observe carefully how other successful managers act and make decisions (develop a role model)
- Develop some clear-cut objectives for the coming fiscal year
- Ask for feedback from subordinates about your impact on them
- Talk with human resources or management development departments to see what developmental activities they may offer

The second lists actions a manager can take to enhance the development of subordinates:

- Provide more orientation about the department's goals and/or problems
- Provide feedback more frequently on a subordinate's performance or growth
- Provide job rotational opportunities
- Provide time for discussions about career paths
- Invite subordinate to meetings not normally attended
- Give subordinate easier or quicker access to needed information

- Encourage subordinate to try out new ideas
- Raise more questions about subordinate's area of work and what is happening
- Provide exposure to other areas or facilities of the company
- Allow more autonomy by giving subordinate more latitude in decision making
- Circulate more letters or reports on a routine basis
- Allow subordinate to represent the department at certain meetings or conferences
- Have subordinate fill in for the manager at vacation time

Step 4: Set Follow-up Date

Setting a follow-up date is important because it says a lot about your sincere interest in your subordinate's progress. More than that, it is an action that can help ensure that the time spent on the initial interview will actually pay off. Each coaching session of the growth sort leads to a further step because coaching is constantly building a stronger, more trusting relationship between the manager and subordinate.

Most successful attempts at changing behavior are the result of a long-term process of trying and adjusting and of more trying and adjusting. Growth is a continual process that needs nurturing and encouragement, and follow-up dates are an excellent means of providing these.

The Change Coaching Model

The Change Coaching Model is designed for use whenever the manager wants to effect change or improvement. The difference between this interview and growth interviews is that here the boss is the initiator of the change. Such discussions may take place during feedback in a performance appraisal; more often they occur during informal discussions about improvement in some aspect of the job.

Coaching to get a subordinate to change is clearly the most difficult kind of coaching because, almost always, the request for changed performance marks the beginning of a defensive reaction by the subordinate. This reaction triggers the conflict.

The model outlined in the following pages is based upon the principles of participative management. It is designed to optimize the likelihood that the subordinate will agree to the requested change and also that he will be committed to carrying it out. There is also an implicit assumption in this procedure that the manager is mature enough to recognize that there are always two sides to a story and that he may have been wrong in his original judgment about the need for the change.

There are eight steps in the Change Coaching Model.

Step 1: State Your Purpose

Most managers start a coaching session with small talk. In general, this is desirable because casual talk is one way of reducing tension. It also gives the subordinate a cue that he is to be an active participant in, rather than a passive receptor of, what the manager has to say. However, in conflict-coaching situations the manager should not begin with small talk unless it occurs spontaneously. Not all small talk reduces anxiety; in fact, when it is extensive or forced, it tends to increase the tension in the air. For example:

MANAGER: Glad you could stop in, Paul.
SUBORDINATE: Well, when you called, I came right down.
MANAGER: Say, how's that new sports car of yours?

It is quite obvious to Paul that he was not invited to the office to talk about his sports car. He knows that something else is "in the wind" and, if he is like most subordinates, his anxiety will gradually increase as he speculates on what is coming next in the discussion.

Thus, while it is desirable to set a casual tone for the discussion, obvious efforts at small talk are not likely to reduce the tension. The question the manager must ask himself is whether he can introduce anything at the outset that (1) will be easy for the subordinate to discuss, or (2) might normally arise in conversation between himself and that employee. When these conditions are met, there is little reason not to use such a topic as an opener. When they are absent, a much more direct beginning is recommended. In these instances, simply state what it is that you want to talk about. For example:

> "I asked you to stop by this afternoon, Paul, because I want to discuss some problems that came up at the operations meeting yesterday."

At this point, Paul knows exactly what the boss is going to talk about. He may not like what he hears, but when the purpose is clearly and frankly stated, he can focus on the topic at hand and not be preoccupied worrying about all the other possible issues the manager might raise.

When a touchy subject must be discussed, some managers attempt to introduce it in a roundabout way, hoping somehow that they will be able to "ease into the topic" or that the subordinate himself will bring it up voluntarily. A good principle to follow is: *The more unpleasant or touchy the topic, the more important it is to state the nature of the discussion at the outset.* Let's take an extreme case of unpleasantness. Suppose you are going to terminate an employee. There is little use in prolonging the agony; it affects both you and your subordinate. You might as well state the purpose right at the beginning: "I called you in this morning because, I'm sorry to say, we are going to have to let you go."

Of course, the subordinate won't like hearing that he is going to be fired any better at the beginning of the discussion than in the middle of it, but there is no point in working up slowly to this issue. It is far better to state the problem at the outset, and then invest the remainder of the time in working through the subordinate's feelings and reactions to what has been said.

Step 2: Describe the Problem

A key factor in determining how constructive a change-coaching discussion will become is how the problem is presented. If you start the discussion by focusing on the individual (as opposed to the job or work), a tremendous barrier is put in the way of continuing the discussion on an objective level. For example, if you say, "Susan, I'm concerned that during the past quarter, three of your key people have resigned," that statement will beget much less defensiveness than if you say, "Susan, you're doing an unsatisfactory job in managing your staff."

If you put a value judgment on something your subordinate does, you are, in effect, criticizing and attacking the subordinate's ego. When criticism occurs, subordinates will engage in efforts to protect themselves. For example, Susan might respond to your comment about her doing an "unsatisfactory job" by stating: "It wasn't my fault they left. You told me to push my people and do whatever it took to get the work out on schedule. I did exactly what you suggested!"

In essence, Step 2 recommends that you describe the problem rather than evaluate the person. Here are some examples of the difference between the two approaches:

Evaluative	*Descriptive*
"You don't plan well."	*"When you plan, I notice you put together a weekly schedule, but not a monthly list of priorities."*
"You did a poor job in conducting the staff meeting this morning."	*"I would like to talk with you about the meeting this morning and, in particular, about what happened when the other participants began directing their questions to me rather than to you."*
"You can't communicate well with your subordinates."	*"When you talk with your subordinates, you often cut them off in the middle of their sentences."*

In each of these examples, the manager gets the point across. In the evaluative approach, however, there is an attack on the person, whereas in the descriptive method the focus is on the event or situation.

Step 3: Listen and Express Understanding

When a subordinate is confronted with a topic or issue that in any way implies a lack of success, some defensiveness will occur. The manner in which the manager handles this defensiveness is the critical, make-or-break point in any counseling discussion.

This step of the model suggests that when the subordinate reacts defensively, usually by responding with excuses or explanations of his conduct or position, the boss must not argue back but instead try to understand the subordinate's point of view. At this moment in the discussion, it is essential not to attack the subordinate's position.

Perhaps an example of a typical manager/subordinate confrontation will help make this point clear:

	Words	*Type of Action*
MANAGER:	John, the cost reports have been late for the past two weeks.	Describes the problem.
SUBORDINATE:	Well, we had two people out sick with the flu. It's been a rough week.	Explains and justifies position.
MANAGER:	I know that makes it tough, but those reports are really needed on time. Why didn't you put some of your staff on overtime?	Rejects one or more of subordinate's explanations.
SUBORDINATE:	A couple of them *were* working over-	Gives additional reasons, perhaps

	time. But you know the push that's been put on us to keep overhead down.	with some hostility.
MANAGER:	You should have let me know you were in a bind. I could have gotten you some help from the purchasing department.	Further attacks by denying subordinate's explanations.
SUBORDINATE:	I never thought of that.	Defends self by retreating.
MANAGER:	Well, that's part of my role—to be of help.	Further attacks.
SUBORDINATE:	Bob is going to be in Thursday and I think Sally can make it by Friday. We'll have the report in on time next week, okay?	Says, in essence: "I'll be cooperative and get the boss off my back."
MANAGER:	Thanks, John. It's important to get those reports to me on time.	Returns to original position.

What is John's attitude as he leaves such a discussion? Did he find the manager helpful? Will he be more willing to share problems with his boss in the future?

While many managers might consider the discussion just cited "successful," the failure to listen and express understanding of the subordinate's viewpoint merely results in time being spent by both parties adjusting their defenses. Neither the manager nor the subordinate is really focusing on the problem in a constructive way. Conceptually, the typical boss-subordinate confrontation follows this pattern:

BOSS: [*Refers to something that is wrong or needs changing.*]
SUBORDINATE: [*Responds defensively, explains and/or justifies his position.*]
BOSS: [*Disagrees with or rejects explanation.*]
SUBORDINATE: [*Introduces more rationalizations and becomes hostile or antagonistic.*]

There is little gained by making, "Yes, but . . ." comments after the subordinate has justified his actions. Such a response only makes it necessary for the employee to renew his defensive effort to protect his ego. Subordinates will not be receptive to the boss's comments when they are busy defending themselves. The manager's alternative to attacking the subordinate's explanation is to listen.

A number of good techniques for listening were presented in Chapter 1. One of the most useful for this segment of the counseling discussion is *restating*. The manager first listens to the subordinate's explanation (justification) and then mirrors back his understanding of what was said. For instance:

SUBORDINATE: If it weren't for the foul-up with the systems department, we would have had the data on time and made a better decision.
MANAGER: You believe that the main reason for making the mistake was that you did not have the information you needed from systems.

Restating at this point in the coaching discussion is helpful for two reasons. First, it keeps the manager from rejecting the subordinate's response and thus minimizes the likelihood of argument. Second, it creates a climate in which the subordinate can elaborate on the situation. As subordinates hear their own words mirrored back by the manager, they often take a "second look" at what they have been saying. The subordinate may come to realize, for example, that the systems department was not the only reason for the delay, and that perhaps he too had some responsibility for the mistake.

Very little is gained by stripping away the subordinate's defenses. It is more important to create a climate in which the subordinate can stop being defensive and begin to explore the problem being presented. This exploration is likely to take place once the subordinate has been permitted to "save face."

Exploring Feelings   Another effective way for the manager to respond to a subordinate's defensiveness is by exploring his feelings about the problem presented. For many managers this action may seem awkward or embarrassing. It is helpful, therefore, to recognize that the reality of the situation is that the subordinate is reacting to his emotions—of feeling hurt, angry, threatened, or diminished—and, so, these feelings might just as well be discussed.

So long as the subordinate's emotions are running strong, objective conversation is next to impossible. After providing negative feedback, it is therefore helpful to ask the subordinate how he *feels* about what was said. This is a particularly useful device when the discussion appears to be going nowhere.

Let's look at an example of a manager asking about feelings. Suppose the manager expresses disappointment over the failure of a subordinate to complete several objectives by the agreed-upon target dates. As the manager expresses his dissatisfaction, the subordinate reacts by putting his head down and responds with brief, terse sentences. In effect, the discussion is not focusing on the problem or possible solutions to it. Instead, the subordinate seems to be retreating from the discussion. Assuming that the manager has first tried to listen and has not rejected the subordinate's justifications, asking about the subordinate's feelings is now quite appropriate. For example:

MANAGER: Bill, we've been talking here about these missed objectives, but we don't seem to be having much of a discussion about the problem or how we can resolve it. Tell me, how do you feel about my bringing up this topic of the missed deadlines on the objectives?

SUBORDINATE: Well, I think that. . . .

MANAGER: No, Bill, not what you think. How do you feel about it?

SUBORDINATE: Well, I think that. . . .

MANAGER: I'm really more interested, Bill, in how you feel than in what you think. Are you angry, are you sad, are you happy? How do you *feel* about my bringing up this topic of the objectives?

SUBORDINATE: Oh, "feel." Well, I guess I feel discouraged about it.

MANAGER: Why do you feel discouraged?

SUBORDINATE: Well, you probably don't remember this, but about a year ago we were discussing the performance of my department, and you talked about the importance of not overstating our objectives. And, you know, this past year I can't think of one time we haven't delivered on schedule what we said we would. And here this week we're a little late on a couple of objectives and you're chewing me out about it. So you wonder why I am discouraged. Well, that's why.

MANAGER: Well, Bill, I'm sorry. You are right. I should have recognized your accomplishments. You really have done a great job during the year.

Notice here that what was blocking the subordinate was a feeling of discouragement, an inner sense of "What's the use?" By allowing the subordinate to reveal his feelings, the manager began to see what the difficulty was and was able to take appropriate remedial steps. If the manager had not asked for feelings, but instead had gone on talking about the importance of achieving objectives on time, eventually the subordinate would have said, "I know you're right and I'll be sure it doesn't happen again." The manager might even have felt at that moment that he had done a good job of counseling. But it must be asked: What goes through that subordinate's mind once he closes the manager's door? What are his attitudes and thoughts? How motivated is that subordinate to really do a better job?

In Step 3, we have been stressing the need to listen to and understand the subordinate's position. There is simply no other viable option. If the manager rejects the subordinate's defenses, it will lead to more defensiveness. On the other hand, if the manager concurs with an excuse that he really does not accept, that too is inappropriate. If one can't agree or disagree, the only option left is to listen!

If the manager listens and encourages the subordinate to express his point of view more fully, one possible consequence is that the subordinate may begin to perceive that his excuses and justifications are not entirely valid, that in fact he is partly to blame. When this happens, the manager can move on to Step 4.

A second possibility is that as the subordinate talks, the manager may learn that he himself was in error. New data may emerge that the manager was unaware of. In such cases, the manager can save himself from the embarrassing position of persisting in a point of view that is inappropriate or incorrect.

A third possible consequence of listening is a standoff. The subordinate does not say anything that convinces the manager that he is wrong in his original assessment of the problem, and the subordinate does not admit to any blame but rather continues to offer excuses and to maintain a defensive posture. When this occurs, a discussion of feelings should be initiated. This procedure will be successful in unblocking the stalemate approximately 80 percent of the time.

Step 4: Get Agreement on the Problem

Despite conscientious efforts by the manager, no change will take place if the subordinate is not prepared to "buy" the idea that he has a problem. This concept applies whether it is a question of handling a drinking problem or changing job behavior. Thus, each step in this counseling process is designed to lead to the point where the subordinate says, "Maybe I was at fault here. Maybe I could have done something different." When this occurs, the manager should quickly agree with the subordinate's acceptance of the problem. This is no time to placate or to beat around the bush.

Unfortunately, getting the subordinate to accept that he has a problem only gets the manager halfway home. There is still the issue of what the problem is. Frequently, what happens is that the manager and subordinate will agree on the presence of a symptom. For example, they may agree that the budget was not made, that the subordinate made an impulsive decision, or that more money was spent than was justified. *If meaningful commitment to change is to occur, the basic problem must be identified and agreed to.* Otherwise, whatever remedial action is decided on is likely to result only in short-term improvement; the basic problem will surface again, perhaps bearing a different symptom. It may be helpful to recognize that there are only a limited number of basic problems, and that most symptoms can be ascribed to one of the following five categories:

1. *Others/outside forces.* Nothing is inherently wrong with the subordinate, but external forces, such as illness or a death in the family, are disrupting his ability to concentrate.
2. *Knowledge/experience.* Subordinate needs to know more about some topic, such as planning, coaching, interviewing, or a specific technology.
3. *Intellectual ability/aptitude.* Subordinate has poor aptitude or capacity for a particular kind of work, for example, numerical aptitude or conceptual skills.
4. *Personality.* Subordinate has some trait or quality that creates problems. For instance, he is impatient, overly aggressive, or stubborn.
5. *Motivational.* Subordinate does not find satisfaction in doing something.

It is recommended that you and your subordinate jointly consider each of these possible problem areas. Once the basic problem has been identified, it will help to determine the nature or possibility of remedial action. Figure 36 lists the major

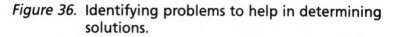

Figure 36. Identifying problems to help in determining solutions.

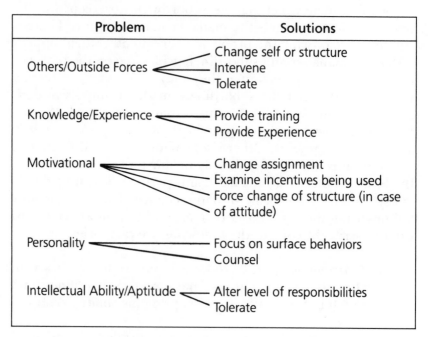

problem areas and the typical actions that can be taken to resolve each basic problem.

Step 5: Get Subordinate's Participation

Once your subordinate accepts that he has a problem, you can move to the next step, gaining his participation in working out a solution to it. The importance of involving the subordinate in this process is a matter of practicality and commitment.

Involving your subordinate in answering the question, "What can we do about the problem?" is practical because it is more likely that the subordinate will accept a solution he has helped develop than one unilaterally decided on by his boss. Even though the manager may believe that his recommendation will be more effective, the odds distinctly favor selecting the subordinate's approach (assuming both ideas have a reasonable chance of succeeding). Gaining commitment is a good reason for placing the burden of determining the solution on the shoulders of the subordinate.

Step 6: Ask Subordinate to Sum Up

Executives often report that despite a seemingly productive discussion, subordinates do not engage in the developmental activity both had apparently agreed upon. The key word here is "apparently." The only positive way of ascertaining your subordinate's precise understanding of what he has agreed to is to have the subordinate sum up his understanding of what is to happen next. You might say, for instance, "Before we break up our meeting, John, what is your understanding of what you're going to do?"

Having your subordinate sum up also provides a good clue as to what extent the subordinate has actually accepted the problem. Most executives will be shocked at their subordinates' responses to this question. Often it will be necessary to go back and again explore whether the subordinate actually accepts that he has a problem. Step 6 is vital to any counseling or delegating situation. It is critical that both parties to a counseling session leave with the same understanding of what will be done and when.

Step 7: Set Follow-up Date

Before your subordinate leaves the counseling discussion, a definite time should be established for the two of you to meet again to discuss progress. Unless this is done, the likelihood of meaningful change occurring is minimal. It should be recognized that it is very difficult for anyone to change a behavior pattern or way of functioning. Usually, considerable trial and error is necessary before people become as skillful and confident with the new approach as they were with the old. When behavior change is attempted, errors, frustrations, and failure should be expected more often than success. Activities and plans of action that seemed easy to accomplish when discussed in the counseling session have a way of turning out to be far more difficult in practice. A follow-up date, therefore, should be set. This date should allow for a period of experimentation, enough time for the subordinate to try out a different way of performing, but not so much that time is wasted when problems are encountered.

In establishing the follow-up date, the stage can be set to make it easy for the subordinate to communicate any problems that are experienced. The manager might say, for example:

> "It may be that the things we talked about doing here will not work out as well in practice as we hope. There may be some problems that we have not foreseen that will make it difficult to implement these changes, so why don't we give it a try between now and June 1 and see how it goes. Suppose we get together again next Friday to see what difficulties you may have run into."

In other words, it is important that the manager make it easy for the subordinate to come back and admit that things are not going as planned. If this step is not taken and the subordinate encounters problems in implementing the desired changes, the likelihood is great that the subordinate will return to the old way of doing things. It is also likely that the subordinate will not tell the manager of his difficulty in making the change.

It is helpful to remember that almost all development is a process of trying and adjusting, trying and adjusting.

Step 8: Hold the Follow-up Session

After your subordinate has had time to try out the new approach, the two of you should sit down and review progress. In most instances, this discussion will necessitate some revision in the original plan. There are four basic parts of any follow-up discussion:

1. A discussion of what progress has been made on the agreed-upon plan. The subordinate should be asked to describe what worked and what did not.
2. Discussion of possible reasons why the new approach was less than successful. Often, at this point, you and your subordinate will realize that the problem you have been attempting to solve is not the real problem. In such cases, you must go back again to Step 2 in the Change Coaching Model.
3. Agreeing on adjustments to and revisions of the original plan.
4. Setting the next follow-up date. Again, it must be emphasized that meaningful behavior or performance changes rarely occur as the result of one or two counseling sessions.

The Performance Appraisal Model

The performance appraisal interview is the formal annual review of a subordinate's performance. Ideally, between the beginning of the rating period and this summary review, the manager will have conducted many discussions concerning the subordinate's progress toward agreed-upon objectives or work improvements. The Conflict Coaching Model is ideal for these kinds of meetings. It is my experience, after having installed more than fifty performance appraisal systems, that improvement is more likely to stem from these interim coaching sessions than from the annual review.

The formal performance appraisal can, however, serve several useful purposes, the most important being that of communication. Subordinates have a right to know where they stand in the boss's judgment. It makes sense to systematically review how things have gone over the past rating period and to set the basis for the next cycle of performance expectations. These reviews also provide an excellent opportunity for reinforcing good performance and effort and for giving positive, motivating feedback. Job expectations are also often clarified when performance appraisals are properly conducted.

Unfortunately, most performance appraisal systems are a great disappointment to those who install them and are equally disliked by those who use them. It is beyond the scope of this interviewing book to cover the most effective ways of structuring performance appraisal systems, but, briefly, here are the reasons why most of them fail:

1. *The results expected are too wide-ranging.* There are expectations, for example, that the performance appraisal system can be used to obtain improved performance and, at the same time, to justify salaries or bonuses. These two objectives are incompatible.

2. *It is not integrated with other major company systems.* There is no tie-in, for instance, between the performance appraisal system and annual fiscal or budget planning. Performance appraisal is perceived as a "program" that is unrelated to how the company is run.

3. *The system involves too much paper work.* The focus is on documentation rather than on meaningful discussions about performance. Performance appraisal seems to be effective in inverse proportion to the amount of paper work involved.

4. *Managers find the process too threatening.* Both managers and subordinates consider the interview "risky" and both embark on it with trepidation. Subordinates rarely enter the meeting with the thought that "this is the day I get help from my boss." It is more often seen as "judgment day."

5. *Personnel are not adequately trained in the use of appraisal feedback.* Training should deal with the development of expectations as well as with effective ways of conducting the feedback discussions. One of the purposes of this book is to help managers with the interview aspects of ongoing feedback and annual reviews.

It is not feasible to provide a specific model for the annual performance appraisal interview because each organization typically has its own procedure and feedback format. The suggestions and generalized model outlined in the following pages can, however, be adapted to fit procedures in use in most organizations.

The three assumptions underlying the suggestions and model are: (1) that the performance appraisal is based upon agreed-upon goals or specific improvements established at the outset of the rating period; (2) that the manager has conducted periodic reviews of progress toward these goals before the final review; and (3) that the desired outcome is better communication about job progress and improved performance.

Suggestion 1: Have Subordinates Provide the Evaluation

As each goal or objective (these two terms will be used interchangeably) is reviewed, it is most helpful to ask the subordinate to give his own perception of how well the goal has been met. This request actively involves the subordinate in the interview, so that he will not merely be playing a passive role, and minimizes the "I'm the boss, you're the subordinate" climate. A "let's-review-how-you-did" approach is more likely to establish an adult, problem-solving atmosphere than when the boss simply tells the subordinate how he has performed.

As subordinates review their perceptions of progress made or not made on each objective, the manager has an excellent opportunity to present his judgments on the matter, to agree or disagree. If the manager agrees with his subordinate's evaluation of progress, there is a further opportunity for reinforcing desired behavior and/or giving approbation for good performance.

Suggestion 2: When Giving Positive Feedback, Be Specific

Positive feedback is most helpful when it is both specific and given close in time to the event being discussed. Most subordinates like it when the boss says they've done a good job, but such feedback will be more meaningful (and thus more likely to reinforce good job behavior) if the manager also indicates exactly what was liked about the performance.

It is the same with gift giving and receiving. For instance, if you give Janet a sweater for her birthday and she says, "Thank you, I really like it," you may wonder if she is saying that merely because she doesn't want to hurt your feelings or because she truly appreciates it. On the other hand, if Janet says *why* she likes it, her appreciation is far more meaningful. Compare this response with the first one: "I really like this sweater; it will go perfectly with a blue skirt I have. Wait a minute, I'll get it and show you—the two together will make a great outfit."

Here's a performance appraisal example:

Not Specific	*Specific*
"You're good at meeting deadlines."	*"I very much like the fact that you have all the cost reports to me two or three days before the monthly budget meeting. It gives me a good opportunity to organize my presentation."*

It is easy to see why this specific positive feedback is likely to result in the subordinate's desire to continue the behavior approved.

Suggestion 3: When Providing Negative Feedback, Be Descriptive

If you disagree with your subordinate's self-appraisal, it is important to *describe* your view of the situation rather than to make a sweeping but too general value judgment. An example of a personal statement would be: "I don't see as much improvement here as you find; you're still insensitive to the feelings of your staff." A better, more descriptive way of conveying the same view would be: "I don't see as much improvement here as you think. Last week, at the staff meeting, you 'chewed out' Sam right in front of everyone."

In neither of these examples will the subordinate like to hear that his boss disagrees. But the degree of defensiveness will be far less in the second scenario. A subordinate may be able to own up to the fact that he did not handle the "Sam situation" properly, but he will not admit to being "insensitive." If Sam denies his insensitivity, it is likely he will tell his boss of other incidents in which he showed great sensitivity. And when this occurs, the appraisal will be at an impasse.

A fuller discussion of the role of descriptive feedback appears earlier in this chapter.

Suggestion 4: Limit the Focus on the Negatives

A central concept of the annual review is to summarize the subordinate's successes and failures. While it is important not to skip over failures, both from the honesty and legal standpoints, too much emphasis on negative factors can result in serious problems. A good relationship with the boss can deteriorate; the motivated can rapidly become demotivated.

It goes something like this. Give a subordinate one criticism and he may be able to accept it, examine it, and perhaps even commit himself to changing and improving. Give him a second criticism and he is apt to find it very difficult to accept; his ego won't take the pounding. Outwardly, he may acknowledge the fault and appear to agree with you, but underneath, his defensive systems are working actively to deny this second assault. Give him a third criticism and he is now likely to reject everything you have said, even the first fault that he initially owned up to. He may even become overtly hostile and blame the problems on you! Most likely, in rejecting what his manager has said, he will simply justify his actions.

It is clear that if the subordinate runs down his list of objectives, he may admit to several failures. If the manager agrees that the objective was not achieved, there is no need to duck affirming the failure. However, each failure is not equally important, so there is no need to dwell on the lesser ones. It is more productive to single out the most important one and then to spend time discussing its implications. This same principle applies when the manager must point out several failures. It is not a question of sugarcoating; it is more a question of how much focus there should be on negatives relative to the positives.

Suggestion 6: Be Honest With Yourself and Subordinate

Considering the current tendency to litigate, it is very important that the appraisal you give as manager be honest and candid. If you do otherwise, you could find yourself in difficulty in court trying to explain how the employee you have discharged managed to get a series of favorable reviews. And that is not a very pleasant situation in which to be.

It's important to be honest, even though at times it can be painful. Remember, you don't do anyone a favor by trying to hide or gloss over mediocre or poor performance. If someone is performing below standard, that person has a right to know. Think of it this way: Wouldn't you want to know it if your boss was displeased with your performance? How else can you make the right decisions about your employment? Unless your boss tells you, you may continue in the unacceptable old ways—and wind up getting fired; you may even pass up other, more suitable opportunities in the erroneous but flattering belief that all is well.

In brief, being honest is only being fair. It helps your subordinate to face and correct the problem—or problems, should that be the case. And, if it finally comes down to a point of discharge, the honest appraisal gives you a solid base upon which to stand.

Suggestion 7: Keep the Interview Brief

The annual performance appraisal is not a good time for counseling or discussing how improvement will take place. The climate is not right. As was mentioned earlier, this interview will be perceived by most subordinates as "judgment day" not "help day." It represents a chance for the boss to let the subordinate know where he stands.

If issues arise that involve "working through" changes in

behavior or performance, most managers will find it more productive to schedule such discussions for another day.

Suggestion 8: Don't Discuss Personality

There are times when personality traits and behavior get in the way of effective performance. Thus, they must be discussed. However, they should not be discussed as an entity apart from performance. If the manager does otherwise, the subordinate's defensiveness will become very strong and the meeting may prove fruitless.

Let's take an example. Suppose one of your subordinates, Mike, did not achieve one or more of his objectives because he was unable to obtain needed data or cooperation from another department. You have observed that Mike tends to walk around with a chip on his shoulder. To put it bluntly, he irritates many people. It is this aggravating manner that results in others not wanting to go out of their way to help him.

If you talk about Mike's irritating manner as a stand-alone topic, Mike is not likely to own up to being irritating. It is too ego damaging. On the other hand, if you talk about the personality trait as a possible factor in his not achieving his objectives, then the probability of both of you constructively discussing this issue is significantly higher. One way the interview might go is like this:

MANAGER: Mike, what do you think prevented you from making this objective?

MIKE: I don't know, but I can tell you the people in the payroll department really let me down. They weren't the least bit cooperative.

MANAGER: Well, there has to be a reason. Most of them are pretty agreeable people.

MIKE: The only thing I can think of is that I lost my patience with them a few times; maybe it bothered them.

MANAGER: Mike, in working with you this past year, it seemed to me that you often spoke to me and others in an impatient, grating way. Almost as if you had a chip on your shoulder. Do you think that could have been a factor in this payroll situation?

MIKE: I don't think I walk around looking for trouble. But you know me. I like to get things done, and when I run into an obstacle, well, I guess I can get a little impatient.

MANAGER: I think that's right. You do show your impatience. Do you think it was a factor here?

Notice how, in this example, Mike gradually comes to accept that he had some responsibility for not attaining his objective. The personality trait becomes a clear obstacle to successful job performance. In this context, the discussion is likely to lead naturally into a conversation of what can be done about it. By contrast, when the trait is brought up out of the context of a job performance problem, it becomes an attack on Mike's ego and the results are then likely to be very different.

Suggestion 9: Have the Subordinate Sign the Appraisal

Chapter 3 dealt with legal risks in recruiting and employment. These same kinds of litigation issues arise from improperly conducted performance appraisals. One way of ensuring the credibility of your contention that the employee was not performing satisfactorily, and was so informed, is to have the subordinate sign a copy of the written appraisal.

Here in brief are the six steps in a Performance Appraisal Model:

1. *Prepare.* Ask the subordinate to complete his copy of the summary evaluation form and to be prepared to discuss progress toward desired objectives. For your part, complete the appraisal form. Consider how you will be descriptive about failures and specific about successes.

2. *Open.* Explain how the review will be conducted. That is, the subordinate will give a self-appraisal of his progress, and differences with the manager's appraisal will then be discussed.

3. *Discuss.* Give positive, specific feedback to reinforce ap-

proved performance or behavior. Explain in a descriptive manner what is unacceptable performance or behavior.

4. *Summarize.* Pull together the entire appraisal, putting positives and negatives in perspective.

5. *Ask for subordinate's reactions.* This is an excellent time to ask about the employee's feelings toward the appraisal. If strong feelings exist, they must be cleared away before a reasoned, objective discussion can take place.

6. *Close.* Invite the subordinate to continue the discussion, if desired, at a later date. Have the subordinate sign the appraisal.

Summary

Four models for developing staff are presented here. The choice of model depends upon the purpose of the interview. The biggest obstacle in effective coaching is the defensiveness that subordinates usually manifest when a manager implies that all is not well. The models are designed to help the manager deal effectively with the defensiveness issue.

When the object is to get the subordinate to commit to change, a most important point to remember is that it is first essential to have the subordinate agree that there is a problem. Without this agreement, plans for improvement become mere words and are rarely translated into job behavior.

Chapter 18

The Termination Interview

Of all the interviews described here, the termination interview is by far the most difficult to conduct. There is no way to make it easy or pleasant for managers to fire someone, even when the employee "deserves it." The purpose of this chapter is to provide a model designed to reduce the stress of conducting it to a minimal level and to make the interview as constructive as possible.

Preparing for the Termination Interview

Preparation for this kind of interview is especially important because it can affect the degree of psychological shock felt by the severed employee as well as whether litigation results from the termination.

The extent to which the termination interview is traumatic for the employee is directly related to how much preconditioning has taken place. For example, in cases where an organization has announced well in advance that a restructuring will occur and that "jobs will be eliminated," the manager will have an easier time telling an employee of his termination than if the interview comes out of the blue. The shock will also be much reduced in cases where the employee already knows (through feedback received in performance appraisals) that he is performing at an unacceptable level.

Often, the psychological shock of a termination is not limited to the terminated employee; the experience can be severely upsetting for the manager, too. But obviously, the greater the preparation, the less stress on the manager doing the terminating.

Without adequate thought and preparation, there is an increasing risk that litigation may result from certain terminations, especially when legally protected classes such as the handicapped, anyone over forty, racial and cultural minorities, and women are involved. In addition, the gradual erosion of the "hire-at-will/fire-at-will" tradition can pose an additional threat when terminating employees (see Chapter 3).

Long-term and Current Preparation

The manager must be concerned with two types of preparation: long-term, which has to do with the employee's previous performance; and current, which has to do with the interview itself.

The long-term effort refers to the feedback provided the employee months earlier, indicating dissatisfaction with his performance on the job. The feedback may have been given via informal ongoing discussions about the need for change and improvement or by means of more formal performance appraisals. Plurals are used here because it usually takes more than one discussion with employees before the message that their work is unsatisfactory is assimilated. Unless the stage is properly set, the consequences of an abrupt or unexpected termination will be predictably unpleasant. There may even be occasions when deferring the termination until adequate feedback has been provided will prove more cost-effective than a sudden termination.

As mentioned, in situations where the termination is not for poor performance, "preselling" the likelihood of termination will ease the termination process. Corporate management often operates on the mistaken assumption that if employees learn in advance of an impending layoff, morale and efficiency will disintegrate or a premature mass exodus will take place. Almost always the reality is that early and frequent warnings about layoffs and reorganizations result in an orderly downsizing. This result is likely whether it is one or two persons or five thousand who are being terminated.

Current preparation concerns itself with two elements: timing and data gathering.

Timing   It is almost classic that firings take place on Friday afternoon and/or just before the boss leaves on vacation or a business trip. The conventional wisdom is that by terminating on Friday afternoon the person will be quickly and quietly removed from the premises (and so won't have a chance to "stir up the troops") and will also have the weekend to cool off in case further contact is necessary. Refining this tactic further, one company even terminated a substantial portion of its work force by telephone! Anyone who has studied the impact of terminations will attest that these approaches are usually counterproductive.

When individuals are summarily cut off, frustration and hostility are the usual by-products. Not only do their experiences have a negative impact on the corporate image but they often spur litigation. If at all possible, it is almost always better to terminate employees early in the week so that the fired individual will not feel completely abandoned and so that there can be opportunities for additional discussion, especially with the boss. Such discussions can often be quite healing once the termination is behind both of them.

Data Gathering   Before plunging into the termination interview, the manager must gather together certain facts and figures. Some of these relate to the employee's past record, others to his future outside the organization. Most will be cited during the interview process. The following is a checklist of the information the manager will need to have on hand:

- Dates of discussions on which requests for improved performance were made
- Copies of performance appraisals in which inadequate performance was delineated

- Specific examples (at least three) of inadequate performance
- All the terms of the severance package (including how long salary, health and insurance plans, and benefits will continue)
- Information on whom the employee should contact and when regarding the exit interview and the signing of final papers (transferring medical insurance or settling pension rights)
- A plan for how the interview will be conducted, in other words, a decision on what reasons to cite for the termination and on whether the manager should conduct the interview alone or in conjunction with others.

The Termination Interview Model

In the overview, the termination interview embodies the same approach and techniques as the job coaching interview (Chapter 17), except that the end goal is different, quite different! There are five steps:

Step 1: Get to the Point of the Interview

Unlike some other interviews, the termination interview is no place for small talk; to engage in it only increases the likelihood of tension and may even induce a sense of betrayal. You might as well get right to the point and say, "I called you in because I am sorry to tell you that we are going to let you go."

Sometimes managers start the interview with open questions such as "How have things been going for you?" or "How do you feel about the job you've been doing?" The manager's hope is that the employee will indicate that he is not doing OK and that he might even volunteer to resign. The odds of such an occurrence are just about nil.

The about-to-be-terminated employee will not like to hear about the firing decision at any point in the discussion but little is to be gained by postponing the bad news. The longer the manager procrastinates, the more awkward the situation becomes.

Step 2: Explain the Reasons for the Termination

Once you have told the employee the purpose of the interview, you should move *immediately* into an explanation of the "whys" of the termination. This explanation should be specific and factual, but need not be harsh. Sometimes managers, being apprehensive that the employee will resist the decision, assume an excessively forceful manner, resulting in a brutal discharge.

The reasons for a termination can be conveyed in a way that increases the probability of acceptance rather than rejection. The acceptance rate will be higher if you:

Convey the reasons for the termination in a calm factual manner. This is possible when the facts have been carefully documented *before* the interview begins. If having notes in front of you will help, by all means use them.

Communicate only the key reasons. There may be many reasons for the termination, but it is not necessary or desirable to run through a litany of the employee's failures. When telling someone that he is fired, to heap on a host of failures is like rubbing salt in the wound.

Use descriptive rather than evaluative language. This concept is discussed at some length in Chapter 17. The idea is to present the reasons for termination in a way that avoids "putting down" the employee yet clearly conveys the performance failure.

An example of *evaluative* language is when the manager says: "Ralph, you were completely irresponsible in not checking out the Jones job." He is being *descriptive* when he puts the same message this way: "Ralph, you did not follow our standard procedure of visiting the installation site on the Jones job to see if everything was working satisfactorily. As you know, they were extremely unhappy and demanded that we remove our switch."

The distinction between the two examples is extremely important. Nothing is gained by rendering negative, global judgments about someone's performance. Ralph is not going to accept that he is "irresponsible"; he can probably cite a dozen instances when he was very responsible. Evaluative comments almost always result in a defensive reaction. Ralph is far more likely to be willing to admit that he failed to check out the installation on the Jones job.

This is not to say that an employee will *like* hearing a descriptively presented reason for his discharge, but only that his defensive reaction will be less. And in a termination interview, that can be a great help.

The reasons for the termination can be kept descriptive by following a few guidelines:

1. *Keep judgments out of your explanation.* Words such as "lazy," "careless," "inconsiderate," and "poor" are almost always tied to a judgment and usually will raise defensiveness.

2. *Stick with the specific behavior or event that spurred the termination.* Describe it. For example: "You failed to meet your sales quota for the past six months." Or, "You said that you had trimmed your operating expenses 10 percent, but the audit showed that they had actually increased 12 percent."

3. *Mention the frequency of the problem.* Whenever it can be shown that the problem or failure occurred a number of times, the terminating reason becomes more understandable and meaningful. It is helpful to be able to say, for instance, that "I spoke with you about this problem three times—last July at the regional meeting, in September during your annual performance appraisal, and a month ago, following the staff meeting." Or, "Six out of the last eight months your inventory reports were late."

4. *Discuss consequences.* The importance of the termination reason will be underscored if negative consequences resulting from the employee's actions can be shown. Perhaps, for instance, in the example just cited, the lateness of the inventory reports resulted in a production shutdown because materials were not in stock when needed.

In addition to the advantage of reducing the employee's defensiveness, descriptively stating the reasons for the termination makes the intent of the interview abundantly clear. This is important, even though you started the interview by saying "We're going to have to let you go," because in an emotionally charged discussion such as this one, an employee's tuning out what he doesn't want to hear is quite common. Objectively stated descriptive reasons help reinforce the point of the interview.

Step 3: Listen to the Employee

No matter how clearly and objectively the reasons for the termination are presented, there is going to be a reaction. That reaction can range widely, from silence to anger to joy. But whatever the reaction, the recommended behavior for the interviewer should be to remain quiet and listen.

Listening at this point in the interview does a number of helpful things. First of all, it allows the terminated employee to react, to express whatever emotions are present. Unless internal feelings are openly expressed, they interfere with objective discussion. There is no point trying to have a logical discussion with someone at a time when he is experiencing strong feelings of hurt or anger. It is quite appropriate to say at this juncture in the interview, "How are you feeling right now about what has happened?"

A second advantage of listening, after giving the termination reasons, is that it helps the interviewer to avoid arguing. There is an old saying that "no one wins an argument." Although it is trite, it also happens to be true in many instances, particularly during a termination interview. To get into an argument at this point can only lead to more defensiveness (this time for both parties), greater hurt, and usually more unacceptance.

The third value of listening is that it helps the employee assimilate the termination. As the discharged employee talks out his thoughts and feelings, there is a strong probability of his eventually admitting to and/or accepting the reasons presented by the manager. The process typically goes like this: First the employee hears about his failure (and firing); he next reacts with defensiveness to protect his sense of self-worth;

then, having "saved face" by expressing one or two justifications, he can now discuss the situation more objectively.

There are several listening techniques that the manager can use to help the terminated employee verbalize his reactions. These are described in Chapter 17. The most important effort of the interviewer, at this point of the discussion, must be focused on not becoming defensive. The listening tool of restating can be most helpful in doing this.

One problem that can occur at this stage of the interview is that the employee may embark on an effort to convince the manager that the termination is not justified or that somehow improvement will not take place, thus making the termination unnecessary. This has to be stopped immediately or else the discussion can become very awkward. For example:

EMPLOYEE: I don't think you have the whole picture. It wasn't all my fault those inventory reports were late. The gang over in data processing were always having trouble with their computers.

MANAGER: I realize that, Martha, but there were a number of opportunities for you to remedy the situation; yet nothing was done.

EMPLOYEE: OK, but now I know better and now I know how to deal with the systems people. I'm sure it won't happen again. You'll see, it's going to work out just fine.

MANAGER: I don't see how you could possibly succeed now when you've had plenty of opportunities in the past to remedy the problem.

EMPLOYEE: Well, things are different now. Just give me the chance and you'll see. . . .

One way to minimize this difficulty, in addition to using good listening tools, is to be clear in your mind, before the interview, that this is *not* a job coaching session. No efforts should be made to diagnose the problem or to discuss how it came about. *The focus at this point should be on now and the future;* otherwise it gives the employee signals that there might be another chance. This effort will often involve use of such phrases as:

"I hear what you are saying, Martha, but I have documented for you the reasons for terminating your employment, and I have already made my decision. Let's talk now about where we go from here."

"I am sorry we disagree about your chances of improving. But I have terminated you, and so right now we need to talk about what's going to happen next."

A second way to avoid the "give me a second chance" trap is to shift the discussion to the severance package. The two examples just cited represent good lead-ins to this stage of the interview.

Step 4: Review the Severance Package

In many organizations, the details of the severance package are conveyed during an exit interview or by a human resources specialist. In these instances, it is relatively simple to say, "Severance arrangements have been made, and if you will contact Dorothy Hinkle, she will fill you in on the details."

An even better way is to indicate that "Since we've almost finished our discussion, I'll call Dorothy right now, and tell her that you'll be down in a few minutes so that you can review the details of your severance package."

If you are the person who will be discussing the severance package, then it is important to have it carefully outlined before the interview begins. Unless the separation arrangements are extremely simple, it is risky to rely on memory; it is safest either to read them or to refer to your notes frequently.

It has been my experience that the greatest problem in reviewing the severance package is the risk of entering into negotiations. Most managers are rather vulnerable at this stage of the interview. There may be a strong underlying desire to have the employee feel better about the situation; or perhaps the manager is experiencing feelings of guilt. As a result, promises may be made that cannot be fulfilled. In any case, *it is important during the interview to make no promises, actual or implied, beyond those severance terms already presented.* It is even risky to say, "I'll look into it for you."

If the interviewer believes that more should be done via the support package, mention of it should be deferred until the necessary approvals are secured and the employee has had time to accept the finality of the termination. This typically means several days (or longer) after the initial interview.

Step 5: Discuss the Employee's Next Steps

As the interview draws to a close, most terminated individuals are at a loss as to what to do next; many may appear disoriented. From both a practical and nurturing standpoint, the manager ought to spend some time talking about what the employee should do next.

There are a lot of little, but nonetheless essential things that the employee will want to know about upon leaving the interview—or at least before long. The manager should therefore be prepared to mention when the employee is expected to clean out his desk and personal belongings, by what date he must leave the premises, and to whom he should turn in any keys in his possession? The employee should also be directed to the services of the outplacement counselor, if such services are wanted, and to the human resources department for signing final papers and clarification of details connected with insurance, benefits, and pension rights.

It is not always helpful to give advice during a stressful interview such as the termination interview, but one exception can be made. Many terminated individuals make future job hunting more difficult by reacting too precipitously to their dismissals. They are apt to call friends and business associates prematurely in an effort to find a new job quickly. It is a good idea to suggest that they not embark on any action until they have first had a chance to look at the situation in perspective. You can safely advise them to take time to consider options, carefully develop a résumé, and plan how best to contact potential sources of employment.

Terminating employment is almost always a painful task. It is to be hoped that the steps outlined in this chapter will provide a framework for a successful and productive termination. It also can be helpful, when conducting this interview, to keep in mind the possibility that even though it is painful at the moment it may ultimately benefit the employee. For many employees the discharge relieves them from an increasingly uncomfortable situation (failure); for some it is the impetus to change to a more appropriate career; for others it may inspire concrete steps toward self-improvement. Firing someone doesn't always have to have a negative end result.

Summary

This chapter deals with the interview that managers most dread—the termination interview. The key to the success of this interview is preparation, the most important aspect of which is to provide specific feedback about the employee's unacceptable performance well before the termination takes place.

It is also important to prepare for what will be said during the interview. Some key items are: justifications for the termination (specific performance failures), terms of the severance package, next steps the employee should take to close out the employment (signing final papers, return of keys, transfer of medical insurance, pension rights), and who should be present during the termination interview.

A five-step model is presented that will apply in most termination situations. It is designed to minimize the manager's stress and to preserve the dignity of the employee. These five steps are: Get to the point at the beginning, explain the reasons for the termination, listen to the employee's reactions, review the severance package, and discuss the employee's next steps. A key point in successful termination interviews is the avoidance of any ambiguity about the manager's intentions. It should be clear throughout the discussion that the decision has already been made. This is no time for equivocation or negotiation.

Chapter 19

The Exit Interview (Voluntary Resignation)

Sooner or later it happens. Someone on your staff announces that he's going to leave. Unless it's someone you wanted to fire anyway, the news almost always comes as a disappointment and creates turmoil. For most managers, the second guessing begins almost immediately: "What could I have done to have prevented this?" Whether or not the employee could have been saved depends, of course, on the reasons for his resignation. Discovering what these are is the purpose of the exit interview. Let us examine the exit interview for voluntary resignation in more detail.

The Nature of Exit Interviews

There are three occasions on which exit interviews are conducted: voluntary resignation, release (termination), and removal from active status such as retirement or a medical leave of absence. The last two, for the most part, are concerned with the organization's separation process (obtaining company keys, having papers signed) and will not be discussed here. It is the discussion with the employee who is voluntarily resigning that is most difficult to conduct and that will be the focus of this chapter. The exit interview for voluntary resignation is extremely difficult to conduct successfully, so let us begin detailing its aspects.

Special Difficulties of the Exit Interview

Exit interviews are much like performance appraisal systems; on the surface they seem to make a lot of sense, yet rarely do they produce the results hoped for. Let's look at some of the difficulties peculiar to this type of interview.

First of all, unlike an employment interview, *most employees don't want to participate in the exit interview* and would avoid it if they could. There is, after all, nothing in it for them. They are leaving the company and just want to get away as simply and quickly as possible.

Second, *employees usually try to deceive the interviewer.* Very few want to stir up trouble or to burn their bridges behind them. It's just too risky. Many enter the interview with the expectation that they are going to be interrogated, and so are apt to be defensive and on guard.

This point is well illustrated by a study conducted by a large aircraft manufacturer.* Employees were given a first exit interview at the time of their quitting and then a second one eleven months later. There was a 40 percent difference between the reasons given at these two interviews! The researchers found that during the first interview almost all the reasons offered by departing employees were related to factors beyond the control of the company, such as "slowness of the industry," "call from an executive recruiter," and "spouse did not like climate." By contrast, the reasons offered nearly a year later were related to internal company problems such as low pay, poor supervision, or unpleasant work environment.

A third reason that tends to make exit interviewing unproductive is that the employee's articulated reason for leaving typically seems so valid that interviewers assume that probing for the underlying motivation is unnecessary. A study of reasons for turnover in a high-tech assembly operation in which I participated shows how mistaken these assumptions can be.

Most of the employees in this high-tech plant were young

---

*Wayne L. McNaughton, "Attitudes of Ex-employees at Intervals After Quitting." *Personal Journal,* Volume 35 (1956).

women, and one of the most frequent reasons given for quitting was "pregnancy." The company managers assumed that as long as they continued to hire women of childbearing age, a certain portion would inevitably leave each year. They accepted it as a given about which they could do very little. In interviewing those leaving, one of the questions asked was, "Is there a reason you chose to become pregnant at this time?" The answers received were an eye-opener. Almost two-thirds (64 percent) said that they had *decided* to become pregnant because of a variety of dissatisfactions at work and that "this was as good a time as any to start raising a family." Pressed further, almost all said they would have stayed if the job had been more satisfying.

A common analogous situation is when employees say they are leaving because a "new opportunity" was brought to their attention. The real question, of course, is why the opportunity caught the employee's attention in the first place.

A final reason why exit interviewing is difficult is that employees often make irrelevant and contradictory comments. The complete picture of an employee's resignation will not usually emerge in a logical sequence; it will evolve piecemeal and must be assembled by the interviewer much like the pieces of a jigsaw puzzle. It is easier for interviewers to accept "more money," "better opportunity," and "wanted to have a family" as valid reasons for leaving than it is to dig for the riskier-to-share but truer reasons.

Thus, the exit interview is extremely difficult to conduct successfully. It is much tougher than most employment interviews. To be successful at it requires sophisticated interviewing skills and a good deal of patience.

In most large organizations the human resources staff will assume responsibility for conducting exit interviews. Such a procedure makes possible an analysis of problems and trends common to a whole division or company, and capitalizes on the skills of experienced interviewers. Individual managers, however, may also find it profitable to interview staff members who resign. This chapter provides a model for the exit interview that was initially designed to be used by human resources professionals but can just as readily be used by operating managers.

"Secrets" for Conducting a Successful Exit Interview

To minimize the difficulties of the exit interview, it may be helpful to be aware of a few fundamental strategies that can serve as guideposts. .

To learn the real reasons for the employee's resignation, it is essential to win the confidence of the employee. Although this may seem self-evident, the idea needs to be kept in the forefront of the interviewer's mind; every action taken during the interview should be geared toward gaining this confidence.

Upon entering the exit interview most employees will already be on the defensive; they expect to be interrogated and are going to be very careful about what they say. The mode of interviewing should be relaxed, informal, and slow-paced. It is important not to push for data. The interviewer should be prepared to back off when meeting resistance and to proceed gently, but can return to any potentially fruitful topic later in the interview.

It takes a while for most people to become comfortable during an exit interview. Therefore, interviewers should not give up too soon. Rather, they should think of themselves as detectives patiently probing the alibi of a suspect. Recalling and emulating how a favorite detective, Columbo perhaps, interviews suspects could be quite helpful. Above all, successful exit interviews require patience and persistence. This is not the kind of interview that will produce accurate information if it is rushed or routinely conducted. And this is true for both professional interviewers and those who are less experienced.

The Exit Interview Model

The Exit Interview Model described here takes into consideration the difficulties discussed and also incorporates the suggestions just made. There are four basic steps.

Step 1: Explore the Employee's Feelings

The most important aspect of the opening of the interview is to explore the employee's feelings. Helping the employee to talk about his feelings is of significant use in psychologically "clearing the air." Once emotions and feelings are lessened, it is easier to discuss issues on a more objective basis.

The discussion of feelings can be made quite relevant and appropriate if the interviewer indicates a personal interest in the employee's feelings about leaving the organization. One way to proceed is to place down on the table any papers being held, such as a notepad or exit interview form, and then to proceed casually and informally. For example:

> "I'm always curious as to what it must feel like to be leaving, especially since you've been here for eight years. How are you feeling about it right now—happy, sad, excited, a little scared, what?"

It is always helpful to mention a range of possible feelings to clarify exactly what is meant by "feelings" and to help employees focus on what they are experiencing. Notice, at this stage of the exit interview, it is important to keep the discussion off the employee's thoughts and to focus instead on his feelings. Sometimes it is necessary to redirect the conversation if the employee responds with what he thinks. For example:

MANAGER: How do you feel about leaving the Boxwood Corporation?"

EMPLOYEE: It wasn't easy for me to do. I thought quite a long time about it. . . .

MANAGER: I'm really interested in how you arrived at your decision, but I was wondering first about your feelings. Are you happy or sad or what?

The employee can be encouraged to elaborate further on what the feelings mentioned are like. Making use of the restating techniques explained in Chapter 1 can be helpful here. If, for example, the employee says that she is "feeling a little angry at this point," the interviewer can ask her to clarify the extent of the angry feeling. For instance:

> "Help me understand a bit about your feeling a little angry. Is it kind of a mild irritation or maybe stronger, like you'd really like to shout about it?"

For nonprofessional interviewers, the recommendation to discuss feelings may seem to be of limited value. They may even experience discomfort with the thought of discussing feelings; after all that's not how they usually communicate. However, it is important to recognize that this step is crucial in any discussion where emotions are high or strong feelings are likely. It represents the best way to get the feelings dissipated and the discussion back on more logical, nonemotional grounds. It is well worth the effort to experiment in trying to understand the employee's feelings. The downside risks are minimal.

Step 2: Explore the Employee's Job Situation

The heart of this model, of course, is the exploration of the employee's attitude to the current job situation and why the decision was made to leave it. But this process cannot be rushed. Thus, a two-step process, which leads deeper and deeper into the topic, is outlined here. First, the "likes" and "dislikes" about the company and job are explored; *only* then should the interviewer ask the direct question: "Why are you leaving?"

Here are a few ways to begin exploring the employee's views of the job he is leaving. A good opening would be:

> "We really want to keep good employees like you, and one of the best ways we can do so is to continually try to improve things around here. So, it would help us a lot if you could tell me what you liked and disliked about working here at the Scott-Niering Company. Let's start with what you liked about working here."

Once the employee begins talking, he can be encouraged to elaborate on his thoughts by the use of such "expanders" as "I see," "uh-huh," "go on," and "I understand."

Confidentiality The primary barrier to frank and open comments about the job or company is the employee's fear that the opinions voiced will be attributed to him and will come back to haunt him in some way, perhaps even jeopardize the references given him at a future date. Therefore, if it is possible (as might be the case with exit interviews conducted by a human resources department) to keep the employee's comments completely confidential and anonymous by using them only with data obtained from others for the purpose of pinpointing problem areas or determining trends, then it would be helpful to add to the opening request for "likes" and "dislikes" about the company with a statement such as:

> "Whatever you tell me will be strictly confidential. We only tabulate the summary data, and your name will never be linked with your comments."

Once three or four "likes" have been elicited, it is time to switch to the slightly more threatening side of the employee's job experience, the "dislikes." This section could be started like this:

> "No place is 100 percent perfect. What might be some of the things here at Scott-Niering that didn't appeal to you?"

It is important to listen to the answers without interruption. No further structuring is usually needed. The answers can be drawn out by using the listening techniques (open questions, silence, expanders, and restating) discussed in Chapter 1.

If the company has developed a separation processing form (for assistance in covering all essential aspects of the separation), a list of possible reasons for the voluntary resignation is typically provided. If none of these are mentioned by the employee, this list can be used as a springboard for bringing forth more information. The interviewer can simply say (referring to the list):

"Would you mind telling me some of your reactions to these areas?"

Denial Sometimes employees avoid getting into any discussion of the negative aspects of their employment by denying their existence. A statement typifying this kind of reaction would be, "I really don't see any problems. . . ." In these instances, the interviewer can attempt to bring the employee into the interview as a "helpmate" by using a sort of team approach. Here is one way to put the interview on this plane:

"I know that none of the items I've mentioned really impacted negatively on you, but let me run a few thoughts past you. Recently, we've had some problems with employees saying that they are not getting sufficient recognition [*or whatever topics seem appropriate*]. Looking at the company, in general, what have you observed about that?"

If this approach works, the interviewer should try to move from the general to the specific by asking:

"Were there times when *you* believed you didn't get enough recognition?"

The interviewer can then proceed to the next topic:

"Another comment we hear a lot these days has to do with the performance appraisals we give. Do you see some people not being fairly evaluated—either overrated or underrated?"

It may be necessary to experiment with a variety of topics to determine which ones produce the most data. Those topics that are actual problem areas in the company usually yield the biggest response. Basically, the idea is to get the employee to discuss negatives from a nonthreatening vantage point, in this way opening the door to meaningful revelations.

Step 3: Directly Explore Why the Employee Is Leaving

Up to this point the Exit Interview Model has guided the manager through a series of steps aimed at creating a climate in which the employee feels reasonably comfortable in sharing his reasons for resigning. It is quite possible, too, that in discussing their feelings or their likes and dislikes about the job and the company, the employees may actually come up with the true reasons for their resignations. Even so, Step 3 is very important. At the least, the data obtained in this segment of the interview may affirm or round out reasons mentioned earlier. But quite often, it is only in this direct questioning segment that the true motivation for the resignation is learned.

A good way to begin this section of the model is with a question such as:

> "Maybe you've already answered this for me, but could you tell me a few of the reasons that might be causing you to leave?"

At this point, the interviewer should be silent until the employee speaks. Even if the climate seems to be getting tense, he should not start talking! Remember, the employee knows it's his turn to talk. He is probably mentally sifting through what he wants to say and what to hold back on. If the interviewer jumps into the conversation, he will lose the opportunity to hear anything meaningful. Two responses to this question are likely:

A *"gutsy," or significant, response* would be one in which the employee indicated, for example, that he "wasn't managed very well." If the response is meaningful, like this one, it should be explored in as much depth as possible, using the usual listening techniques presented in Chapter 1.

But often the first reason presented is one that sounds good but is not in fact the real reason. A useful question to deal with this contingency would be:

> "Can you think of any other possible reasons for your
> leaving, even if they are minor, that would be helpful for
> us to know about?"

Once again, silence is the best strategy at this point. And it
may eventually yield some other reason, possibly one the employee considered too petty or sensitive to mention on the first
go-round. Once the employee has said all he is going to share,
it is time for the interviewer to summarize his understanding of
what has been brought to light.

This action gives the interviewer one last chance to get
from the employee greater clarification, further embellishment
of earlier responses, or even new input. An easy way to lead
into this step is to say:

> "Let me see if I understand. The main reasons you're
> leaving are [*reasons to be mentioned as succinctly as possible*]. Is
> that right?"

The other kind of response the interviewer could get to
this segment of questioning is a "*packaged,*" *or* "*pap,*" *response*—
or still further denial. When no meaningful reasons are prof-
fered, a few actions can still be taken. For instance, a final pass
at hearing something significant can be made by summarizing
the situation. This is not done in a condemnatory tone, but
simply as a statement of fact:

> "What you've been saying then is that the only reason
> you are leaving is because 'it's time to move on' [*or whatever
> reason the employee has given*].
> "As you see it then, there really isn't anything you can
> share with me that will help us understand your resigna-
> tion."

If nothing significant comes from this attempt at summarization, it is worth trying a completely different tack. For example:

> "How did you learn about the new job you're going
> to?"

One of two answers is likely: Either the employee himself sought out the job, or he was recruited or otherwise told about the opening. The question provides a springboard for one more attempt because whatever answer is given, it is possible to explore further by asking:

> "But at least you were receptive to this new situation. What do you believe that you'll have there that we are not able to offer you?"

This question could at last yield a meaningful response.

Step 4: Close by Mentioning the Next Steps

In moving to the close, the interviewer should thank the employee for whatever help has been given and then say:

> "Is there anything else you can think of that we haven't talked about that would help me to make recommendations to the company, especially for ways that we could improve?"

If something is forthcoming, it should of course be explored and the employee again thanked for his cooperation.

The interviewer will formally end the interview by mentioning the next steps in the separation process.

A summary of the Exit Interview Model is shown in Figure 37. It may be helpful to keep this inconspicuously on your desk for easy reference until you become comfortable with the flow of the model.

For Human Resources Professionals

As mentioned earlier, the Exit Interview Model presented here was originally designed for use by personnel department interviewers. Those experienced in exit interviewing will fully understand why the interview described slowly "builds" so as to allow employees to feel comfortable enough to share data they initially intended to keep to themselves.

Figure 37. Outline of exit interview model.

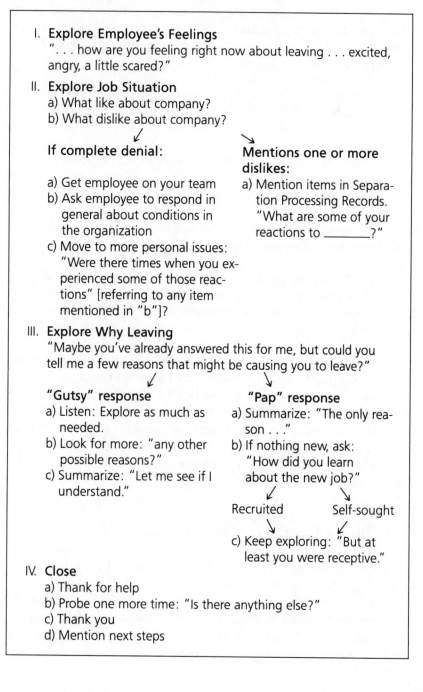

I. **Explore Employee's Feelings**
". . . how are you feeling right now about leaving . . . excited, angry, a little scared?"

II. **Explore Job Situation**
a) What like about company?
b) What dislike about company?

If complete denial:	**Mentions one or more dislikes:**
a) Get employee on your team	a) Mention items in Separation Processing Records. "What are some of your reactions to _____?"
b) Ask employee to respond in general about conditions in the organization	
c) Move to more personal issues: "Were there times when you experienced some of those reactions" [referring to any item mentioned in "b"]?	

III. **Explore Why Leaving**
"Maybe you've already answered this for me, but could you tell me a few reasons that might be causing you to leave?"

"Gutsy" response	**"Pap" response**
a) Listen: Explore as much as needed.	a) Summarize: "The only reason . . ."
b) Look for more: "any other possible reasons?"	b) If nothing new, ask: "How did you learn about the new job?"
c) Summarize: "Let me see if I understand."	Recruited Self-sought
	c) Keep exploring: "But at least you were receptive."

IV. **Close**
a) Thank for help
b) Probe one more time: "Is there anything else?"
c) Thank you
d) Mention next steps

Several human resources groups with whom I have worked have successfully taught this model to their operating managers. However, if both line managers and human resources personnel follow the same interview model, the exit process will become repetitive and at least part of it quite redundant.

It has been my experience that personnel departments should have the primary responsibility for conducting the company's exit interviews. The professional interviewing skills reside there, and it is usually easier for an employee to talk openly to a human resources representative than to his boss, especially if the boss is one of the reasons the employee is leaving. Moreover, the expectation of most employees is that they will be speaking with personnel for debriefing and the normal steps in closing out their employment. Even more important, the centralizing of exit interviewing makes possible an analysis of the reasons for voluntary resignations. There can be significant payback to the company if negative trends are uncovered and remedial action taken.

Payback is not easy to attain, however. Here are a few critical "musts" to follow if rewards are to be reaped from an exit interviewing:

1. *For exit interviewing to be productive, the process should be used continuously and with all leaving employees.* In organizations in which exit interviews are conducted on a "catch as catch can" basis, they will soon be avoided, and the data obtained will obviously be of questionable value. A clear-cut policy requiring all individuals leaving the company to be processed through human resources ought to be established. Such a policy should not be difficult to establish because the necessity for closing out records, arranging for the transfer of medical insurance, and other programs brings departing employees to the human resources department to begin with. The problem stems from the inability of the company, or the human resources department, to decide on a definite commitment of the time, effort, and money required by exit interviews (apart from the routine mechanics of the separation process).

2. *Exit interview formats (reporting sheets) should be developed so that the tabulation of data can be readily accomplished.* Consistency in the types of data recorded is essential. In Figure 38 is shown

Figure 38. Sample of an exit interview processing form.

SEPARATION PROCESSING RECORD		CONFIDENTIAL

THIS SECTION TO BE COMPLETED BY SUPERVISOR AND RETURNED TO PERSONNEL

Employee Name	Position	Expense Center
Number of Unused Vacation Days	Last Working Day Scheduled	Date Notice Given

1. Your understanding why employee is leaving_____

_____

2. Comment of employee's work performance in your unit_____

_____

_____

Return this form along with employee profile and letter of resignation (if applicable) one week prior to termination date to Location Personnel. | Supervisor's Signature   Date

TO BE COMPLETED BY PERSONNEL

REASON FOR SEPARATION

VOLUNTARY RESIGNATIONS

- ☐ 401 Dissatisfaction with pay
- ☐ 402 Dissatisfaction with working conditions
- ☐ 403 Dissatisfaction with opportunity for advancement
- ☐ 404 Dissatisfaction with type of work
- ☐ 405 Dissatisfaction with hours of work
- ☐ 406 Dissatisfaction with fellow employees
- ☐ 407 Dissatisfaction with supervision
- ☐ 408 Dissatisfaction with location
- ☐ 410 Dissatisfaction with company policies
- ☐ 415 Irresistible offer
- ☐ 416 Career redirection
- ☐ 501 Transportation problems
- ☐ 502 Relocation
- ☐ 504 Returning to school
- ☐ 507 Health problems
- ☐ 508 Leaving labor market
- ☐ 509 Family problems
- ☐ 510* Other reason

RELEASES

- ☐ 601 Unsatisfactory performance
- ☐ 605 Refused transfer
- ☐ 608* Unaccpetable conduct (Refer to Manager's Guide, re: Disciplinary procedures, and indicate specific classification below)
- ☐ 609 Excessive absenteeism
- ☐ 612* Other employee-related reason
- ☐ 613 Mutual agreement
- ☐ 651 Discontinuation of function
- ☐ 652 Reduction in force
- ☐ 653 Temporary layoff
- ☐ 654 Reduction in force—Profit Sharing eligible

REMOVALS FROM ACTIVE STATUS TRANSACTION CODES

- ☐ 701 Normal retirement
- ☐ 702 Early retirement
- ☐ 753 Educational leave with pay
- ☐ 754 Personal leave of absence with pay
- ☐ 773 Educational leave, no pay
- ☐ 774 Personal leave of absence, no pay
- ☐ 775 Medical leave of absence, no pay

*(Explanation of 510, 608, and 612 where applicable)

_____

_____

_____

_____

	Very Satisfied	Satisfied	Dissatisfied	Very Dissatisfied

TO BE COMPLETED BY PERSONNEL

Name

(This interview should be complete and informative. It is an excellent means of obtaining the employee's opinions, complaints, and suggestions. A statement should be made of the reason for the separation of the employee: reason for leaving, or the company's reason for involuntary release. To be of value in the future, the information must be clear, complete, and open. Employees are to be reminded of the Confidentiality and Invention Agreement signed by them, if pertinent, and their responsibilities and obligations are to be reiterated.)

Check which best characterizes employee's feelings about the following aspects of experience with the company.

	Very Satisfied	Satisfied	Dissatisfied	Very Dissatisfied
Nature of the job	☐	☐	☐	☐
Utilization of skills and experiences	☐	☐	☐	☐
Supervision	☐	☐	☐	☐
Coaching and counseling	☐	☐	☐	☐
Performance appraisals	☐	☐	☐	☐
Training and development programs	☐	☐	☐	☐
Opportunities for advancement	☐	☐	☐	☐
Salary treatment	☐	☐	☐	☐
Company benefits	☐	☐	☐	☐
Overall, XYZ as a company to work for	☐	☐	☐	☐

In your comments below, include the following:
• Employees new situation
• Primary reason(s) employee is leaving the company.
• Employee's suggestions for improvement.

_____
_____
_____
_____
_____
_____

Use additional paper if necessary

NOTIFICATION | **INFORMATION TO EMPLOYEE**

☐ Payroll
☐ Credit Union
☐ Library
☐ Travel Desk (Return company credit cards to Travel Services (K-1-1)
☐ Patent Dept. (Research Division Only)
☐ Security Services (Return Access Card to Security Services)
☐ Health Services

☐ Unemployment Insurance Form BC-10
☐ Group Insurance Conversion Forms
☐ Retirement Plan
☐ Profit Sharing, 401K, IRA, ESOP
☐ C.O.B.R.A. Letter
☐ Authorization for Release of Information
☐ "Employee Separating from Company" letter sent

DATE _____

IDENTIFICATION CARD AND EMPLOYEE HANDBOOK RETURNED TO | KEYS RETURNED TO | INTERVIEWER | DATE an effective exit interview format used by the human resources group at a major pharmaceutical company. It provides both easily tabulated "check-off" items and an opportunity for the interviewer to write qualifiable interpretations and commentary.

3. *A policy should be determined concerning the management of "confidential" or "off-the-record" information.* Quite often, during the course of an exit interview, the employee will preface the sharing of some information by the question, "Is this strictly between you and me?" In most cases, it is recommended that the policy be to honor confidentiality but not to lose the potential value of the input. This can be accomplished by telling the employee that his name will definitely not be linked with the information provided, but that it may be combined with data from other informants so that it can be tabulated. It is often possible, too, that once the information has been shared, the employee will exhibit a greater willingness to release the interviewer from the confidentiality promise. If this result is considered desirable, a question such as this is often effective:

> "What you have just shared with me is really important. It is a shame I can't talk to others about it. Are you still unwilling to let me say anything about it, or would it be OK if I discussed it with the vice-president of marketing?"

The important point here is that all exit interviewers understand the policy and that it be applied consistently.

Options for Enhancing Validity of Exit Interview Data

In addition to the techniques described in this chapter for conducting an exit interview, organizations desiring the most accurate assessment of the causes of turnover should also consider two other approaches.

One option is to send a questionnaire inquiring about the reasons for the resignation. It should be mailed not sooner than two months from the employee's departure from the company; three to five months seems to work best.

The second option is to hire a consultant to do the exit interviews. In a study cited in Appendix B, it was found that a significant amount of additional, negative data was obtained by an outside consultant compared to the information gleaned by company interviewers.

Summary

Exit interviews are conducted for three basic purposes: voluntary resignation, termination, and removal from active status. This chapter has focused on the exit interview for voluntary resignation because it is very difficult to conduct successfully. Most employees do not want to "burn their bridges" and are therefore reluctant to share any reasons for leaving a company that could come back to haunt them.

The Exit Interview Model presented here is designed to cope with the employee's reluctance to reveal the true reasons for resigning. The model stresses the importance of gaining good rapport with the employee and of helping that individual to feel comfortable in the interview situation.

Appendix A

A List of Tested Questions

The following chart is arranged so that the reader can easily find questions that are appropriate for use in hiring interviews. In addition, the columns at the right will help the reader identify questions that are likely to yield information about one or more of the four basic factors:

K Aptitude or knowledge factor
I Intellectual factor
P Personality factor
M Motivational factor

Thus, the reader who wants to obtain relatively few inputs about intellectual functioning should select some questions from the **I** column and weave them into the next interview. The interviewer should not try to build an interview around these questions. They are offered only as a resource from which a few may be drawn from application in the tested questions step of the Evaluation Model or as ideas in the broad-brush questions of the campus interview model. Usually some experimentation is necessary before the interviewer evolves the most productive repertoire of tested questions.

	Probable Hypothesis			
	K	**I**	**P**	**M**

I. Years Before High School

	K	I	P	M
Did you do anything in the years before high school that you are particularly proud of?		x		x
As you look back on those years (before high school), was there anything you learned then that you see carrying over to your adult life today?	x	x	x	x
During those years before high school, were there any activities you particularly enjoyed, apart from those in school? What was there about ____that made it appealing?				x
In your earlier schooling, were there any natural talents or abilities you displayed that your teachers or parents commented about? What part, if any, do they play in your work success today?		x	x	

II. High School

	K	I	P	M
What degree of difficulty did you encounter in making your grades in school?	x	x		x
During high school, what did you think you wanted to do when you got out into the workaday world?				x
What did you enjoy doing after school?				x
What would you say you learned from your high school experiences that you see carried over to your adult life today?			x	x

III. College or Other Studies

	K	I	P	M
What do you believe is the basic purpose of a college education?	x	x		x
What do you think is the most valuable contribution it will make to your life?	x	x		

	Probable Hypothesis			
	K	**I**	**P**	**M**
How did you view the importance of grades in college?			x	x
What led you to choose ____College?				x
What prompted you to pick ____for your major subject?		x		x
If you had an opportunity to relive your college years, what might you do differently? Why?				x
What subjects did you do best in? Why?	x	x		
What subjects did you do poorest in? Why?	x	x		
What was there about the subjects in your major that made them appealing?		x		x
What did you learn from your extracurricular experiences that you see helping you today as an adult?	x	x		
What motivated you to seek a college degree?				x
What elective courses did you take? Why did you choose those particular ones?	x	x		x
If you had any part-time jobs while in school, which one or ones did you find most interesting? Why?				x
What would you say is the most important thing you learned from your college career?	x		x	
There is an opinion that student extracurricular activities infringe too much on valuable study time. What do you think about this?			x	x

IV. Work Experience (summer and full-time)

What changes, if any, have you ever made in your approach to others in order to become better accepted work?			x	

	Probable Hypothesis			
	K	I	P	M
What kind of people do you like to work with? What makes them pleasant to work with?			x	x
What kind of people do you find most difficult to work with? What is there about them you would like to change?			x	x
In your last job, what would you say were the main drawbacks to pursuing that kind of job as a career?	x			x
Starting with your last job, can you tell me about any of your achievements that were recognized by your superiors?	x	x		
Can you give me an example or two of your ability to manage or supervise others?	x		x	
What are some things you would like to avoid in a job? Why?				x
In your previous job, what kind of pressures did you encounter?			x	
What would you say is the most important thing you are looking for in an employer?			x	x
How do you feel about travel? On the average, how many nights a week would you be willing to be away from home?				x
What are some of the things on your job you think you have done particularly well or in which you have achieved the greatest success? Why do you feel this way?	x	x	x	x
What were some of the things in your last job that you found difficult to do?	x	x		
What are some of the problems you encounter in doing your job? Which one frustrates you the most? What do you usually do about it?			x	x

	Probable Hypothesis			
	K	**I**	**P**	**M**
How do you feel about the progress you have made with your present company?				x
In what ways do you think your present job has prepared you to take on even greater responsibilities?	x	x	x	
What would you say was the most, or least, promising job you ever had? Why do you feel this way?				x
What has been your greatest frustration or disappointment on your present job and why do you feel this way?				x
What are some of the reasons prompting you to consider leaving your present job?				x
What are some things you particularly liked about your last job?				x
Most jobs have pluses and minuses. What were some of the minuses in your last job?				x
Do you consider your progress on the job representative of your ability? Why?	x	x		x
What are some of the things about which you and your supervisor might occasionally disagree?			x	
How do you feel about the way you or others in the department were managed by your supervisor?			x	
In what ways has your supervisor helped you to further develop your capabilities?	x			
What are some of the things your boss did that you particularly liked or disliked? Why did you feel this way?			x	x
How do you think your boss rated your work performance? What were some of the things he indicated you could improve upon?	x	x	x	

	Probable Hypothesis			
	K	**I**	**P**	**M**

V. Military Career

What, if anything, would you say you learned from your military service? — K: x, P: x

	K	I	P	M
What, if anything, would you say you learned from your military service?	x		x	
I know a number of appeals are often made to keep people in the service; how did you evaluate the situation—leaving versus staying in?				x
How do you feel about the military's authority structure?			x	

VI. Reactions to the Job and Company

	K	I	P	M
What do you see in this job that makes it appealing to you that you do (did) not have in your present (last) job?				x
How do you evaluate our company as a place in which to build your future?				x
I know you don't have a good perspective of this job yet—not being in it—but from your present vantage point, what would you say there is about the job that is particularly appealing to you?	x		x	x
What would you say might not be highly desirable?	x		x	x
What is it that you are looking for in a company?				x

VII. Goals and Ambitions

	K	I	P	M
Where do you see yourself going from here? You may not have any particular goal at this time, but if you do, what might you be thinking about?				x
What is your long-term career objective?				x

	Probable Hypothesis			
	K	**I**	**P**	**M**
What do you think you need to develop yourself in to be ready for such a spot?	x	x	x	
What do you have going for you that might make you successful in such a job?	x	x	x	
What are some things you would want to avoid in future jobs? Why?	x		x	x
Do you have any particular salary goals or targets [If the candidate describes some, ask why he or she arrived at them.] What makes you think you will be able to earn that kind of income in _____years?	x	x	x	x
What kinds of job or career objectives do you have?				x
Who or what in your life would you say influenced you most with regard to your career objectives?	x		x	x
Can you pinpoint anything specific in your past experience that affected your present career objectives?	x		x	x
What are your salary expectations? What do you consider a fair salary progression from date of employment on?				x
How does your family feel about your career plans?			x	x

VIII. Self-Assessment

	K	**I**	**P**	**M**
What would you say there is about you that accounts for your progress to date?	x	x	x	x
We've talked a lot thus far about your education and work experience. But how about yourself—your other strengths and weaknesses? What are some of the good qualities or traits you possess?			x	x

	Probable Hypothesis			
	K	**I**	**P**	**M**
How about the other side of the coin? Apart from knowledge or experience, what traits or qualities do you think could be strengthened or improved upon?			x	x
What would you say are some of the basic factors that motivate you?				x
What kinds of things do you feel most confident in doing?	x	x	x	
What do you feel somewhat less confident about doing?	x	x	x	
What are some of the things you are either doing now or have thought about doing that are self-development activities?	x	x	x	x
In what way(s) do you think you have grown most in the past two to three years?	x	x		x
Can you describe for me a difficult obstacle you have had to overcome? How did you handle it? How do you think this experience affected your personality or ability? [The second and third questions usually are answered without asking.]		x	x	x
How would you describe yourself as a person?	x	x	x	x
If you had your life to live over again, what things would you do differently?	x			x
What do you think are the most important characteristics and abilities a person must possess to become a successful _____? How do you rate yourself in these areas?	x	x	x	x
Do you consider yourself a self-starter? If so, explain why.				x
What things in life that you have been asked to do have you found the hardest?	x	x	x	x

	Probable Hypothesis			
	K	**I**	**P**	**M**
What would you consider your greatest achievement to date? Why?	x	x	x	x
What things give you the greatest satisfaction?				x
What things frustrate you the most?			x	
How do you usually cope with them?	x		x	

IX. Leisure-Time Activities

What do you enjoy doing in your off hours?				x
What is there about _____that is appealing to you?		x	x	x
What do you like to avoid getting involved in during your off hours?			x	x
Are there any talents that you use during your leisure time that you have not been able to apply in a work situation?	x	x	x	x

Appendix B

Some Interesting Research About Interviewing

How Good Is the Interview as an Assessment Tool?

Until recently, much of the research concerning the effectiveness of the interview for predicting job behavior has shown disappointing results. Investigators often found little relationship between the ratings generated by interviewers and actual on-the-job performance. It is interesting to note, however, that most of the researchers did not concern themselves with the skills of the interviewers. In fact, in many studies in which the interview turned out to be a relatively ineffective assessment device, the interviewers were not particularly well trained. And even in those studies that reported the interviewers to have had some fundamental interview training, the interviewers were rarely required to follow a specified technique or procedure. It is not surprising, therefore, that many of the studies showed the interview to be a rather limited tool for assessing others. By contrast, when an experienced, skillful interviewer makes an assessment, he can demonstrate good predictive accuracy.*

Because the available research data seem to be ambiguous and at times conflicting, I conducted two studies designed to help clarify the issues. The purpose of these research projects was to compare the effectiveness of interviewers before and after training. They represent an attempt to ascertain if nonprofessional interviewers (operating managers) can learn and apply specific interview procedures. If

*E. E. Ghiselli,"The Validity of a Personnel Interview," *Personnel Psychology* No. 4 (1966): 389–394.

the participant can apply the techniques successfully, then the value of the interview as a tool for managers can be demonstrated. Furthermore, if managers learn to use particular techniques and if they are effective, then certain predictable results should occur.

- The trained interviewers should be consistent with one another in their judgments—at least more consistent than when judgments are rendered by untrained interviewers.
- Trained interviewers should have a good "batting average" in evaluating candidates. The accuracy of their predictions should be higher than the accuracy of those who are untrained.

An Experiment in Consistency

In the first study, the research was designed to ascertain whether or not those trained in interviewing were more consistent with each other in their evaluations than those not trained. In this project, two different adult college classes were exposed to a brief résumé and a fifty-minute tape recording of an interview. This tape was made during an actual interview that had been conducted by the author. The applicant was a twenty-four-year-old male candidate for a sales representative job with a large consumer marketing company.

The classes were approximately the same size and were comprised largely of middle management business and professional men attending evening university courses in business subjects. The students in Class I were enrolled in a course on interviewing. Of the thirty-eight members of this class, only five were employed in personnel departments or had extensive interviewing experience prior to attending the class. Class II was comprised of a similar group of business and professional personnel. These men and women had signed up for a course in personnel administration.

Both classes were independently exposed to the résumé and the tape recording. Each student was also given a job description of the sales representative position. The students in each class were subsequently asked to evaluate the qualifications of the candidate for the sales representative position on a seven-point scale, as shown in the following table.

Point Value	Description
7	Superior
6	Above average
5	Average to above average
4	Average
3	Average to below average
2	Below average
1	Poor

The findings of this study were most interesting. Before training, Class I and Class II were approximately equal in how they evaluated the candidate. That is, the mean rating of the students in Class I was 4.6 (average to above average), while the mean for Class II was 4.8. Both classes were also approximately the same in the extent to which their respective raters differed in their opinions. The more the ratings cluster around the mean, the more consistent, of course, are the ratings. For the two classes studied, the standard deviation (SD) provides an index of the range of scores. The higher the SD, the more the majority of the raters vary from the mean. As can be noted in Figure 39, the SD for both classes was approximately equal, 3.1 and 2.8, respectively. Thus it can be said that both classes were basically equal in their assessment capabilities.

Six weeks after the first evaluations, the same tape and résumé were provided for a second time to both classes. In the interval, Class I had been trained in the interview techniques described in this book; Class II continued its regular studies in personnel administration (not including interviewing). Notice the column headed "Second Interview" in Figure 39. For Class I, the interview-trained class, the range of ratings decreased from 3.1 to 1.2. This finding shows a marked increase in intrarater consistency between the first and second interviews. For Class II, however, the noninterview-trained group, the variability remained high at 2.9. The likelihood of such a difference occurring between Class I and Class II as a result of chance is less than one in a hundred. It is quite evident, therefore, that those trained in the interview techniques were more consistent in their ratings than those who were untrained.

It is interesting to note the differences in mean (average scores) obtained by the two classes. After listening to the tape for a second time, members of Class I were much more critical in their ratings of

---

Figure 39. Comparison of the variability of ratings for groups trained and not trained in interview techniques.

Class	Measure	First Interview	Interviewer-Trained	Second Interview	Interviewer-Trained
I $N=38$	Mean Rating	4.6	No	3.4	Yes
	Range (SD)	3.1		1.2	
II $N=31$	Mean Rating	4.8	No	4.5	No
	Range (SD)	2.8		2.9	

the candidate than before the training. In other words, after interview training, the Class I students not only agreed more consistently with each other but they also tended to view the candidate as less well qualified than they had on the first assessment. For Class II students, on the other hand, consistency and qualifications ratings were almost the same after the second interview as after the first.

An Experiment in Predictability

A second study was conducted to determine how accurate the interview might be as a tool for predicting on-the-job performance. In this instance, an attempt was also made to evaluate the effectiveness of the techniques outlined in this book.

The situation that permitted the study was a major chemical corporation's acquisition of a smaller high-technology company. Many of the acquired firm's manufacturing and research facilities were to be integrated into an already existing division of the chemical firm. Because it was necessary to merge the manpower of the two groups, an evaluation of managerial and professional talent in the acquired company had to be made. To accomplish the assessment, two teams of five men were selected to interview the personnel. These interviewers were, with the exception of one man on each team, operating managerial personnel with strong chemical engineering backgrounds. (Technical sophistication was thought to be an important ingredient in establishing rapport and meaningful communication between the interviewers and the acquired company's staff.) Each team included a personnel department representative who had extensive interviewing experience.

In conducting the evaluation interviews, the teams followed no consistent pattern. Sometimes two or three members of the team would jointly interview a candidate; sometimes the interviews were conducted on a one-to-one basis. However, for each candidate assessed, the members of the interviewing team met as a group and arrived at some composite evaluation. For these evaluations, a six-point scale of management acceptability (shown in Figure 40) was used.

In the first round of assessments, sixty-six males were evaluated. The evaluation ratings were then correlated with the acquired company's performance ratings from the previous three years. As Figure 41 shows, the correlation of the evaluation ratings of the two groups with job-rated performances was low: .25 and .22, respectively. Because it had been anticipated that a much higher degree of concurrence would be found between former performance records and the team assessments, I was authorized to train one of the interviewing teams. The situation represented a unique opportunity to put the trained-interviewer theory to a test.

In this research project, Team A was trained; Team B was not. After Team A had been given three days of training, a second round of evaluations was begun. This time, 104 people (ninety-nine males and five females) were assessed. The results were exciting. As can be seen in Figure 41, Team A almost doubled its predictive accuracy, while the untrained team remained at approximately the same level. Here was convincing evidence of the greater consistency and validity of the ratings given by those trained in interviewing techniques. The findings also demonstrate that in a relatively short period managers can learn to predict, with reasonable accuracy, on-the-job performance.

Figure 40. Six-point evaluative scale for managerial talent.

Points	Descriptive Rating	Qualifiable Job Level
6	Extraordinary managerial talent—ready for top-echelon management	Division Head
5	Very good managerial talent—ready for upper middle management	Department Head
4	Good managerial talent—ready for middle management assignment	Section Head
3	Good in managerial talent—ready for supervisory level assignment	Supervisor
2	Fair managerial talent—marginally effective at directing others	_____
1	Poor—limited skill for supervisory assignment	_____

It now seems increasingly evident that simply sitting down and talking with candidates about themselves and their qualifications is not likely to produce consistent or valid findings. An interviewer must follow procedures that have been tested and proved effective. This book has described one such set of techniques or procedures. They need not be slavishly followed; they can be adapted to the interviewer's own personality and the circumstances of the interview. It is important, however, that certain fundamental principles be adhered to and certain procedural steps followed. In other chapters of this book, a step-by-step method is described. The approach should lend itself well to many different kinds of interviews, although it is geared, essentially, to helping executives make hire/not-hire decisions about job applicants and candidates for promotion.

Figure 41. Effect of interview training on predictive
accuracy of interviewers.

Team	Number Evaluated	First Round Assessments	Inter-viewers Trained	Number Evaluated	Second Round Assessments	Inter-viewers Trained
A	31	.25*	No	54	.44*	Yes
B	35	.22*	No	50	.26*	No

*Indicates correlations between interview ratings and management performance ratings.

Other Interesting Research on Interviews

As was mentioned elsewhere, almost all of the models and recommendations presented in this book have emanated from my trial-and-error experiences over an extended period of time. I have seen them work quite well in a variety of business and government situations. However, for those interested in the technical underpinnings and for my professional colleagues, I have outlined below research findings which lend support to the techniques and procedures described in this book. This summary, in no way, represents a complete survey of professional literature; it merely focuses on items that are relevant and interesting (at least they are to me).

Company-Conducted Exit Interviews—How Good?

The results of this study confirm other research that suggests that exit interviews, conducted by company management, yield qualitatively different information than those obtained either by follow-up questionnaires or by exit interviews conducted by an outside consultant. It was found that data obtained by the outside consultant provided far more negative information about management than was obtained either by the company exit interview or the company questionnaire.

The researchers concluded that:

Because of the importance of understanding the factors associated with attrition and the powerful distortion through the in-house exit interview procedure, supplementary means of data collection regarding attrition are extremely important. A systematic survey of departing employees is one approach which can help, but supplementary follow-up interviews by an outside consultant should probably also be part of the data collection procedure.[1]

Impact of Positive and Negative Interview Information on Employment Decisions

There are a number of studies indicating that interviewers are more sensitive to negative information than positive information. Also, that negative data tends to have a strong weight in making an evaluation.[2]

Effects of Interview Length and Applicant Quality on Interview Decision Time

In a study done with thirty males and thirty females, it became apparent that the point at which decisions are made (hire/not-hire) depends on the quality of the applicant and the perceived amount of time available to conduct the interview. When more time is alloted to conduct the interview, interviewers are less likely to make early or premature decisions. This suggests that there is some value in structuring longer interview periods of time. It will take most interviewers at least forty-five minutes to go through the Evaluation Model described in this book.

A second finding was that the decision is deferred for a longer period of time for good quality applicants than for those of poorer quality. Many interviewers continue the interview longer before they make a positive decision, waiting for negative data to come up. Often it is not until the end of the interview, on very high-quality candidates, that the "hire" decision is made.[3]

Biasing of Interview Impressions Because of Prior Input

In an experiment in which the subjects were given the opportunity to read a letter of reference before examining written interview transcripts, it was found that those interviewers who had read relatively unfavorable letters of references were most likely to give the applicant less credit for past successes and to hold the applicant more personally responsible for past failures. The results also indicated that the final decision to accept or reject an applicant is closely related to these kinds of interpretations of past behaviors.[4]

This study supports, as others have, that discussion of candidates before the interview, particularly if the discussion has negative implications, does hamper objectivity in assessing the candidate.

The Effect of Preinterview Impressions on Types of Questions Asked

In the study cited below, it was found that both male and female interviewers plan to ask significantly more questions seeking negative information when planning to interview a "low suitability applicant" compared with a "high suitability applicant" when preparing to interview someone of the opposite sex.

The investigators speculate that the "going easy" on a person of the opposite sex may reflect certain social norms and are operative in opposite-sex interviews, or that equal employment issues in today's society make interviewers of opposite-sex candidates attempt to behave equitably, or at least present the appearance of being more than fair.[5]

This data was done on college-aged candidates and may not be relevant to older applicants, but the findings are quite interesting.

Validity of What-Would-You-Do-If . . . -Type Questions in Employment Interviews

In the study cited below, an attempt was made to observe the validity of an interview that is structured so that applicants are asked a question about how they would handle various job responsibilities. The answers were then assigned a score, based on defined, benchmark answers. There is a positive, significant correlation between what people said they would do and how they performed on the job. Interestingly enough, when questions were based on actual prior experience, rather than "what would you do?" the relationships between past experiences and job performance were low (.14).[6]

This finding gives further support to the value of the self-appraisal question for understanding how a person is likely to perform on the job.

The Tendency to Inflate One's Capability When Doing Self-Assessments

In this study, 351 applicants were asked to rate on a scale of 0–4 the extent to which they had experience and/or skill in performing various tasks related to the job in question. Findings indicated that "inflation bias in the context of personal selection is extensive and tends to reduce the validity of the selection process when self-examinations of skills and abilities are used." This finding has also been supported by earlier research.

This finding is important to people using self-appraisal questions, as recommended in this book. It reemphasizes the importance of getting at the "how and why" one performs, rather than the "what." There is high risk in asking a person to rate how competent they are on a particular task. It is quite a different thing, however, to follow up that question with a self-appraisal question, such as: "Well, you said you did well at this particular task, what is there about you or your skills that you would say makes you good and effective at it?" It is in the applicant's responses about the "hows and whys" that the assessor is more likely to pick up those who are distorting the truth of their abilities.[7]

The Value of Interviewer Training

As was pointed out in the study by the author cited earlier in this section, it was suggested that interviewer consistency can be improved with training. Also, following training on selected rating dimensions, the interviewers' predictive validities improved.[8]

How Much Do You Tell Someone About the Job Before He or She Starts the Job?

In a study in which realistic job previews were presented, the findings suggest that the effect of these job previews is modest but nevertheless encouraging. The researchers found that realistic job previews appear to lower the initial expectations about the job or the organization and, as could be expected, increased the number of candidates who voluntarily dropped out for the consideration for the job. However, for those who did not drop out, realistic job previews seemed to increase intial levels of organizational commitment and job satisfaction, and even slightly improved the likelihood of their not quitting.[9]

This finding suggests that, as part of the employment process, it might be productive, especially at the end of the interview, to review the dimensions of the job in a realistic fashion.

What Recruiting Source Is Best?

For many years, literature suggested that employees who were hired via informal methods (employee referral, self-initiated contacts, and friends or relatives familiar with the organization) were likely to stay longer with the organization than employees hired through use of more formal recruiting methods (newspaper advertisements, college recruiting, or employment agencies). More recently, however, research data suggests that the effectiveness of various recruiting sources is more complex than thought. The recruiting sources may be differentially effective to the extent that they reach different populations. For example, in jobs in which there is historically high turnover and/or many leave because of disatisfaction with current salary or compensation, the impact of referral source is greatly diminished.[10]

How Much Attention Should Be Placed on Nonverbals in an Interview?

It is often said that we are more influenced by nonverbal behavior than by the words being spoken. This is especially true when the words are in conflict with the observed behavior. In an interview, our judgment of another can be influenced strongly by nonverbal behavior. A number of studies have shown that applicants who have displayed positive nonverbal behavior such as good eye contact, high energy level, and good voice modulation were evaluated better than those who did not display such behavior. Another study showed that applicants who engaged in eye contact were judged as being more alert, assertive, dependable, confident, responsible, and as having more initiative. Applicants rated highly on these attributes were also evaluated most likely to be hired.

So, it appears that eye contact and other nonverbal behaviors tend to bias the interview in a very favorable manner. Whether or not the interviewer's interpretation of these nonverbal cues is valid, however, has not been carefully studied. In one investigation it was demonstrated that nonverbal cues seem to be a rather accurate predictor of social skills, but not at all good at predicting one's motivation to work. The conclusion is, that we need to be careful not to be unduly biased by nonverbal behavior and attribute capability in areas other than social skill.[11]

Value of Feedback About Job Performance

This study confirms other research that supports the finding that *timely* and *specific* feedback to individuals is beneficial to task performance. It further revealed that it is important to provide feedback on all of the important aspects of the task (quality and quantity, for example). The data further suggests that it is most helpful if feedback is independently provided for each important aspect of the job. In other words, it is better to talk about quality separately from quantity rather than merge them together in a single discussion. Here, again we see that ongoing feedback about work is more helpful than summary appraisals.[12]

How Valid Are Self-Evaluations of Ability?

The authors reviewed fifty-five studies in which self-evaluations were compared with measures of actual performance. The mean correlation of these studies was .29. The research showed that persons with high intelligence, high achievement status, and internal focus of control were more accurate in their evaluations.

These findings lend support to use of the Hypothesis Method described in this book. This specialized, structured approach to seeking behavioral data about job applicants gains additional credence by the researcher's comments that:

> . . . in the self-evaluation studies reviewed, the provision of self-evaluation was more incidental than systematic, *and it may be that more careful structuring of these self-evaluation experiences may help elicit valid self-evaluation.*[13]

In a different study, the authors found that their

> . . . findings partially bear out the promise of self-assessment as a valuable tool in personnel selection . . . (and) favor the notion that

individuals possess the capability to reliably evaluate themselves in a manner similar to that of others and in a way that can predict subsequent performance.[14]

Validity of Tested Questions

Using tested questions of the how-would-you-handle type, a number of recent studies have shown that when applicants are asked to describe how they think they would respond to certain job-related situations—even if they have never done that kind of thing before—significantly predictive validities have come from analyzing responses to these kinds of questions. Usually they are in the format of a situational interview in which benchmark responses have been established, and the applicant's responses are given a numerical value according to these "benchmarks." The findings here indicate that it is helpful to use tested questions of the sort in which applicants are asked to describe how they would handle various job-related circumstances. This kind of information, added to the data obtained by the Hypothesis Method, has the potential for enhancing interview accuracy.[15]

Notes

1. *Journal of Applied Psychology,* vol. 60, no. 4 (1975).

2. Blackeney, R. N., and McNaughton, J. F. "Effects of Temporal Placement of Unfavorable Information on Decision-Making During the Selection Interview," *Journal of Applied Psychology,* vol. 55, no. 2 (1971): 138–142; Springbett, B. M. "Factors Affecting the Final Decision in the Employment Interview," *Canadian Journal of Psychology,* vol. 12, no. 1 (1958): 13–22; Sydiaha, D. Bales. "Interaction Process Analysis of the Personnel Selection Interview," *Journal of Applied Psychology,* vol. 45, no. 4 (1961): 393–401.

3. Tullar, William W., et al. "Effects of Interview Length and Applicant Quality on the Interview Decision Time," *Journal of Applied Psychology,* vol. 64, no. 6 (1979): 669–674.

4. Tucker, David H., and Rowe, Patricia M. "Relationships Between Expectancy, Casual Attributions, and Final Hiring Decisions in the Employment Interview," *Journal of Applied Psychology,* vol. 64, no. 1 (1979): 27–34.

5. Binning, John F., et al. "Effects of Preinterview Impressions on

Questioning Strategies in Same- and Opposite-Sex Employment Interviews," *Journal of Applied Psychology*, vol. 73, no. 1 (1988): 30–37.

6. Latham, Gary P., and Saari, Lise M. "Do People Do What They Say? Further Studies on the Situational Interview," *Journal of Applied Psychology*, vol. 69, no. 4 (1984): 569–573.

7. Danderson, Cathy D., et al. "Inflation Bias in Self-Assessment Examinations: Implications for Valid Employee Selection," *Journal of Applied Psychology*, vol. 69, no. 4 (1984): 574–580.

8. Dougherty, Thomas W., et al. "Policy Capturing in the Employment Interview," *Journal of Applied Psychology*, vol. 71, no. 1 (1986): 9–15.

9. Premack, Steven L., and Wanous, John P. "A Meta-Analysis of Realistic Job Preview Experiments," *Journal of Applied Psychology*, vol. 70, no. 4 (1985): 706–719; Dean, R. A., and Wanous, J. P. "The Effects of Realistic Job Previews on Hiring Bank Tellers," *Journal of Applied Psychology*, vol. 69, no. 1 (1984): 61–68; Krausz, M., and Fox, S. "Two Dimensions of a Realistic Job Preview and Their Impact Upon Initial Expectations, Expectation Fulfillment, Satisfaction and Intentions to Quit," *Journal of Occupational Behavior*, vol. 2, no. 2 (1981): 211–216; Raphael, M. A. "Work Previews Can Reduce Turnover and Improve Performance," *Personnel Journal*, vol. 54, no. 1 (1975): 97–98; Wanous, J. P. "Effects of a Realistic Job Preview on Job Acceptance, Job Attitudes, and Job Survival," *Journal of Applied Psychology*, vol. 58, no. 3 (1973): 32–35.

10. Swaroff, Philip G., et al. "Recruiting Sources: Another Look," *Journal of Applied Psychology*, vol. 70, no. 4 (1985): 720–728; Gannon, M. J. "Sources of Referral and Employee Turnover," *Journal of Applied Psychology*, vol. 55, no. 1 (1971): 226–228.

11. Giford, Robert, et al. "Nonverbal Cues in the Employment Interview: Links Between Applicant Qualities and Interviewer Judgments," *Journal of Applied Psychology*, vol. 70, no. 4 (1985): 729–736.

12. Ilgen, Daniel R., and Moore, Carol F. "Types and Choices of Performance Feedback," *Journal of Applied Psychology*, vol. 72, no. 3 (1987): 401–406.

13. Mabe, Paul A., and West, Stephen G. "Validity of Self-Evaluation of Ability: A Review and Meta-Analysis," *Journal of Applied Psychology*, vol. 67, no. 3 (1982): 280–296.

14. Fox, Shaul, and Dinur, Yossi. "Validity and Self-Assessment: A Field Evaluation," *Personnel Psychology*, vol. 41, no. 3 (1988): 581–592.
15. Weekley, Jeff A., and Geir, Joseph A. "Reliability and Validity of the Situational Interview for a Sales Position," *Journal of Applied Psychology*, vol. 72, no. 3 (1987): 480.

Appendix C

Format for Developing Behavioral Specifications

Job Title _____ Grade level _____

Department _____ Reports to _____

(Job Title)

KNOWLEDGE/EXPERIENCE FACTOR

Are there any *essential* kinds of information (or tasks) the incumbent must know (or know how to do) in order to perform the job?

    1. Must know _____

    2. Must know _____

    3. Must know _____

    4. Must know _____

Are there any kinds of work experience lacking which the incumbent could not perform the job?

    1. Must have _____

    2. Must have _____

3. Must have _____

4. Must have _____

INTELLECTUAL FACTOR

Are any specific intellectual aptitudes (such as mathematical, mechanical, conceptual, or artistic ability) necessary for the job?

1. Must have aptitude for _____ __

_____

2. Must have aptitude for _____

_____

How complex are the problems to be solved? What must the incumbent demonstrate he/she can do intellectually (for example, work with abstract concepts, examine problems from a broad perspective)?

1. Must be able to solve problems involving _____

_____

2. Must be able to solve problems involving _____

_____

How must the incumbent go about problem solving (for example, make quick decisions, be concerned with details)?

1. Must have thinking pattern that permits incumbent to

_____

PERSONALITY FACTOR

Are there certain personality characteristics that are critical for success in this job (for example, decisiveness, patience)?

1. Incumbent must be _____

2. Incumbent must be _____

3. Incumbent must be _____

What kind of interpersonal behavior is required in the job?

Up the line _____

_____

_____

Down the line _____

_____

_____

Outside firm (customers) _____

_____

_____

MOTIVATIONAL FACTOR

Is there any activity the incumbent should enjoy doing in order to find satisfaction in this job?

1. Must like to _____

2. Must like to _____

3. Must like to _____

Is there anything the incumbent definitely should not dislike doing (for example, travel, meet deadlines under pressure)?

1. Must not dislike _____

2. Must not dislike _____

Does the job make any unusual energy demands (such as long hours, constant travel)?

1. Incumbent must be able to _____

2. Incumbent must be able to _____

How critical is overt drive? Must incumbent push over, through, or around many obstacles?

1. Must have the drive to _____

2. Must have the drive to _____

Appendix D

The Impact of the New Immigration Law

In 1986, President Reagan signed into law a piece of legislation that affects every employer, whether it be a mom-and-pop operation or General Motors. It's called the Immigration Reform and Control Act of 1986, and, in a sense, makes every employer an arm of the Immigration and Naturalization Service (INS). The law states that, beginning November 6, 1986, all new employees, including U.S. citizens, must provide their employers with proof of their eligibility to work. *It prohibits employers from knowingly hiring an undocumented alien* and further stipulates that employers cannot, without violation, continue to employ an undocumented alien.

Fortunately for employers, the law has a grandfather clause exempting all employees, residing in the United States legally or illegally, who were on the payroll prior to November 6, 1986. The current burden is left by employers in screening new hires.

Checking Hiring Eligibility

According to the law, new hires must present to the employer some document that establishes their identity and eligibility to work. For most companies, checking on documentation can be facilitated by requiring applicants to present their documents *before* the employment interview. In large organizations with a human resources department, a sign prominently displayed at the receptionist's desk can speed up the documentation step in the screening process. One sign observed at a large insurance company read:

366

All applicants must provide proof of eligibility to work (U.S. passport, driver's license, social security card, etc.).

Some state employment agencies, as a matter of routine, screen out ineligible job candidates. In these cases, those who have passed the screen can use a letter of certification received from the state agency as their means of documentation. Companies dealing with this type of applicant, for their own protection, should make sure that the letter certifying eligibility is on official agency stationary, embossed with an agency stamp, and signed by an agency official. If the candidate is hired, the letter should be kept on file and treated in the same manner as the usual means of verifying compliance with the law.

The INS lists thirty-two types of documentation it considers acceptable, but the most commonly used are a U.S. passport or the combination of driver's license (establishing identity) and social security card (establishing work eligibility). For further details on other acceptable documents, the INS's *Employer's Handbook,* available at INS regional and district offices as well as at Regional Government Printing Offices, should be consulted.

The means of verifying compliance with the law is the I-9 Form (shown in Figure 42), a relatively simple one-page document. The INS estimates that the cost to employers is about $2.50 per hire (15 minutes completion time at $10 per hour); the Small Business Administration puts the cost at $10 per transaction (cost of form, filling it out, and storing it). But whatever the cost, employers must complete I-9 Forms on all new hires and employees hired after November 6, 1986.

As can be noted, the employee (or job applicant) fills out the upper half; the employer, after having examined the documents, completes and signs the bottom portion. The I-9 Form is to be kept on file for three years, or for one year following termination, whichever is later. Most legal advisers recommend that the forms be kept permanently. Currently, there is no statute of limitation included in the law.

An obvious repository for the I-9 Form is the employee's personnel file. However, because the I-9 Form contains data about the employee's age and national origin, access should be controlled to avoid any possibility of the information being used to discriminate. An even better solution is to establish a separate, confidential file. This arrangement has the added advantage of keeping government inspectors from tying up personnel folders.

Figure 42. I-9 Form.

EMPLOYMENT ELIGIBILITY VERIFICATION (Form I-9)

1 EMPLOYEE INFORMATION AND VERIFICATION: (To be completed and signed by employee.)

Name (Print or Type) Last	First	Middle	Birth Name
Address: Street Name and Number	City	State	ZIP Code
Date of Birth (Month Day Year)		Social Security Number	

I attest, under penalty of perjury, that I am (check a box):

☐ 1. A citizen or national of the United States.

☐ 2. An alien lawfully admitted for permanent residence (Alien Number A _____).

☐ 3. An alien authorized by the Immigration and Naturalization Service to work in the United States (Alien Number A _____ ,
or Admission Number _____ , expiration of employment authorization, if any _____).

I attest, under penalty of perjury, the documents that I have presented as evidence of identity and employment eligibility are genuine and relate to me. I am aware that federal law provides for imprisonment and/or fine for any false statements or use of false documents in connection with this certificate.

Signature	Date (Month/Day/Year)

PREPARER TRANSLATOR CERTIFICATION (To be completed if prepared by person other than the employee). I attest, under penalty of perjury, that the above was prepared by me at the request of the named individual and is based on all information of which I have any knowledge.

Signature	Name (Print or Type)		
Address (Street Name and Number)	City	State	Zip Code

2 EMPLOYER REVIEW AND VERIFICATION: (To be completed and signed by employer.)

Instructions:

Examine one document from List A and check the appropriate box, **OR** examine one document from List B **and** one from List C and check the appropriate boxes.
Provide the **Document Identification Number** and **Expiration Date** for the document checked.

List A Documents that Establish Identity and Employment Eligibility	List B Documents that Establish Identity	and	List C Documents that Establish Employment Eligibility
☐ 1. United States Passport ☐ 2. Certificate of United States Citizenship ☐ 3. Certificate of Naturalization ☐ 4. Unexpired foreign passport with attached Employment Authorization ☐ 5. Alien Registration Card with photograph	☐ 1. A State-issued driver's license or a State-issued I.D. card with a photograph, or information, including name, sex, date of birth, height, weight, and color of eyes. (Specify State)._____ ☐ 2. U.S. Military Card ☐ 3. Other (Specify document and issuing authority) _____		☐ 1. Original Social Security Number Card (other than a card stating it is not valid for employment) ☐ 2. A birth certificate issued by State, county, or municipal authority bearing a seal or other certification ☐ 3. Unexpired INS Employment Authorization Specify form #_____
Document Identification #_____	**Document Identification** #_____		**Document Identification** #_____
Expiration Date (if any)	**Expiration Date (if any)**		**Expiration Date (if any)**

CERTIFICATION: I attest, under penalty of perjury, that I have examined the documents presented by the above individual, that they appear to be genuine and to relate to the individual named, and that the individual, to the best of my knowledge, is eligible to work in the United States.

Signature	Name (Print or Type)	Title
Employer Name	Address	Date

Form I-9 (05 07 87)
OMB No. 1115-0136

U.S. Department of Justice
Immigration and Naturalization Service

Protecting Against Fake or Forged Documents

Fortunately, the law does not require employers to be experts at determining fakes or forged documents. The law appears to be fulfilled if upon examining the documents the employer believes that "each appears on its face to be genuine." For most employers, the best safeguard against penalties is to photocopy the documents presented. The law allows employers to photocopy these particular documents provided they are kept with the I-9 Form. This is true even when the documents carry "unlawful to photocopy" warnings.

There are a number of advantages to making copies to support the I-9 Form. First, it shows good faith on the part of the employer; it is tangible proof of an effort to comply with the law. Second, it provides substantial legal protection in the event the undocumented employee is indicted and then claims that the employer never verified his or her eligibility. Finally, if the employer does not hire a job candidate because the documents failed to pass the "appears genuine" review, the photocopies are available to provide justification for the organization's decision.

A word of caution about photocopying eligibility/immigration documents is in order here. *It is important to set up procedures to ensure that photocopying is done consistently for all employees.* Unless this is done, there is a risk that someone may claim that a promotion decision (or other management action) was based on discrimination against national origin. If documentation is available for some candidates but not for this particular individual, it may look as though no copies were made because of an intent to discriminate against the claimant.

Penalties and Exceptions

The INS has the primary responsibility for reviewing I-9 Forms. However, it has been reported that wage-and-hour inspectors from the U.S. Department of Labor are also checking these forms as part of their regular audits.

The civil penalties for *knowingly* hiring unauthorized aliens are graduated: For a first violation, the fine is $250 to $2,000 per alien; for a second, $2,000 to $5,000 per alien; and for a third, $3,000 to $10,000 per alien. Additional criminal fines can be levied on employers who engage in a "pattern or practice" of hiring undocumented aliens; provisions for issuing restraining orders and for imprisoning law breakers for up to six months are also incorporated in the Immigration Reform Act.

There are some exceptions to the 1986 law. For example, employers are not responsible for completing I-9s for contract employees such as temporaries. However, an employer may not *knowingly* make use of a contract agency to obtain the services of an undocumented alien. To be on the safe side, it is recommended that in agreements with providers of contract help a clause be included stipulating that the contractor will be liable for verifying the eligibility of all workers referred to the company. Even safer is to require that contractors provide copies of the I-9 Forms for all referred employees.

Appendix E

A Sample Format for Requesting Transcripts

Date: _____

To: Registrar

Please furnish a transcript of my record, at their expense, to:
[Company Name and Address]

_____

_____

_____

☐ I am a candidate for a _____
(degree)

_____   _____
(major)   (expected graduate date)

☐ I received a _____

_____   _____
(major)   (date)

Signature: _____
Address: _____

_____

Appendix F

A Handout for Employment Interviewers

This concerns interview statements that can endanger our company's rights.

The Problem: Recent trends in the courts have made significant inroads on the company's right to terminate employment at its own discretion. These court decisions have resulted in "wrongful discharge" claims that have resulted in settlements in excess of $400,000.

Most of the aforementioned claims were based on oral statements made during employment interviews by well-meaning interviewers—usually extolling the virtues of the organization. Listed below are phrases that should be avoided; most of those shown have been presented in courts to successfully win judgments against the employer.

Avoid making statements such as:

"You'll be with us as long as you do your job."
"You'll be joining us as a permanent employee."
"In this company, you'll have lots of job security."
"This is a job in which you can stay and grow."
"You'll never be terminated without just cause."
"You're hired, pending satisfactory performance."
"Your salary will be $___ annually." (Quote salary on a weekly or monthly basis to avoid any implication that employment is for a year's duration.)

After each interview:

1. Review your interview discussion. Were any promises made—implied or otherwise—that need to be corrected or revoked in a subsequent letter or formal offer of employment?

2. Record on your interview notes that all "employment-at-will precautions were complied with." Such written documentation provides a tangible defense against an employee's version of what was implied, should a wrongful discharge claim be filed some years hence.

Selected Reading

The following books, dealing with various kinds of interviews and with different interviewing techniques and systems, should be of help to the business manager.

Carroll, Stephen J., and Schneier, Craig E. *Performance Appraisal and Review Systems.* Glenview, Ill.: Scott, Foresman, 1982.

DeVries, David L. et al. *Performance Appraisal on the Line.* New York: John Wiley and Sons, 1981.

Drake, John D. *The Campus Interview.* New York: Harcourt Brace Jovanovich, 1981.

———. *Counseling Techniques for the Non-Personnel Executive.* New York: Harcourt Brace Jovanovich, 1974.

Gaylin, Willard. *Feelings.* New York: Ballantine Books, 1980.

Gould, Richard. *Sacked.* New York: John Wiley, 1986.

Kahn, Steven C. et al. *Personnel Director's Legal Guide.* New York: Warren, Gorham & Lamont, 1984.

Kennedy, Jim. *Getting Behind the Résumé.* Paramus, N.J.: Prentice-Hall, 1987.

Moses, Joseph L, and Byham, William C. *Applying the Assessment Center Method.* New York: Pergamon Press, 1977.

Morin, William J., and Yorks, Lyle. *Outplacement Techniques.* New York: AMACOM, 1982.

Plachy, Roger J. *Performance Management: Getting Results From Your Performance Planning & Appraisal System.* New York: AMACOM, 1988.

Tracey, William R. *Critical Skills: The Guide to Top Performance for Human Resources Managers.* New York: AMACOM, 1988.

Index

labor pool, 17
language discrimination, 43
laws, immigration, 366–380
layoffs, 311–312
legal risks
  in advertising, 23
  in performance appraisal, 308
  interview guidelines and, 41–43
legal risks in employment interviewing, 28–51
  discrimination, 33–46
  negligent hiring, 46–50
  wrongful dismissal, 29–32
leisure-time activities, 153
  tested questions on, 346
letters
  in college recruitment process, 58, 61
  of certification, from state employment agencies, 367
  offering, 66–69
  turndown, 66
liability, *see* legal risks
life areas, 140–153
  college, 142
  high school, 141–142
  military experience, 142–143
  work experience, 143–145
listening, 1–14, 116, 291–296
  accepting responses and, 5
  and feelings, 5–10
  without interruption, 214
  nonjudgmental, 284
  questions and, 2–5
long-range potential, 206
Lopez, Felix M., on behavioral specifications, 243

make or break questions, 82
management

participative, 288
publicizing openings in, 26
managers
  interview with, 271
  involvement of, in selling candidate, 263
  personnel, 271
  recruiting, 52–54
  relationship with subordinates, 283
  role of, 272
  and subordinates' development, 286–287
manpower needs, forecasting, 55
market research, job opening advertising as, 23
M.B.A. graduates, 120
military experience, 142–143
  tested questions on, 343
misstatements, intentional, 8
mistakes, by interviewers, 115–122
model
  for college recruitment interviews, 77–89
  for exit interview, 324–331
  for screening interview, 109–114
  teaching, for job coaching, 278–281
morale, 32
  job posting and, 27
motivation, 142, 147
  and job coaching, 277
  problems with, 297
motivational factor, 134–139, 247–248

National Organization for Women, 36, 37–38

soft closing method, to terminating interview, 113
Spencer Stuart & Associates, 19
sponsors, in college recruitment, 63
spouse
  employment opportunities for, 268
  program for, 269–270
  selling the candidate and, 264
state employment agencies, certification letter from, 367
state human rights commissions, 34
statements, oral, as enforceable contracts, 32
steering committee, for college recruitment, 53
strengths, 202
  compensating, 175
  of job applicant, 118
strengths and weaknesses
  in reference checks, 232
  self-assessment of, 149–153
stress, 11
stress interviewing, 156
strike replacements, employment-at-will and, 31
studies, tested questions on, 339–340
subordinates
  development of, managers and, 286–287
  evaluation of, 303
  participation by, 298
  relationship with manager, 283
subpoena, and wrongful dismissal, 30
success in job, personality in, 98, 100

summarization, in teaching model, 280
summer employment, 144
system, in evaluation, 168–170

target schools, for college recruitment, 54, 55
teaching model, for job coaching, 278–281
technical competence, 127
technical qualifications, 242–243
technological expertise, screening interview for, 105
telegraphing intent, 118–119, 172, 213
"tell me" approach, 212
temperament, 133–134
tension, reducing, 288
termination interview, 310–319
  data collection for, 312–313
  language in, 314–315
  model for, 313–320
  preparation for, 310–313
  severance package in, 318–319
  timing of, 312
termination of employees, 288
  reasons for, 314–316
tested questions, 154, 221–222, 338–346, 359
tests
  of knowledge and experience factor, 127
  situational, and future job behavior, 156–157
thoughts, processing, 129–130
threatening questions, 165–167
threat level, 158–165
  atmosphere and, 159
  compliments and, 164–165